Collins

World Factfile

Afghanistan Islamic State of Afghanistan

Area Sq Km **652 225**
Area Sq Miles **251 825**

Population **28 150 000**
Capital **Kābul**

Currency **Afghani**
Languages **Dari, Pushtu, Uzbek, Turkmen**

Religions **Sunni Muslim, Shi'a Muslim**
Organizations **UN**

Population

Total population **28 150 000**
Population change **N/A**
Urban population **N/A**
Total fertility rate **6.6 births per woman**
Population aged 0–14 **N/A**
Population aged over 65 **N/A**
2050 projected population **97 324 000**

Communications

Main telephone lines
0.3 per 100 people
Cellular mobile subscribers
8.1 per 100 people
Internet users
172 per 10 000 people
International dialling code **93**
Time zone **+4.5**

Economy

Total Gross National
Income (GNI) **N/A**
GNI per capita **N/A**
Debt service ratio **0.1% of GNI**
Total debt service **9 260 000 US$**
Aid receipts **35.7% of GNI**
Military spending **9.9% of GDP**

Environment

Forest area **1.3%**
Annual change in
forest area **-3.1%**
Protected land area **0.3%**
CO_2 emissions **N/A**

Social Indicators

Infant mortality rate
165 per 1 000 live births
Life expectancy **44.2**
Literacy rate **N/A**
Access to safe water **39%**
Doctors **0.2 per 1 000 people**

A landlocked country in central Asia with central highlands bordered by plains in the north and southwest, and by the mountains of the Hindu Kush in the northeast. The climate is dry continental. Over the last thirty years war has disrupted the economy, which is highly dependent on farming and livestock rearing. Most trade is with the former USSR, Pakistan and Iran.

Minaret of Jam, Afghanistan

Area Sq Km **28 748**
Area Sq Miles **11 100**

Population **3 155 000**
Capital **Tirana (Tiranë)**

Currency **Lek**
Languages **Albanian, Greek**

Religions **Sunni Muslim,**
Orthodox,
Roman Catholic
Organizations **NATO, UN**

Total population **3 155 000**
Population change **0.3%**
Urban population **46.7%**
Total fertility rate **1.9 births per woman**
Population aged 0–14 **24.2%**
Population aged over 65 **9.3%**
2050 projected population **3 458 000**

Communications

Main telephone lines
11.3 per 100 people
Cellular mobile subscribers
60.4 per 100 people
Internet users
1 498 per 10 000 people
International dialling code **355**
Time zone **+1**

Total Gross National
Income (GNI) **9 295 US$M**
GNI per capita **3 840 US$**
Debt service ratio **1.4% of GNI**
Total debt service **132 034 000 US$**
Aid receipts **3.5% of GNI**
Military spending **1.6% of GDP**

Environment

Forest area **29.0%**
Annual change in
forest area **0.6%**
Protected land area **0.7%**
CO_2 emissions **1.1 metric**
tons per capita

Social Indicators

Infant mortality rate
13 per 1 000 live births
Life expectancy **76.6**
Literacy rate **99.0%**
Access to safe water **96%**
Doctors **1.15 per 1 000 people**

Albania lies in the western Balkan
Mountains in southeastern Europe,
bordering the Adriatic Sea. It is
mountainous, with coastal plains where
half the population lives. The economy
is based on agriculture and mining.
Albania is one of the poorest countries
in Europe and relies heavily on foreign
aid.

Archaeological site of Butrint, Albania

Algeria People's Democratic Republic of Algeria

Area Sq Km **2 381 741**
Area Sq Miles **919 595**

Population **34 895 000**
Capital **Algiers (Alger)**

Currency **Algerian dinar**
Languages **Arabic, French, Berber**

Religions **Sunni Muslim**
Organizations **OPEC, UN**

Population

Total population **34 895 000**
Population change **1.5**
Urban population **65.2%**
Total fertility rate **2.4 births per woman**
Population aged 0–14 **27.7%**
Population aged over 65 **4.6%**
2050 projected population **49 500 000**

Communications

Main telephone lines
8.5 per 100 people
Cellular mobile subscribers
63.0 per 100 people
Internet users
738 per 10 000 people
International dialling code **213**
Time zone **+1**

Economy

Total Gross National
Income (GNI) **101 206 US$M**
GNI per capita **4 260 US$**
Debt service ratio **12.4% of GNI**
Total debt service **13 351 425 000 US$**
Aid receipts **0.2% of GNI**
Military spending **2.7% of GDP**

Environment

Forest area **1.0%**
Annual change in
forest area **1.2%**
Protected land area **5.0%**
CO_2 emissions **4.2 metric tons per capita**

Social Indicators

Infant mortality rate
33 per 1 000 live births
Life expectancy **72.3**
Literacy rate **75.4%**
Access to safe water **85%**
Doctors **1.13 per 1 000 people**

Algeria, the second largest country in Africa, lies on the Mediterranean coast of northwest Africa and extends southwards to the Atlas Mountains and the dry sandstone plateau and desert of the Sahara.

The climate ranges from Mediterranea on the coast to semi-arid and arid inland. The most populated areas are the coastal plains and the fertile northern slopes of the Atlas Mountain Oil, natural gas and related products account for over ninety-five per cent o export earnings. Agriculture employs about a quarter of the workforce, producing mainly food crops. Algeria's main trading partners are Italy, France and the USA.

Ancient Timgad, Algeria

Area Sq Km **197**
Area Sq Miles **76**

Currency **United States dollar**
Languages **Samoan, English**

Population **67 000**
Capital **Fagatogo**

Religions **Protestant,
Roman Catholic**

...ing in the south Pacific ...cean, American Samoa ...nsists of five main islands ...d two coral atolls. The largest island is Tutuila. Tuna and tuna products are the main exports, and the main trading partner is the USA.

Ofu, American Samoa

Andorra Principality of Andorra

Area Sq Km **465**
Area Sq Miles **180**

Population **86 000**
Capital **Andorra la Vella**

Currency **Euro**
Languages **Spanish, Catalan,
French**

Religions **Roman Catholic**
Organizations **UN**

Total population **86 000**
Population change **2.0%**
Urban population **88.9%**
Total fertility rate **N/A**
Population aged 0–14 **N/A**
Population aged over 65 **N/A**
2050 projected population **58 000**

Communications
Main telephone lines
51.3 per 100 people
Cellular mobile subscribers
96.9 per 100 people
Internet users
3 257 per 10 000 people
International dialling code **376**
Time zone **+1**

Environment
Forest area **34.0%**
Annual change in
forest area **0.0%**
Protected land area **7.0%**
CO2 emissions **N/A**

Total Gross National
Income (GNI) **N/A**
GNI per capita **N/A**
Debt service ratio **N/A**
Total debt service **N/A**
Aid receipts **N/A**
Military spending **N/A**

Social Indicators
Infant mortality rate
3 per 1 000 live births
Life expectancy **N/A**
Literacy rate **N/A**
Access to safe water **100%**
Doctors **3.64 per 1 000 people**

A landlocked state in southwest Europe, Andorra lies in the Pyrenees mountain range between France and Spain. It consists of deep valleys and gorges, surrounded by mountains. Tourism, encouraged by the development of ski resorts, is the mainstay of the economy. Banking is also an important economic activity.

6 Angola Republic of Angola

Area Sq Km **1 246 700**
Area Sq Miles **481 354**

Population **18 498 000**
Capital **Luanda**

Currency **Kwanza**
Languages **Portuguese, Bantu, local languages**

Religions **Roman Catholic, Protestant, traditional beliefs**
Organizations **OPEC, SADC, U**

Population

Total population **18 498 000**
Population change **2.6%**
Urban population **56.7%**
Total fertility rate **5.8 births per woman**
Population aged 0–14 **45.3%**
Population aged over 65 **2.5%**
2050 projected population **43 501 000**

Communications

Main telephone lines **0.6 per 100 people**
Cellular mobile subscribers **14.3 per 100 people**
Internet users **60 per 10 000 people**
International dialling code **244**
Time zone **+1**

Environment

Forest area **47.4%**
Annual change in forest area **-0.2%**
Protected land area **10.1%**
CO_2 emissions **0.5 metric tons per capita**

Economy

Total Gross National Income (GNI) **32 646 US$M**
GNI per capita **3 450 US$**
Debt service ratio **10.8% of GNI**
Total debt service **4 296 094 000 US$**
Aid receipts **0.4% of GNI**
Military spending **5.4% of GDP**

Social Indicators

Infant mortality rate **116 per 1 000 live births**
Life expectancy **47.3**
Literacy rate **N/A**
Access to safe water **53%**
Doctors **0.08 per 1 000 people**

Angola lies on the Atlantic coast of south central Africa. Its small northern province, Cabinda, is separated from the rest of the country by part of the Democratic Republic of the Congo. Much of Angola is high plateau. In the west is a narrow coastal plain and in the southwest is desert. The climate is equatorial in the north but desert in the south. Over eighty per cent of the population relies on subsistence agriculture. Angola is rich in minerals (particularly diamonds), and oil accounts for approximately ninety per cent of export earnings.
The USA, South Korea and Portugal are its main trading partners.

Epupa waterfall, Angola

Area Sq Km **155**	Currency **East Caribbean dollar**
Area Sq Miles **60**	Languages **English**

Population **15 000**	Religions **Protestant,**
Capital **The Valley**	**Roman Catholic**

nguilla lies at the northern nd of the Leeward Islands in he eastern Caribbean. Tourism and fishing form the basis of the economy.

Anguilla

Antigua and Barbuda

Area Sq Km **442**	Population **88 000**	Currency **East Caribbean dollar**	Religions **Protestant,**
Area Sq Miles **171**	Capital **St John's**	Languages **English, creole**	**Roman Catholic**
			Organizations **CARICOM, Comm., UN**

Population

Total population **88 000**
Population change **0.8%**
Urban population **30.5%**
Total fertility rate **N/A**
Population aged 0–14 **N/A**
Population aged over 65 **N/A**
2050 projected population **112 000**

Communications

Main telephone lines **45.5 per 100 people**
Cellular mobile subscribers **133.6 per 100 people**
Internet users **6 424 per 10 000 people**
International dialling code **1 268**
Time zone **-4**

Environment

Forest area **21.4%**
Annual change in forest area **0.0%**
Protected land area **0.0%**
CO_2 emissions **5.1 metric tons per capita**

Economy

Total Gross National Income (GNI) **929 US$M**
GNI per capita **13 620 US$**
Debt service ratio **N/A**
Total debt service **N/A**
Aid receipts **0.4% of GNI**
Military spending **N/A**

Social Indicators

Infant mortality rate **10 per 1 000 live births**
Life expectancy **N/A**
Literacy rate **N/A**
Access to safe water **91%**
Doctors **N/A**

The state comprises the islands of Antigua, Barbuda and the tiny rocky outcrop of Redonda, in the Leeward Islands in the eastern Caribbean. Antigua, the largest and most populous island, is mainly hilly scrubland, with many beaches. The climate is tropical, and the economy relies heavily on tourism. Most trade is with other eastern Caribbean states and the USA.

Argentina Argentine Republic

Area Sq Km **2 766 889**
Area Sq Miles **1 068 302**

Population **40 276 000**
Capital **Buenos Aires**

Currency **Argentinian peso**
Languages **Spanish, Italian, Amerindian languages**

Religions **Roman Catholic, Protestant**
Organizations **UN**

Population

Total population **40 276 000**
Population change **0.9%**
Urban population **92.0%**
Total fertility rate **2.3 births per woman**
Population aged 0–14 **25.4%**
Population aged over 65 **10.5%**
2050 projected population **51 382 000**

Communications

Main telephone lines **24.2 per 100 people**
Cellular mobile subscribers **80.5 per 100 people**
Internet users **2 091 per 10 000 people**
International dialling code **54**
Time zone **-3**

Economy

Total Gross National Income (GNI) **201 347 US$M**
GNI per capita **7 200 US$**
Debt service ratio **9.1% of GNI**
Total debt service **18 993 819 000 US$**
Aid receipts **0.1% of GNI**
Military spending **0.9% of GDP**

Environment

Forest area **12.1%**
Annual change in forest area **-0.4%**
Protected land area **6.3%**
CO_2 emissions **3.9 metric tons per capita**

Social Indicators

Infant mortality rate **15 per 1 000 live births**
Life expectancy **75.2**
Literacy rate **97.6%**
Access to safe water **96%**
Doctors **N/A**

Argentina, the second largest state in South America, extends from Bolivia to Cape Horn and from the Andes mountains to the Atlantic Ocean. It has four geographical regions: subtropical forests and swampland in the northeast; temperate fertile plains or Pampas in the centre; the wooded foothills and valleys of the Andes in the west; and the cold, semi-arid plateaus of Patagonia in the south. The highest mountain in South America, Cerro Aconcagua, is in Argentina. Nearly ninety per cent of the population lives in towns and cities. The country is rich in natural resources including petroleum, natural gas, ores and precious metals. Agricultural products dominate exports, which also include motor vehicles and crude oil. Most trade is with Brazil and the USA.

Buenos Aires, Argentina

Area Sq Km **29 800**
Area Sq Miles **11 506**

Population **3 083 000**
Capital **Yerevan (Erevan)**

Currency **Dram**
Languages **Armenian, Azeri**

Religions **Armenian Orthodox**
Organizations **CIS, UN**

Total population **3 083 000**
Population change **0.2%**
Urban population **63.9%**
Total fertility rate **1.7 births per woman**
Population aged 0–14 **20.5%**
Population aged over 65 **11.6%**
2050 projected population **2 506 000**

Communications

Main telephone lines
19.7 per 100 people
Cellular mobile subscribers
10.5 per 100 people
Internet users
575 per 10 000 people
International dialling
code **374**
Time zone **+4**

Total Gross National
Income (GNI) **5 788 US$M**
GNI per capita **3 350 US$**
Debt service ratio **2.6% of GNI**
Total debt service **167 008 000 US$**
Aid receipts **3.3% of GNI**
Military spending **2.8% of GDP**

Environment

Forest area **10.0%**
Annual change in
forest area **-1.5%**
Protected land area **8.7%**
CO_2 emissions **1.4 metric
tons per capita**

Social Indicators

Infant mortality rate
22 per 1 000 live births
Life expectancy **73.6**
Literacy rate **99.5%**
Access to safe water **92%**
Doctors **3.7 per 1 000 people**

A landlocked state in southwest Asia,
Armenia lies in the south of the
Lesser Caucasus mountains. It is a
mountainous country with a continental
climate. One-third of the population
lives in the capital, Yerevan (Erevan).
Exports include diamonds, scrap metal
and machinery. Many Armenians
depend on remittances from abroad.

Tatev Monastery, Armenia

Aruba Self-governing Netherlands Territory

Area Sq Km **193**
Area Sq Miles **75**

Currency **Aruban florin**
Languages **Papiamento, Dutch, English**

Population **107 000**
Capital **Oranjestad**

Religions **Roman Catholic, Protestant**

The most southwesterly of the islands in the Lesser Antilles in the Caribbean, Aruba lies just off the coast of Venezuela. Tourism, offshore finance and oil refining are the most important sectors of the economy. The USA is the main trading partner.

Aruba church

 Ascension Part of the United Kingdom Overseas Territory of St Helena, Ascension and Tristan da Cunha

Area Sq Km **88**
Area Sq Miles **34**

Population **1 100**
Capital **Georgetown**

A volcanic island in the south Atlantic Ocean about 1 300 kilometres (800 miles) northwest of St Helena. Once part of the dependancy of St Helena, a consititutional change in September 2009 saw Ascension (along with Tristan da Cunha) become recognised in the territory's name in its own right. The economy is based on military and communications installations, tourism, and offshore banking.

Long Beach, Ascension Island

Area Sq Km **207 600**
Area Sq Miles **80 155**

Population **9 634 000**
Capital **Minsk**

Currency **Belarus rouble**
Languages **Belorussian, Russian**

Religions **Belorussian Orthodox, Roman Catholic**
Organizations **CIS, UN**

Population

Total population **9 634 000**
Population change **-0.2%**
Urban population **73.5%**
Total fertility rate **1.3 births per woman**
Population aged 0–14 **14.8%**
Population aged over 65 **13.8%**
2050 projected population **7 017 000**

Communications

Main telephone lines
34.7 per 100 people
Cellular mobile subscribers
61.4 per 100 people
Internet users
5 647 per 10 000 people
International dialling code **375**
Time zone **+2**

Economy

Total Gross National Income (GNI) **33 760 US$M**
GNI per capita **5 380 US$**
Debt service ratio **2.0% of GNI**
Total debt service **733 327 000 US$**
Aid receipts **0.2% of GNI**
Military spending **1.7% of GDP**

Environment

Forest area **38.0%**
Annual change in forest area **0.1%**
Protected land area **5.2%**
CO2 emissions **6.5 metric tons per capita**

Social Indicators

Infant mortality rate
12 per 1 000 live births
Life expectancy **70.2**
Literacy rate **99.7%**
Access to safe water **100%**
Doctors **4.78 per 1 000 people**

Belarus, a landlocked state in eastern Europe, consists of low hills and plains, with many lakes, rivers and, in the south, extensive marshes. Forests cover approximately one-third of the country. It has a continental climate. Agriculture contributes one-third of national income, with beef cattle and grains as the major products. Manufacturing industries produce a range of items, from construction equipment to textiles. The Russian Federation and Ukraine are the main trading partners.

Mir Castle, Belarus

Belgium Kingdom of Belgium

Area Sq Km **30 520**
Area Sq Miles **11 784**

Population **10 647 000**
Capital **Brussels (Bruxelles)**

Currency **Euro**
Languages **Dutch (Flemish),**
French (Walloon),
German

Religions **Roman Catholic,**
Protestant
Organizations **EU, NATO,**
OECD, UN

Population

Total population **10 647 000**
Population change **0.7%**
Urban population **97.4%**
Total fertility rate **1.8 births per woman**
Population aged 0–14 **16.9%**
Population aged over 65 **17.2%**
2050 projected population **10 302 000**

Communications

Main telephone lines
45.2 per 100 people
Cellular mobile subscribers
92.6 per 100 people
Internet users
5 260 per 10 000 people
International dialling code **32**
Time zone **+1**

Economy

Total Gross National
Income (GNI) **405 419 US$M**
GNI per capita **44 330 US$**
Debt service ratio **N/A**
Total debt service **N/A**
Aid receipts **N/A**
Military spending **1.1% of GDP**

Environment

Forest area **22.1%**
Annual change in
forest area **0.0%**
Protected land area **3.2%**
CO_2 emissions **9.8 metric tons per capita**

Social Indicators

Infant mortality rate
4 per 1 000 live births
Life expectancy **80.2**
Literacy rate **N/A**
Access to safe water **N/A**
Doctors **4.23 per 1 000 people**

Belgium lies on the North Sea coast of western Europe. Beyond low sand dunes and a narrow belt of reclaimed land, fertile plains extend to the Sambre-Meuse river valley. The land rises to the forested Ardennes plateau in the southeast. Belgium has mild winters and cool summers. It is densely populated and has a highly urbanized population. With few mineral resources, Belgium imports raw materials for processing and manufacture. The agricultural sector is small, but provides for most food needs. A large services sector reflects Belgium's position as the home base for over eight hundred international institutions. The headquarters of the European Union are in the capital, Brussels.

Grand Place, Brussels, Belgium

Area Sq Km **22 965**
Area Sq Miles **8 867**

Population **307 000**
Capital **Belmopan**

Currency **Belize dollar**
Languages **English, Spanish, Mayan, creole**

Religions **Roman Catholic, Protestant**
Organizations **CARICOM, Comm., UN**

Population

Total population **307 000**
Population change **2.1%**
Urban population **51.7%**
Total fertility rate **2.9 births per woman**
Population aged 0–14 **35.8%**
Population aged over 65 **4.1%**
2050 projected population **442 000**

Communications

Main telephone lines **12.3 per 100 people**
Cellular mobile subscribers **44.1 per 100 people**
Internet users **1 236 per 10 000 people**
International dialling code **501**
Time zone **-6**

Economy

Total Gross National Income (GNI) **1 114 US$M**
GNI per capita **3 820 US$**
Debt service ratio **12.3% of GNI**
Total debt service **134 775 000 US$**
Aid receipts **0.7% of GNI**
Military spending **N/A**

Environment

Forest area **72.5%**
Annual change in forest area **0.0%**
Protected land area **35.8%**
CO_2 emissions **2.8 metric tons per capita**

Social Indicators

Infant mortality rate **22 per 1 000 live births**
Life expectancy **76.2**
Literacy rate **N/A**
Access to safe water **91%**
Doctors **1.05 per 1 000 people**

Belize lies on the Caribbean coast of central America and includes numerous cays and a large barrier reef offshore. The coastal areas are flat and swampy. To the southwest are the Maya Mountains. Tropical jungle covers much of the country and the climate is humid tropical, but tempered by sea breezes. A third of the population lives in the capital. The economy is based primarily on agriculture, forestry and fishing, and exports include raw sugar, orange concentrate and bananas.

Xunantunich, Belize

Benin Republic of Benin

Area Sq Km **112 620**
Area Sq Miles **43 483**

Population **8 935 000**
Capital **Porto-Novo**

Currency **CFA franc**
Languages **French, Fon, Yoruba, Adja, local languages**

Religions **Traditional beliefs, Roman Catholic, Sunni Muslim**
Organizations **UN**

Population

Total population **8 935 000**
Population change **3.2%**
Urban population **41.2%**
Total fertility rate **5.5 births per woman**
Population aged 0–14 **43.2%**
Population aged over 65 **3.2%**
2050 projected population **22 123 000**

Communications

Main telephone lines
0.9 per 100 people
Cellular mobile subscribers
12.1 per 100 people
Internet users
144 per 10 000 people
International dialling code **229**
Time zone **+1**

Environment

Forest area **21.3%**
Annual change in forest area **-2.5%**
Protected land area **23.6%**
CO_2 emissions **0.3 metric tons per capita**

Economy

Total Gross National Income (GNI) **4 665 US$M**
GNI per capita **690 US$**
Debt service ratio **1.8% of GNI**
Total debt service **82 763 000 US$**
Aid receipts **8.0% of GNI**
Military spending **N/A**

Social Indicators

Infant mortality rate
78 per 1 000 live births
Life expectancy **61.6**
Literacy rate **40.5%**
Access to safe water **67%**
Doctors **0.04 per 1 000 people**

Benin is in west Africa, on the Gulf of Guinea. The climate is tropical in the north, equatorial in the south. The economy is based mainly on agricultur and transit trade. Agricultural products account for two-thirds of export earnings. Oil, produced offshore, is als a major export.

Ganvié, Benin

Area Sq Km **54**
Area Sq Miles **21**

Currency **Bermuda dollar**
Languages **English**

Population **65 000**
Capital **Hamilton**

Religions **Protestant,
Roman Catholic**

the Atlantic Ocean to the
st of the USA, Bermuda
mprises a group of small
ands with a warm and humid

climate. The economy is based
on international business and
tourism.

Hamilton, Bermuda

Bhutan Kingdom of Bhutan

Area Sq Km **46 620**
Area Sq Miles **18 000**

Population **697 000**
Capital **Thimphu**

Currency **Ngultrum,
Indian rupee**
Languages **Dzongkha, Nepali,
Assamese**

Religions **Buddhist, Hindu**
Organizations **UN**

Bhutan lies in the eastern Himalaya mountains, between China and India. It is mountainous in the north, with fertile valleys. The climate ranges between permanently cold in the far north and subtropical in the south. Most of the population is involved in livestock rearing and subsistence farming. Bhutan is the world's largest producer of cardamom. Tourism is an increasingly important foreign currency earner.

Total population **697 000**
Population change **1.6%**
Urban population **34.5%**
Total fertility rate **2.7 births per woman**
Population aged 0–14 **31.3%**
Population aged over 65 **4.7%**
2050 projected population **4 393 000**

Environment

Forest area **68.0%**
Annual change in forest area **0.3%**
Protected land area **26.4%**
CO2 emissions **0.6 metric tons per capita**

Total Gross National Income (GNI) **928 US$M**
GNI per capita **1 900 US$**
Debt service ratio **1.1% of GNI**
Total debt service **10 105 000 US$**
Aid receipts **10.2% of GNI**
Military spending **N/A**

Communications

Main telephone lines **3.8 per 100 people**
Cellular mobile subscribers **9.8 per 100 people**
Internet users **357 per 10 000 people**
International dialling code **975**
Time zone **+6**

Social Indicators

Infant mortality rate **56 per 1 000 live births**
Life expectancy **66.2**
Literacy rate **52.8**
Access to safe water **62%**
Doctors **0.02 per 1 000 people**

Bolivia Republic of Bolivia

Area Sq Km **1 098 581**
Area Sq Miles **424 164**

Population **9 863 000**
Capital **La Paz/Sucre**

Currency **Boliviano**
Languages **Spanish, Quechua, Aymara**

Religions **Roman Catholic, Protestant, Baha'i**
Organizations **UN**

Population

Total population **9 863 000**
Population change **1.7%**
Urban population **65.6%**
Total fertility rate **3.5 births per woman**
Population aged 0–14 **36.7%**
Population aged over 65 **4.7%**
2050 projected population **14 908 000**

Communications

Main telephone lines **7.1 per 100 people**
Cellular mobile subscribers **30.8 per 100 people**
Internet users **620 per 10 000 people**
International dialling code **591**
Time zone **-4**

Economy

Total Gross National Income (GNI) **10 293 US$M**
GNI per capita **1 460 US$**
Debt service ratio **4.0% of GNI**
Total debt service **430 341 000 US$**
Aid receipts **5.4% of GNI**
Military spending **1.5% of GDP**

Environment

Forest area **54.2%**
Annual change in forest area **-0.5%**
Protected land area **20.2%**
CO2 emissions **1.0 metric tons per capita**

Social Indicators

Infant mortality rate **48 per 1 000 live births**
Life expectancy **65.5**
Literacy rate **90.7%**
Access to safe water **85%**
Doctors **1.22 per 1 000 people**

Bolivia is a landlocked state in central South America. Most Bolivians live on the high plateau within the Andes mountains. The lowlands range between dense rainforest in the northeast and semi-arid grasslands in the southeast. Bolivia is rich in minerals (zinc, tin and gold), and sales generate approximately half of export income. Natural gas, timber and soya beans are also exported. The USA is the main trading partner.

Alpacas, Sajama National Park, Bolivia

Area Sq Km **288**
Area Sq Miles **111**

Population **12 103**
Capital **Kralendijk**

n island in the Caribbean
ea off the north coast of
enezuela, known for its
ne beaches; tourism is the
ainstay of the economy.

Designated a Netherlands
Special Municipality after the
dissolution of the Netherlands
Antilles in October 2010, of
which it was formerly a part.

Coral reef, Bonaire

Bosnia-Herzegovina Republic of Bosnia and Herzegovina

Area Sq Km **51 130**
Area Sq Miles **19 741**

Population **3 767 000**
Capital **Sarajevo**

Currency **Marka**
Languages **Bosnian, Serbian,
Croatian**

Religions **Sunni Muslim,
Orthodox, Roman
Catholic, Protestant**
Organizations **UN**

Population

Total population **3 767 000**
Population change **-0.1%**
Urban population **47.4%**
Total fertility rate **1.2 births per woman**
Population aged 0–14 **15.7%**
Population aged over 65 **13.8%**
2050 projected population **3 170 000**

Communications

Main telephone lines
25.3 per 100 people
Cellular mobile subscribers
48.3 per 100 people
Internet users
2 428 per 10 000 people
International dialling code **387**
Time zone **+1**

Bosnia-Herzegovina lies in the western
Balkan Mountains of southern Europe,
on the Adriatic Sea. It is mountainous,
with ridges running northwest–
southeast. The main lowlands are
around the Sava valley in the north.
Summers are warm, but winters can be
very cold. The economy relies heavily on
overseas aid.

Economy

Total Gross National
Income (GNI) **12 689 US$M**
GNI per capita **4 510 US$**
Debt service ratio **4.6% of GNI**
Total debt service **589 095 000 US$**
Aid receipts **4.2% of GNI**
Military spending **1.6% of GDP**

Environment

Forest area **42.7%**
Annual change in
forest area **0.0%**
Protected land area **0.5%**
CO2 emissions **6.9 metric
tons per capita**

Social Indicators

Infant mortality rate
13 per 1 000 live births
Life expectancy **75.2**
Literacy rate **N/A**
Access to safe water **97%**
Doctors **1.42 per 1 000 people**

Botswana Republic of Botswana

Area Sq Km **581 370**
Area Sq Miles **224 468**

Population **1 950 000**
Capital **Gaborone**

Currency **Pula**
Languages **English, Setswana, Shona, local languages**

Religions **Traditional beliefs, Protestant, Roman Catholic**
Organizations **Comm., SADC, UN**

Population

Total population **1 950 000**
Population change **1.2%**
urban **59.6%**
Total fertility rate **2.9 births per woman**
Population aged 0–14 **33.7%**
Population aged over 65 **3.7%**
2050 projected population **1 658 000**

Communications

Main telephone lines **7.8 per 100 people**
Cellular mobile subscribers **46.8 per 100 people**
Internet users **455 per 10 000 people**
International dialling code **267**
Time zone **+2**

Environment

Forest area **21.1%**
Annual change in forest area **-1.0%**
Protected land area **30.8%**
CO_2 emissions **2.5 metric tons per capita**

Economy

Total Gross National Income (GNI) **10 358 US$M**
GNI per capita **6 470 US$**
Debt service ratio **0.6% of GNI**
Total debt service **54 861 000 US$**
Aid receipts **0.7% of GNI**
Military spending **3.0% of GDP**

Social Indicators

Infant mortality rate **33 per 1 000 live births**
Life expectancy **50.6**
Literacy rate **82.9%**
Access to safe water **95%**
Doctors **0.4 per 1 000 people**

Botswana is a landlocked state in southern Africa. Over half of the country lies within the Kalahari Desert, with swamps to the north and salt-pans to the northeast. Most of the population lives near the eastern border. The climate is subtropical, but drought-prone. The economy was founded on cattle rearing, and although beef remains an important export, the economy is now based on mining. Diamonds account for seventy per cent of export earnings. Copper-nickel matte is also exported. Most trade is with members of the South African Customs Union.

Okavango Delta, Botswana

Area Sq Km **8 514 879**
Area Sq Miles **3 287 613**

Population **193 734 000**
Capital **Brasília**

Currency **Real**
Languages **Portuguese**

Religions **Roman Catholic, Protestant**
Organizations **UN**

Population

Total population **193 734 000**
Population change **1.0%**
urban **85.6%**
Total fertility rate **1.9 births per woman**
Population aged 0–14 **26.4%**
Population aged over 65 **6.6%**
2050 projected population **253 105 000**

Communications

Main telephone lines **20.5 per 100 people**
Cellular mobile subscribers **52.9 per 100 people**
Internet users **2 255 per 10 000 people**
International dialling code **55**
Time zone **-2 to -5**

Environment

Forest area **56.5%**
Annual change in forest area **-0.6%**
Protected land area **17.9%**
CO2 emissions **1.7 metric tons per capita**

Economy

Total Gross National Income (GNI) **892 639 US$M**
GNI per capita **7 350 US$**
Debt service ratio **6.0% of GNI**
Total debt service **62 144 534 000 US$**
Aid receipts **0.0% of GNI**
Military spending **1.5% of GDP**

Social Indicators

Infant mortality rate **20 per 1 000 live births**
Life expectancy **72.5**
Literacy rate **90.0%**
Access to safe water **90%**
Doctors **1.15 per 1 000 people**

Brazil, in eastern South America, covers almost half of the continent, and is the world's fifth largest country. The northwest contains the vast basin of the Amazon, while the centre-west is largely a vast plateau of savanna and rock escarpments. The northeast is mostly semi-arid plateaus, while to the east and south are rugged mountains, fertile valleys and narrow, fertile coastal plains. The Amazon basin is hot, humid and wet; the rest of the country is cooler and drier, with seasonal variations. The northeast is drought-prone. Most Brazilians live in urban areas along the coast and on the central plateau. Brazil has well-developed agricultural, mining and service sectors, and the economy is larger than that of all other South American countries combined. Brazil is the world's biggest producer of coffee, and other agricultural crops include grains and sugar cane. Mineral production includes iron, aluminium and gold. Manufactured goods include food products, transport equipment, machinery and industrial chemicals. The main trading partners are the USA and Argentina. Despite its natural wealth, Brazil has a large external debt and a growing poverty gap.

Christ the Redeemer, Rio de Janeiro, Brazil

British Indian Ocean Territory United Kingdom Overseas Territory

Area Sq Km **60**
Area Sq Miles **23**

Population **uninhabited**

The territory consists of the Chagos Archipelago in the central Indian Ocean. The islands are uninhabited apart from the joint British-US military base on Diego Garcia.

Coconut plantaion, Diego Garcia, British Indian Ocean Territory

 Brunei Brunei Darussalam

Area Sq Km **5 765**
Area Sq Miles **2 226**

Population **400 000**
Capital **Bandar Seri Begawan**

Currency **Brunei dollar**
Languages **Malay, English, Chinese**

Religions **Sunni Muslim, Buddhist, Christian**
Organizations **APEC, ASEAN, Comm., UN**

Population

Total population **400 000**
Population change **1.9%**
Urban population **74.8%**
Total fertility rate **2.3 births per woman**
Population aged 0–14 **27.3%**
Population aged over 65 **3.3%**
2050 projected population **681 000**

Environment

Forest area **52.8%**
Annual change in forest area **-0.7%**
Protected land area **61.5%**
CO_2 emissions **15.8 metric tons per capita**

Communications

Main telephone lines
21.0 per 100 people
Cellular mobile subscribers
78.9 per 100 people
Internet users
4 169 per 10 000 people
International dialling code **673**
Time zone **+8**

Economy

Total Gross National Income (GNI) **10 287 US$M**
GNI per capita **26 740 US$**
Debt service ratio **N/A**
Total debt service **N/A**
Aid receipts **N/A**
Military spending **2.4% of GDP**

Social Indicators

Infant mortality rate
8 per 1 000 live births
Life expectancy **77.3**
Literacy rate **94.9%**
Access to safe water **N/A**
Doctors **1.14 per 1 000 people**

The southeast Asian oil-rich state of Brunei lies on the northwest coast of the island of Borneo, on the South China Sea. Its two enclaves are surrounded by the Malaysian state of Sarawak. Tropical rainforest covers over two-thirds of the country. The economy is dominated by the oil and gas industries.

Area Sq Km **110 994**
Area Sq Miles **42 855**

Population **7 545 000**
Capital **Sofia (Sofiya)**

Currency **Lev**
Languages **Bulgarian, Turkish, Romany, Macedonian**

Religions **Bulgarian Orthodox, Sunni Muslim**
Organizations **EU, NATO, UN**

Population

Total population **7 545 000**
Population change **-0.5%**
Urban population **71.1%**
Total fertility rate **1.4 births per woman**
Population aged 0–14 **13.4%**
Population aged over 65 **17.3%**
2050 projected population **5 065 000**

Communications

Main telephone lines
31.3 per 100 people
Cellular mobile subscribers
107.6 per 100 people
Internet users
2 166 per 10 000 people
International dialling code **359**
Time zone **+2**

Economy

Total Gross National Income (GNI) **30 669 US$M**
GNI per capita **5 490 US$**
Debt service ratio **8.7% of GNI**
Total debt service **2 743 215 000 US$**
Aid receipts **N/A**
Military spending **2.3% of GDP**

Environment

Forest area **33.4%**
Annual change in forest area **1.4%**
Protected land area **10.1%**
CO_2 emissions **5.7 metric tons per capita**

Social Indicators

Infant mortality rate
10 per 1 000 live births
Life expectancy **72.7**
Literacy rate **98.3%**
Access to safe water **99%**
Doctors **3.66 per 1 000 people**

Bulgaria, in southern Europe, borders the western shore of the Black Sea. The Balkan Mountains separate the Danube plains in the north from the Rhodope Mountains and the lowlands in the south. The economy has a strong agricultural base. Manufacturing industries include machinery, consumer goods, chemicals and metals. Most trade is with the Russian Federation, Italy and Germany.

Alexander Nevski Church, Sofia, Bulgaria

Burkina Faso Democratic Republic of Burkina Faso

Area Sq Km **274 200**
Area Sq Miles **105 869**

Population **15 757 000**
Capital **Ouagadougou**

Currency **CFA franc**
Languages **French, Moore (Mossi), Fulani, local languages**

Religions **Sunni Muslim, traditional beliefs, Roman Catholic**
Organizations **UN**

Population

Total population **15 757 000**
Population change **2.9%**
Urban population **19.6%**
Total fertility rate **6.0 births per woman**
Population aged 0–14 **46.2%**
Population aged over 65 **2.0%**
2050 projected population **39 093 000**

Communications

Main telephone lines **0.7 per 100 people**
Cellular mobile subscribers **7.5 per 100 people**
Internet users **59 per 10 000 people**
International dialling code **226**
Time zone **GMT**

Environment

Forest area **24.8%**
Annual change in forest area **-0.3%**
Protected land area **14.0%**
CO_2 emissions **0.1 metric tons per capita**

Economy

Total Gross National Income (GNI) **6 249 US$M**
GNI per capita **480 US$**
Debt service ratio **0.8% of GNI**
Total debt service **51 765 000 US$**
Aid receipts **14.0% of GNI**
Military spending **1.4% of GDP**

Social Indicators

Infant mortality rate **104 per 1 000 live births**
Life expectancy **52.2**
Literacy rate **28.7%**
Access to safe water **61%**
Doctors **0.05 per 1 000 people**

Burkina Faso, a landlocked country in west Africa, lies within the Sahara desert to the north and semi-arid savanna to the south. Rainfall is erratic, and droughts are common. Livestock rearing and farming are the main activities, and cotton, livestock, groundnuts and some minerals are exported. Burkina Faso relies heavily on foreign aid, and is one of the poorest and least developed countries in the world.

Banfora waterfalls, Burkina Faso

Area Sq Km **27 835**
Area Sq Miles **10 747**

Population **8 303 000**
Capital **Bujumbura**

Currency **Burundian franc**
Languages **Kirundi (Hutu, Tutsi), French**

Religions **Roman Catholic, traditional beliefs, Protestant**
Organizations **UN**

Population

Total population **8 303 000**
Population change **3.0%**
Urban population **10.4%**
Total fertility rate **4.7 births per woman**
Population aged 0–14 **39.0%**
Population aged over 65 **2.8%**
2050 projected population **25 812 000**

Communications

Main telephone lines **0.4 per 100 people**
Cellular mobile subscribers **2.0 per 100 people**
Internet users **77 per 10 000 people**
International dialling code **257**
Time zone **+2**

Environment

Forest area **5.9%**
Annual change in forest area **-5.2%**
Protected land area **6.0%**
CO_2 emissions **0.0 metric tons per capita**

Economy

Total Gross National Income (GNI) **815 US$M**
GNI per capita **140 US$**
Debt service ratio **4.5% of GNI**
Total debt service **39 523 000 US$**
Aid receipts **52.8% of GNI**
Military spending **5.5% of GDP**

Social Indicators

Infant mortality rate **108 per 1 000 live births**
Life expectancy **50.6**
Literacy rate **N/A**
Access to safe water **79%**
Doctors **0.03 per 1 000 people**

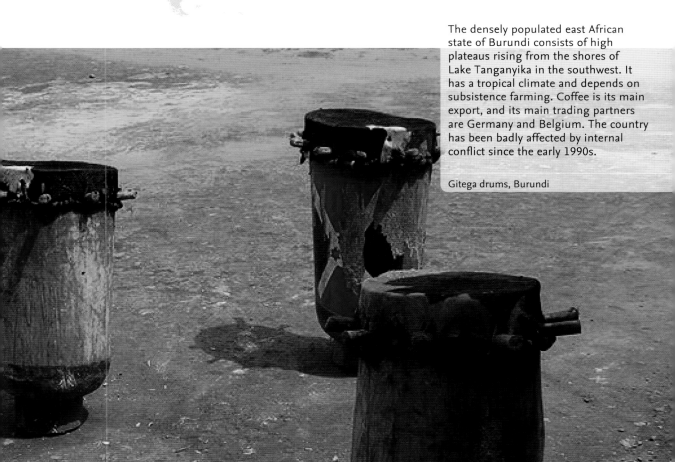

The densely populated east African state of Burundi consists of high plateaus rising from the shores of Lake Tanganyika in the southwest. It has a tropical climate and depends on subsistence farming. Coffee is its main export, and its main trading partners are Germany and Belgium. The country has been badly affected by internal conflict since the early 1990s.

Gitega drums, Burundi

Area Sq Km **181 035**
Area Sq Miles **69 884**

Population **14 805 000**
Capital **Phnom Penh**

Currency **Riel**
Languages **Khmer, Vietnamese**

Religions **Buddhist, Roman Catholic, Sunni Muslim**
Organizations **ASEAN, UN**

Population

Total population **14 805 000**
Population change **1.7%**
Urban population **21.6%**
Total fertility rate **3.2 births per woman**
Population aged 0–14 **34.1%**
Population aged over 65 **3.4%**
2050 projected population **25 972 000**

Communications

Main telephone lines
0.2 per 100 people
Cellular mobile subscribers
7.9 per 100 people
Internet users
31 per 10 000 people
International dialling code **855**
Time zone **+7**

Social Indicators

Infant mortality rate
70 per 1 000 live births
Life expectancy **59.5**
Literacy rate **76.3%**
Access to safe water **41%**
Doctors **0.16 per 1 000 people**

Economy

Total Gross National
Income (GNI) **6 990 US$M**
GNI per capita **600 US$**
Debt service ratio **0.4% of GNI**
Total debt service **30 584 000 US$**
Aid receipts **7.7% of GNI**
Military spending **1.7% of GDP**

Environment

Forest area **59.2%**
Annual change in
forest area **-2.0%**
Protected land area **23.5%**
CO_2 emissions **0.0 metric tons per capita**

Angkor Wat, Cambodia

Cambodia lies in southeast Asia on the Gulf of Thailand, and occupies the Mekong river basin, with the Tônlé Sap (Great Lake) at its centre. The climate is tropical monsoon. Forests cover half the country. Most of the population lives on the plains and is engaged in farming (chiefly rice growing), fishing and forestry. The economy is recovering slowly following the devastation of civil war in the 1970s.

Area Sq Km **475 442**
Area Sq Miles **183 569**

Population **19 522 000**
Capital **Yaoundé**

Currency **CFA franc**
Languages **French, English, Fang, Bamileke, local languages**

Religions **Roman Catholic, traditional beliefs, Sunni Muslim, Protestant**
Organizations **Comm., UN**

Population

Total population **19 522 000**
Population change **2.0%**
Urban population **56.8%**
Total fertility rate **4.3 births per woman**
Population aged 0–14 **41.1%**
Population aged over 65 **3.6%**
2050 projected population **26 891 000**

Communications

Main telephone lines **0.8 per 100 people**
Cellular mobile subscribers **18.9 per 100 people**
Internet users **223 per 10 000 people**
International dialling code **237**
Time zone **+1**

Environment

Forest area **45.6%**
Annual change in forest area **-1.0%**
Protected land area **8.6%**
CO_2 emissions **0.2 metric tons per capita**

Economy

Total Gross National Income (GNI) **18 060 US$M**
GNI per capita **1 150 US$**
Debt service ratio **2.9% of GNI**
Total debt service **518 897 000 US$**
Aid receipts **9.3% of GNI**
Military spending **1.4% of GDP**

Social Indicators

Infant mortality rate **87 per 1 000 live births**
Life expectancy **50.4**
Literacy rate **N/A**
Access to safe water **66%**
Doctors **0.19 per 1 000 people**

Cameroon is in west Africa, on the Gulf of Guinea. The coastal plains and southern and central plateaus are covered with tropical forest. Despite oil resources and favourable agricultural conditions Cameroon still faces problems of underdevelopment. Oil, timber and cocoa are the main exports. France is the main trading partner.

Musgum house, Cameroon

Area Sq Km **9 984 670**
Area Sq Miles **3 855 103**

Population **33 573 000**
Capital **Ottawa**

Currency **Canadian dollar**
Languages **English, French, local languages**

Religions **Roman Catholic, Protestant, Orthodox, Jewish**
Organizations **APEC, Comm., NATO, OECD, UN**

Population

Total population **33 573 000**
Population change **1.0%**
Urban population **80.4%**
Total fertility rate **1.6 births per woman**
Population aged 0–14 **16.8%**
Population aged over 65 **13.6%**
2050 projected population **42 844 000**

Communications

Main telephone lines **64.5 per 100 people**
Cellular mobile subscribers **57.6 per 100 people**
Internet users **6 789 per 10 000 people**
International dialling code **1**
Time zone **-3.5 to -8**

Economy

Total Gross National Income (GNI) **1 196 626 US$M**
GNI per capita **41 730 US$**
Debt service ratio **N/A**
Total debt service **N/A**
Aid receipts **N/A**
Military spending **1.2% of GDP**

Environment

Forest area **34.1%**
Annual change in forest area **0.0%**
Protected land area **5.2%**
CO_2 emissions **16.6 metric tons per capita**

Social Indicators

Infant mortality rate **5 per 1 000 live births**
Life expectancy **80.6**
Literacy rate **N/A**
Access to safe water **100%**
Doctors **1.91 per 1 000 people**

The world's second largest country, Canada covers the northern two-fifths of North America and has coastlines on the Atlantic, Arctic and Pacific Oceans.

In the west are the Coast Mountains, the Rocky Mountains and interior plateaus. In the centre lie the fertile Prairies. Further east, covering about half the total land area, is the Canadian Shield, a relatively flat area of infertile lowlands around Hudson Bay, extending to Labrador on the east coast. The Shield is bordered to the south by the fertile Great Lakes-St Lawrence lowlands. In the far north climatic conditions are polar, while the rest has a continental climate. Most Canadians live in the urban areas of the Great Lakes-St Lawrence basin. Canada is rich in mineral and energy resources. Only five per cent of land is arable. Canada is among the world's leading producers of wheat, of wood from its vast coniferous forests, and of fish and seafood from its Atlantic and Pacific fishing grounds. It is a major producer of nickel, uranium, copper, iron ore, zinc and other minerals, as well as oil and natural gas. Its abundant raw materials are the basis for many manufacturing industries. Main exports are machinery, motor vehicles, oil, timber, newsprint and paper, wood pulp and wheat. Since the 1989 free trade agreement with the USA and the 1994 North America Free Trade Agreement, trade with the USA has grown and now accounts for around seventy-five per cent of imports and around eighty-five per cent of exports.

The Rockies, Canada

Area Sq Km **4 033**
Area Sq Miles **1 557**

Population **506 000**
Capital **Praia**

Currency **Cape Verde escudo**
Languages **Portuguese, creole**

Religions **Roman Catholic, Protestant**
Organizations **UN**

Infant mortality rate **24 per 1 000 live births**
Life expectancy **71.2**
Literacy rate **83.8%**
Access to safe water **80%**
Doctors **0.49 per 1 000 people**

Total population **506 000**
Population change **1.4%**
Urban population **59.6%**
Total fertility rate **2.8 births per woman**
Population aged 0–14 **36.9%**
Population aged over 65 **4.3%**
2050 projected population **1 002 000**

Main telephone lines **13.8 per 100 people**
Cellular mobile subscribers **21.0 per 100 people**
Internet users **636 per 10 000 people**
International dialling code **238**
Time zone **-1**

Total Gross National Income (GNI) **1 105 US$M**
GNI per capita **3 130 US$**
Debt service ratio **2.9% of GNI**
Total debt service **31 361 000 US$**
Aid receipts **12.6% of GNI**
Military spending **0.7% of GDP**

Forest area **20.7%**
Annual change in forest area **0.4%**
Protected land area **N/A**
CO_2 emissions **0.6 metric tons per capita**

Cape Verde is a group of semi-arid volcanic islands lying off the coast of west Africa. The economy is based on fishing and subsistence farming but relies on emigrant workers' remittances and foreign aid.

Cayman Islands United Kingdom Overseas Territory

Area Sq Km **259**
Area Sq Miles **100**

Currency **Cayman Islands dollar**
Languages **English**

Population **56 000**
Capital **George Town**

Religions **Roman Catholic, Protestant**

group of islands in the aribbean, northwest of maica. There are three main lands: Grand Cayman, Little ayman and Cayman Brac. The

Cayman Islands are one of the world's major offshore financial centres. Tourism is also important to the economy.

Shipwreck, Cayman Brac, Cayman Islands

Central African Republic

Area Sq Km **622 436**
Area Sq Miles **240 324**

Population **4 422 000**
Capital **Bangui**

Currency **CFA franc**
Languages **French, Sango, Banda, Baya, local languages**

Religions **Protestant, Roman Catholic, trad. beliefs, Muslim**
Organizations **UN**

Population

Total population **4 422 000**
Population change **1.8%**
Urban population **38.6%**
Total fertility rate **4.6 births per woman**
Population aged 0–14 **40.9%**
Population aged over 65 **3.9%**
2050 projected population **6 747 000**

Communications

Main telephone lines **0.3 per 100 people**
Cellular mobile subscribers **2.5 per 100 people**
Internet users **32 per 10 000 people**
International dialling code **236**
Time zone **+1**

Environment

Forest area **36.5%**
Annual change in forest area **-0.1%**
Protected land area **15.2%**
CO2 emissions **0.1 metric tons per capita**

Economy

Total Gross National Income (GNI) **1 499 US$M**
GNI per capita **410 US$**
Debt service ratio **4.7% of GNI**
Total debt service **70 406 000 US$**
Aid receipts **9.0% of GNI**
Military spending **1.1% of GDP**

Social Indicators

Infant mortality rate **113 per 1 000 live births**
Life expectancy **44.7**
Literacy rate **N/A**
Access to safe water **75%**
Doctors **0.08 per 1 000 people**

A landlocked country in central Africa, the Central African Republic is mainly savanna plateau, drained by the Ubangi and Chari river systems, with mountains to the east and west. The climate is tropical, with high rainfall. Most of the population lives in the south and west, and a majority of the workforce is involved in subsistence farming. Some cotton, coffee, tobacco and timber are exported, but diamonds account for around half of export earnings.

Ubangi River, Central African Republic

Area Sq Km **1 284 000**
Area Sq Miles **495 755**

Population **11 206 000**
Capital **Ndjamena**

Currency **CFA franc**
Languages **Arabic, French, Sara, local languages**

Religions **Sunni Muslim, Roman Catholic, Protestant, traditional beliefs**
Organizations **UN**

Population

Total population **11 206 000**
Population change **2.8%**
Urban population **26.7%**
Total fertility rate **6.2 births per woman**
Population aged 0–14 **45.8%**
Population aged over 65 **2.9%**
2050 projected population **31 497 000**

Communications

Main telephone lines **0.1 per 100 people**
Cellular mobile subscribers **4.7 per 100 people**
Internet users **60 per 10 000 people**
International dialling code **235**
Time zone **+1**

Environment

Forest area **9.5%**
Annual change in forest area **-0.7%**
Protected land area **9.1%**
CO_2 emissions **0.0 metric tons per capita**

Economy

Total Gross National Income (GNI) **4 708 US$M**
GNI per capita **530 US$**
Debt service ratio **1.3% of GNI**
Total debt service **67 834 000 US$**
Aid receipts **5.5% of GNI**
Military spending **0.9% of GDP**

Social Indicators

Infant mortality rate **124 per 1 000 live births**
Life expectancy **50.6**
Literacy rate **31.8%**
Access to safe water **42%**
Doctors **0.04 per 1 000 people**

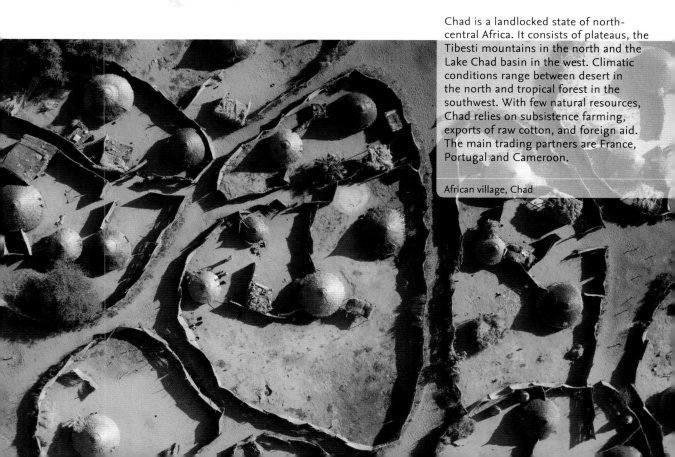

Chad is a landlocked state of north-central Africa. It consists of plateaus, the Tibesti mountains in the north and the Lake Chad basin in the west. Climatic conditions range between desert in the north and tropical forest in the southwest. With few natural resources, Chad relies on subsistence farming, exports of raw cotton, and foreign aid. The main trading partners are France, Portugal and Cameroon.

African village, Chad

Chile Republic of Chile

Area Sq Km **756 945**
Area Sq Miles **292 258**

Population **16 970 000**
Capital **Santiago**

Currency **Chilean peso**
Languages **Spanish, Amerindian languages**

Religions **Roman Catholic, Protestant**
Organizations **APEC, UN**

Population

Total population **16 970 000**
Population change **1.0%**
Urban population **88.4%**
Total fertility rate **1.9 births per woman**
Population aged 0–14 **23.2%**
Population aged over 65 **8.8%**
2050 projected population **20 657 000**

Communications

Main telephone lines
20.2 per 100 people
Cellular mobile subscribers
75.6 per 100 people
Internet users
2 524 per 10 000 people
International dialling code **56**
Time zone **+4**

Environment

Forest area **21.5%**
Annual change in forest area **0.4%**
Protected land area **3.7%**
CO2 emissions **4.1 metric tons per capita**

Economy

Total Gross National Income (GNI) **111 869 US$M**
GNI per capita **9 400 US$**
Debt service ratio **10.9% of GNI**
Total debt service **13 792 891 000 US$**
Aid receipts **0.1% of GNI**
Military spending **3.6% of GDP**

Social Indicators

Infant mortality rate
8 per 1 000 live births
Life expectancy **78.4**
Literacy rate **96.5%**
Access to safe water **95%**
Doctors **1.09 per 1 000 people**

Chile lies along the Pacific coast of the southern half of South America. Between the Andes in the east and the lower coastal ranges is a central valley, with a mild climate, where most Chileans live. To the north is the arid Atacama Desert and to the south is cold, wet forested grassland. Chile has considerable mineral resources and is the world's leading exporter of copper. Nitrates, molybdenum, gold and iron ore are also mined. Agriculture (particularly viticulture), forestry and fishing are also important to the economy.

Ahu Tongariki, Easter Island, Chile

Area Sq Km **9 620 671**
Area Sq Miles **3 714 562**

Population **1 353 265 000**
Capital **Beijing (Peking)**

Currency **Yuan, Hong Kong dollar, Macao pataca**
Languages **Mandarin, Wu, Cantonese, Hsiang, regional languages**

Religions **Confucian, Taoist, Buddhist, Christian, Muslim**
Organizations **APEC, UN**

Population

Total population **1 353 265 000**
Population change **0.6%**
Urban population **43.1%**
Total fertility rate **1.7 births per woman**
Population aged 0–14 **20.5%**
Population aged over 65 **7.9%**
2050 projected population **1 402 062 000**

Communications

Main telephone lines **27.8 per 100 people**
Cellular mobile subscribers **34.8 per 100 people**
Internet users **1 035 per 10 000 people**
International dialling code **86**
Time zone **+8**

Economy

Total Gross National Income (GNI) **2 620 951 US$M**
GNI per capita **2 940 US$**
Debt service ratio **1.0% of GNI**
Total debt service **27 876 906 000 US$**
Aid receipts **0.1% of GNI**
Military spending **1.9% of GDP**

Environment

Forest area **21.2%**
Annual change in forest area **2.2%**
Protected land area **15.4%**
CO_2 emissions **4.3 metric tons per capita**

Social Indicators

Infant mortality rate **19 per 1 000 live births**
Life expectancy **73.0**
Literacy rate **93.3%**
Access to safe water **77%**
Doctors **1.51 per 1 000 people**

China, the world's most populous and fourth largest country, occupies a large part of east Asia, borders fourteen states and has coastlines on the Yellow, East China and South China Seas. It has a huge variety of landscapes. The southwest contains the high Plateau of Tibet, flanked by the Himalaya and Kunlun Shan mountains. The north is mountainous with arid basins and extends from the Tien Shan and Altai Mountains and the vast Taklimakan Desert in the west to the plateau and Gobi Desert in the centre-east. Eastern China is predominantly lowland and is divided broadly into the basins of the Yellow River (Huang He) in the north, the Yangtze (Chang Jiang) in the centre and the Pearl River (Xi Jiang) in the southeast. Climatic conditions and vegetation are as diverse as the topography: much of the country experiences temperate conditions, while the southwest has an extreme mountain climate and the southeast enjoys a moist, warm subtropical climate. Nearly seventy per cent of China's huge population lives in rural areas, and agriculture employs around half of the working population. The main crops are rice, wheat, soya beans, peanuts, cotton, tobacco and hemp. China is rich in coal, oil and natural gas and has the world's largest potential in hydroelectric power. It is a major world producer of iron ore, molybdenum, copper, asbestos and gold. Economic reforms from the early 1980's led to an explosion in manufacturing development concentrated on the 'coastal economic open region'. The main exports are machinery, textiles, footwear, toys and sports goods. Japan and the USA are China's main trading partners.

Great Wall, China

Colombia Republic of Colombia

Area Sq Km **1 141 748**
Area Sq Miles **440 831**

Population **45 660 000**
Capital **Bogotá**

Currency **Colombian peso**
Languages **Spanish, Amerindian languages**

Religions **Roman Catholic, Protestant**
Organizations **UN**

Population

Total population **45 660 000**
Population change **1.2%**
Urban population **74.5%**
Total fertility rate **2.5 births per woman**
Population aged 0–14 **29.6%**
Population aged over 65 **5.4%**
2050 projected population **65 679 000**

Communications

Main telephone lines **17.0 per 100 people**
Cellular mobile subscribers **64.3 per 100 people**
Internet users **1 449 per 10 000 people**
International dialling code **57**
Time zone **-5**

Environment

Forest area **54.7%**
Annual change in forest area **-0.1%**
Protected land area **25.5%**
CO2 emissions **1.4 metric tons per capita**

Economy

Total Gross National Income (GNI) **141 982 US$M**
GNI per capita **4 660 US$**
Debt service ratio **7.2% of GNI**
Total debt service **10 639 506 000 US$**
Aid receipts **0.8% of GNI**
Military spending **3.5% of GDP**

Social Indicators

Infant mortality rate **17 per 1 000 live births**
Life expectancy **72.8**
Literacy rate **92.7%**
Access to safe water **93%**
Doctors **1.43 per 1 000 people**

Medellín, Colombia

Colombia, in northwest South America, has coastlines on the Pacific and the Caribbean. Most Colombians live in high valleys and plateaus within the Andes. To the southeast are grasslands and the forests of the Amazon. The climate is tropical, varying with altitude. Only five per cent of land is cultivable. Colombia is the world's second largest producer of coffee and the largest producer of emeralds. Also important are sugar, bananas, cotton and flowers for export; and coal, nickel, gold, silver and platinum. Oil and its products are the main export. The main trade partner is the USA. Internal violence - both politically motivated and drugs-related - continues to hinder development.

Area Sq Km **1 862**
Area Sq Miles **719**

Population **676 000**
Capital **Moroni**

Currency **Comoros franc**
Languages **Comorian, French, Arabic**

Religions **Sunni Muslim, Roman Catholic**
Organizations **UN**

Population

Total population **676 000**
Population change **2.4%**
Urban population **28.1%**
Total fertility rate **4.3 births per woman**
Population aged 0–14 **38.2%**
Population aged over 65 **3.1%**
2050 projected population **1 781 000**

Communications

Main telephone lines **2.3 per 100 people**
Cellular mobile subscribers **4.5 per 100 people**
Internet users **256 per 10 000 people**
International dialling code **269**
Time zone **+3**

Social Indicators

Infant mortality rate **49 per 1 000 live births**
Life expectancy **65.1**
Literacy rate **75.1%**
Access to safe water **86%**
Doctors **0.15 per 1 000 people**

Economy

Total Gross National Income (GNI) **406 US$M**
GNI per capita **750 US$**
Debt service ratio **0.9% of GNI**
Total debt service **3 616 000 US$**
Aid receipts **7.6% of GNI**
Military spending **N/A**

Environment

Forest area **3.0%**
Annual change in forest area **-7.4%**
Protected land area **N/A**
CO_2 emissions **0.1 metric tons per capita**

This state, in the Indian Ocean off the east African coast, comprises three volcanic islands of Ngazidja (Grande Comore), Nzwani (Anjouan) and Mwali (Mohéli), and some coral atolls. These tropical islands are mountainous, with poor soil and few natural resources. Subsistence farming predominates. Vanilla, cloves and ylang-ylang (an essential oil) are exported, and the economy relies heavily on workers' remittances from abroad.

Waterfall, Comoros

Congo Republic of the Congo

Area Sq Km **342 000**
Area Sq Miles **132 047**

Population **3 683 000**
Capital **Brazzaville**

Currency **CFA franc**
Languages **French, Kongo, Monokutuba, local languages**

Religions **Roman Catholic, Protestant, trad. beliefs, Sunni Muslim**
Organizations **UN**

Population
Total population **3 683 000**
Population change **1.8%**
Urban population **61.3%**
Total fertility rate **4.4 births per woman**
Population aged 0–14 **40.7%**
Population aged over 65 **3.8%**
2050 projected population **13 721 000**

Communications
Main telephone lines **0.4 per 100 people**
Cellular mobile subscribers **12.3 per 100 people**
Internet users **170 per 10 000 people**
International dialling code **242**
Time zone **+1**

Environment
Forest area **65.8%**
Annual change in forest area **-0.1%**
Protected land area **14.3%**
CO_2 emissions **0.6 metric tons per capita**

Economy
Total Gross National Income (GNI) **3 806 US$M**
GNI per capita **1 970 US$**
Debt service ratio **2.7% of GNI**
Total debt service **101 220 000 US$**
Aid receipts **N/A**
Military spending **1.1% of GDP**

Social Indicators
Infant mortality rate **79 per 1 000 live births**
Life expectancy **53.7**
Literacy rate **N/A**
Access to safe water **58%**
Doctors **0.2 per 1 000 people**

Congo, in central Africa, is mostly a forest or savanna-covered plateau drained by the Ubangi-Congo river systems. Sand dunes and lagoons line the short Atlantic coast. The climate is hot and tropical. Most Congolese live in the southern third of the country.

Half of the workforce are farmers, growing food and cash crops including sugar, coffee, cocoa and oil palms. Oil and timber are the mainstays of the economy, and oil generates over fifty per cent of export revenues.

Gorillas, Congo

Area Sq Km **2 345 410**
Area Sq Miles **905 568**

Population **66 020 000**
Capital **Kinshasa**

Currency **Congolese franc**
Languages **French, Lingala, Swahili, Kongo, local languages**

Religions **Christian, Sunni Muslim**
Organizations **SADC, UN**

Population

Total population **66 020 000**
Population change **2.9%**
Urban population **34.0%**
Total fertility rate **6.3 births per woman**
Population aged 0–14 **47.0%**
Population aged over 65 **2.6%**
2050 projected population **177 271 000**

Communications

Main telephone lines
0.0 per 100 people
Cellular mobile subscribers
7.4 per 100 people
Internet users
30 per 10 000 people
International dialling code **243**
Time zone **+1 to +2**

Environment

Forest area **58.9%**
Annual change in forest area **-0.2%**
Protected land area **8.6%**
CO_2 emissions **0.0 metric tons per capita**

Economy

Total Gross National Income (GNI) **7 742 US$M**
GNI per capita **150 US$**
Debt service ratio **3.9% of GNI**
Total debt service **319 345 000 US$**
Aid receipts **25.2% of GNI**
Military spending **0.0% of GDP**

Social Indicators

Infant mortality rate
108 per 1 000 live births
Life expectancy **46.4**
Literacy rate **N/A**
Access to safe water **46%**
Doctors **0.11 per 1 000 people**

This central African state, formerly Zaire, consists of the basin of the Congo river flanked by plateaus, with high mountain ranges to the east and a short Atlantic coastline to the west. The climate is tropical, with rainforest close to the Equator and savanna to the north and south. Fertile land allows a range of food and cash crops to be grown, chiefly coffee. The country has vast mineral resources, with copper, cobalt and diamonds being the most important.

Lake Mweru, Democratic Republic of the Congo

Cook Islands New Zealand Overseas Territory

Area Sq Km **293**
Area Sq Miles **113**

Currency **New Zealand dollar**
Languages **English, Maori**

Population **20 000**
Capital **Avarua**

Religions **Protestant,**
Roman Catholic

These consist of groups of coral atolls and volcanic islands in the southwest Pacific Ocean. The main island is Rarotonga.

Distance from foreign markets and restricted natural resources hinder development.

Shell fans, Cook Islands

 Costa Rica Republic of Costa Rica

Area Sq Km **51 100**
Area Sq Miles **19 730**

Population **4 579 000**
Capital **San José**

Currency **Costa Rican colón**
Languages **Spanish**

Religions **Roman Catholic,**
Protestant
Organizations **UN**

Social Indicators

Infant mortality rate
10 per 1 000 live births

Life expectancy
78.8

Literacy rate
95.9%

Access to safe water **97%**

Doctors **1.32 per 1 000 people**

Population

Total population **4 579 000**

Population change **1.4%**

Urban population **63.3%**

Total fertility rate **2.1 births per woman**

Population aged 0–14 **26.4%**

Population aged over 65 **6.2%**

2050 projected population **6 426 000**

Communications

Main telephone lines
30.7 per 100 people

Cellular mobile subscribers
32.8 per 100 people

Internet users
2 761 per 10 000 people

International dialling code **506**

Time zone **-6**

Economy

Total Gross National Income (GNI) **21 894 US$M**

GNI per capita **6 060 US$**

Debt service ratio **2.8% of GNI**

Total debt service **597 316 000 US$**

Aid receipts **0.1% of GNI**

Military spending **N/A**

Environment

Forest area **46.8%**

Annual change in forest area **0.1%**

Protected land area **21.8%**

CO2 emissions **1.7 metric tons per capita**

Costa Rica, in central America, has coastlines on the Caribbean Sea and Pacific Ocean. From tropical coastal plains, the land rises to mountains and a temperate central plateau, where most of the population lives. The economy depends on agriculture and tourism, with ecotourism becoming increasingly important. Main exports are textiles, coffee and bananas, and almost half of all trade is with the USA.

Area Sq Km **322 463**
Area Sq Miles **124 504**

Population **21 075 000**
Capital **Yamoussoukro**

Currency **CFA franc**
Languages **French, creole, Akan, local languages**

Religions **Sunni Muslim, Roman Catholic, traditional beliefs, Protestant**
Organizations **UN**

Population

Total population **21 075 000**
Population change **2.3%**
Urban population **48.8%**
Total fertility rate **4.6 births per woman**
Population aged 0–14 **40.9%**
Population aged over 65 **3.8%**
2050 projected population **33 959 000**

Communications

Main telephone lines
1.4 per 100 people
Cellular mobile subscribers
22.0 per 100 people
Internet users
163 per 10 000 people
International dialling code **225**
Time zone **GMT**

Environment

Forest area **32.7%**
Annual change in forest area **0.1%**
Protected land area **12.2%**
CO_2 emissions **0.5 metric tons per capita**

Economy

Total Gross National Income (GNI) **16 578 US$M**
GNI per capita **980 US$**
Debt service ratio **0.8% of GNI**
Total debt service **126 329 000 US$**
Aid receipts **1.6% of GNI**
Military spending **1.6% of GDP**

Social Indicators

Infant mortality rate
89 per 1 000 live births
Life expectancy **57.8**
Literacy rate **N/A**
Access to safe water **84%**
Doctors **0.12 per 1 000 people**

Côte d'Ivoire (Ivory Coast) is in west Africa, on the Gulf of Guinea. In the north are plateaus and savanna; in the south are low undulating plains and rainforest, with sand-bars and lagoons on the coast. Temperatures are warm, and rainfall is heavier in the south. Most of the workforce is engaged in farming. Côte d'Ivoire is a major producer of cocoa and coffee, and agricultural products (also including cotton and timber) are the main exports. Oil and gas have begun to be exploited.

Abidjan, Côte d'Ivoire

Croatia Republic of Croatia

Area Sq Km **56 538**
Area Sq Miles **21 829**

Population **4 416 000**
Capital **Zagreb**

Currency **Kuna**
Languages **Croatian, Serbian**

Religions **Roman Catholic, Serbian Orthodox, Sunni Muslim**
Organizations **NATO, UN**

Population

Total population **4 416 000**
Population change **0.0%**
Urban population **57.3%**
Total fertility rate **1.4 births per woman**
Population aged 0–14 **15.3%**
Population aged over 65 **17.2%**
2050 projected population **3 686 000**

Communications

Main telephone lines
40.1 per 100 people
Cellular mobile subscribers
96.5 per 100 people
Internet users
3 698 per 10 000 people
International dialling code **385**
Time zone **+1**

Economy

Total Gross National
Income (GNI) **41 348 US$M**
GNI per capita **13 570 US$**
Debt service ratio **18.5% of GNI**
Total debt service **7 680 306 000 US$**
Aid receipts **0.5% of GNI**
Military spending **1.6% of GDP**

Environment

Forest area **38.2%**
Annual change in
forest area **0.1%**
Protected land area **5.6%**
CO_2 emissions **5.2 metric tons per capita**

Social Indicators

Infant mortality rate
5 per 1 000 live births
Life expectancy **75.7**
Literacy rate **98.7%**
Access to safe water **100%**
Doctors **2.66 per 1 000 people**

The southern European state of Croatia has a long coastline on the Adriatic Sea, with many offshore islands. Coastal areas have a Mediterranean climate; inland is cooler and wetter. Croatia was once strong agriculturally and industrially, but conflict in the early 1990s, and associated loss of tourist revenue, caused economic problems from which recovery has been slow.

Dubrovnik, Croatia

Area Sq Km **110 860**
Area Sq Miles **42 803**

Population **11 204 000**
Capital **Havana (La Habana)**

Currency **Cuban peso**
Languages **Spanish**

Religions **Roman Catholic,**
Protestant
Organizations **UN**

Social indicators

Infant mortality rate
5 per 1 000 live births
Life expectancy
78.3
Literacy rate
99.8%
Access to safe water **91%**
Doctors **5.91 per 1 000 people**

Population

Total population **11 204 000**
Population change **-0.1%**
Urban population **75.7%**
Total fertility rate **1.5 births per woman**
Population aged 0–14 **18.1%**
Population aged over 65 **11.6%**
2050 projected population **9 749 000**

Communications

Main telephone lines
8.6 per 100 people
Cellular mobile subscribers
1.4 per 100 people
Internet users
213 per 10 000 people
International dialling code **53**
Time zone **-5**

Economy

Total Gross National
Income (GNI) **N/A**
GNI per capita **N/A**
Debt service ratio **N/A**
Total debt service **N/A**
Aid receipts **N/A**
Military spending **N/A**

Environment

Forest area **24.7%**
Annual change in
forest area **2.2%**
Protected land area **1.4%**
CO_2 emissions **2.2 metric
tons per capita**

The country comprises the island of Cuba
(the largest island in the Caribbean), and
many islets and cays. A fifth of Cubans
live in and around Havana. Cuba is slowly
recovering from the withdrawal of aid
and subsidies from the former USSR.
Sugar remains the basis of the economy,
although tourism is developing and is,
together with remittances from workers
abroad, an important source of revenue.

Curaçao Self-governing Netherlands Territory

Area Sq Km **444**
Area Sq Miles **171**

Population **140 796**
Capital **Willemstad**

n island in the Caribbean
ea off the north coast of
enezuela, it is the largest
nd most populous island of
e Netherlands Antilles. Oil
fining and tourism form the
asis of the economy.

Designated a Self-governing
Netherlands Territory after the
dissolution of the Netherlands
Antilles in October 2010, of
which it was formerly a part.

Fort Beekenburg, Caracas Bay Island, Curaçao

Area Sq Km **9 251**
Area Sq Miles **3 572**

Population **871 000**
Capital **Nicosia (Lefkosia)**

Currency **Euro**
Languages **Greek, Turkish, English**

Religions **Greek Orthodox, Sunni Muslim**
Organizations **Comm., EU, UN**

Population

Total population **871 000**
Population change **1.0%**
Urban population **69.9%**
Total fertility rate **1.5 births per woman**
Population aged 0–14 **18.2%**
Population aged over 65 **12.8%**
2050 projected population **1 174 000**

Communications

Main telephone lines **48.3 per 100 people**
Cellular mobile subscribers **102.8 per 100 people**
Internet users **4 222 per 10 000 people**
International dialling code **357**
Time zone **+2**

Economy

Total Gross National Income (GNI) **17 948 US$M**
GNI per capita **22 950 US$**
Debt service ratio **N/A**
Total debt service **N/A**
Aid receipts **N/A**
Military spending **1.4% of GDP**

Environment

Forest area **18.9%**
Annual change in forest area **0.2%**
Protected land area **9.7%**
CO_2 emissions **8.4 metric tons per capita**

Social Indicators

Infant mortality rate **3 per 1 000 live births**
Life expectancy **79.3**
Literacy rate **97.7%**
Access to safe water **100%**
Doctors **2.3 per 1 000 people**

The eastern Mediterranean island of Cyprus has hot dry summers and mild winters. The economy of the Greek south is based mainly on specialist agriculture and tourism, though shipping and offshore banking are also major sources of income. The Turkish north depends on agriculture, tourism and aid from Turkey. Cyprus joined the European Union in May 2004.

Paphos, Cyprus

Area Sq Km **78 864**
Area Sq Miles **30 450**

Population **10 369 000**
Capital **Prague (Praha)**

Currency **Koruna**
Languages **Czech, Moravian, Slovakian**

Religions **Roman Catholic, Protestant**
Organizations **EU, NATO, OECD, UN**

Population

Total population **10 369 000**
Population change **0.9%**
Urban population **73.5%**
Total fertility rate **1.4 births per woman**
Population aged 0–14 **14.1%**
Population aged over 65 **14.7%**
2050 projected population **8 452 000**

Communications

Main telephone lines **28.3 per 100 people**
Cellular mobile subscribers **116.4 per 100 people**
Internet users **3 469 per 10 000 people**
International dialling code **420**
Time zone **+1**

Economy

Total Gross National Income (GNI) **131 404 US$M**
GNI per capita **16 600 US$**
Debt service ratio **N/A**
Total debt service **N/A**
Aid receipts **N/A**
Military spending **1.7% of GDP**

Environment

Forest area **34.3%**
Annual change in forest area **0.1%**
Protected land area **16.1%**
CO_2 emissions **11.7 metric tons per capita**

Social Indicators

Infant mortality rate **3 per 1 000 live births**
Life expectancy **76.7**
Literacy rate **N/A**
Access to safe water **100%**
Doctors **3.58 per 1 000 people**

The landlocked Czech Republic in central Europe consists of rolling countryside, wooded hills and fertile valleys. The climate is continental. The country has substantial reserves of coal and lignite, timber and some minerals, chiefly iron ore. It is highly industrialized, and major manufactured goods include industrial machinery, consumer goods, cars, iron and steel, chemicals and glass. Germany is the main trading partner. The Czech Republic joined the European Union in May 2004.

Prague, Czech Republic

Denmark Kingdom of Denmark

Area Sq Km **43 075**
Area Sq Miles **16 631**

Population **5 470 000**
Capital **Copenhagen (København)**

Currency **Danish krone**
Languages **Danish**

Religions **Protestant**
Organizations **EU, NATO, OECD, UN**

Population

Total population **5 470 000**
Population change **0.7%**
Urban population **86.7%**
Total fertility rate **1.9 births per woman**
Population aged 0–14 **18.4%**
Population aged over 65 **15.9%**
2050 projected population **5 851 000**

Communications

Main telephone lines
56.9 per 100 people
Cellular mobile subscribers
107.0 per 100 people
Internet users
5 823 per 10 000 people
International dialling code **45**
Time zone **+1**

Economy

Total Gross National
Income (GNI) **283 316 US$M**
GNI per capita **59 130 US$**
Debt service ratio **N/A**
Total debt service **N/A**
Aid receipts **N/A**
Military spending **1.4% of GDP**

Environment

Forest area **11.8%**
Annual change in
forest area **0.6%**
Protected land area **5.8%**
CO2 emissions **8.5 metric tons per capita**

Social Indicators

Infant mortality rate
4 per 1 000 live births
Life expectancy **78.3**
Literacy rate **N/A**
Access to safe water **100%**
Doctors **3.59 per 1 000 people**

Copenhagen, Denmark

In northern Europe, Denmark occupies the Jutland (Jylland) peninsula and nearly five hundred islands in and between the North and Baltic Seas. The country is low-lying, with long, indented coastlines. The climate is cool and temperate, with rainfall throughout the year. A fifth of the population lives in and around the capital, Copenhagen (København), on the largest of the islands, Zealand (Sjælland). The country's main natural resource is its agricultural potential: two-thirds of the total area is fertile farmland or pasture. Agriculture is high-tech, and with forestry and fishing employs only around six per cent of the workforce. Denmark is self-sufficient in oil and natural gas, produced from fields in the North Sea. Manufacturing, largely based on imported raw materials, accounts for over half of all exports, which include machinery, food, furniture, and pharmaceuticals. The main trading partners are Germany and Sweden.

Area Sq Km **23 200**
Area Sq Miles **8 958**

Population **864 000**
Capital **Djibouti**

Currency **Djibouti franc**
Languages **Somali, Afar, French, Arabic**

Religions **Sunni Muslim, Christian**
Organizations **UN**

Population

Total population **864 000**
Population change **1.8%**
Urban population **87.3%**
Total fertility rate **3.9 births per woman**
Population aged 0–14 **36.6%**
Population aged over 65 **3.2%**
2050 projected population **1 547 000**

Communications

Main telephone lines **1.6 per 100 people**
Cellular mobile subscribers **6.4 per 100 people**
Internet users **136 per 10 000 people**
International dialling code **253**
Time zone **+3**

Social Indicators

Infant mortality rate **84 per 1 000 live births**
Life expectancy **54.8**
Literacy rate **N/A**
Access to safe water **73%**
Doctors **0.18 per 1 000 people**

Economy

Total Gross National Income (GNI) **864 US$M**
GNI per capita **1 130 US$**
Debt service ratio **2.6% of GNI**
Total debt service **22 564 000 US$**
Aid receipts **14.0% of GNI**
Military spending **N/A**

Environment

Forest area **0.2%**
Annual change in forest area **0.0%**
Protected land area **N/A**
CO_2 emissions **0.5 metric tons per capita**

Djibouti lies in northeast Africa, on the Gulf of Aden at the entrance to the Red Sea. Most of the country is semi-arid desert with high temperatures and low rainfall. More than two-thirds of the population live in the capital. There is some camel, sheep and goat herding, but with few natural resources the economy is based on services and trade. Djibouti serves as a free trade zone for northern Africa, and the capital's port is a major transhipment and refuelling destination. It is linked by rail to Addis Ababa in Ethiopia.

Dominica Commonwealth of Dominica

Area Sq Km **750**
Area Sq Miles **290**

Population **67 000**
Capital **Roseau**

Currency **East Caribbean dollar**
Languages **English, creole**

Religions **Roman Catholic, Protestant**
Organizations **CARICOM, Comm., UN**

Social Indicators

Infant mortality rate **9 per 1 000 live births**
Life expectancy **N/A**
Literacy rate **N/A**
Access to safe water **97%**
Doctors **N/A**

Population

Total population **67 000**
Population change **0.5%**
Urban population **73.9%**
Total fertility rate **N/A**
Population aged 0–14 **N/A**
Population aged over 65 **N/A**
2050 projected population **98 000**

Communications

Main telephone lines **29.4 per 100 people**
Cellular mobile subscribers **58.7 per 100 people**
Internet users **3 722 per 10 000 people**
International dialling code **1 767**
Time zone **-4**

Economy

Total Gross National Income (GNI) **300 US$M**
GNI per capita **4 770 US$**
Debt service ratio **6.9% of GNI**
Total debt service **21 255 000 US$**
Aid receipts **7.0% of GNI**
Military spending **N/A**

Environment

Forest area **61.3%**
Annual change in forest area **-0.6%**
Protected land area **26.5%**
CO_2 emissions **1.6 metric tons per capita**

Dominica is the most northerly of the Windward Islands, in the eastern Caribbean. It is very mountainous and forested, with a coastline of steep cliffs. The climate is tropical and rainfall is abundant. Approximately a quarter of Dominicans live in the capital. The economy is based on agriculture, with bananas (the major export), coconuts and citrus fruits the most important crops. Tourism is a developing industry.

Dominican Republic

Area Sq Km **48 442**
Area Sq Miles **18 704**

Population **10 090 000**
Capital **Santo Domingo**

Currency **Dominican peso**
Languages **Spanish, creole**

Religions **Roman Catholic, Protestant**
Organizations **UN**

Social Indicators

Infant mortality rate **31 per 1 000 live births**
Life expectancy **72.3**
Literacy rate **89.1%**
Access to safe water **95%**
Doctors **1.88 per 1 000 people**

Population

Total population **10 090 000**
Population change **1.1%**
Urban population **69.0%**
Total fertility rate **2.4 births per woman**
Population aged 0–14 **31.8%**
Population aged over 65 **5.9%**
2050 projected population **12 668 000**

Communications

Main telephone lines **9.9 per 100 people**
Cellular mobile subscribers **51.1 per 100 people**
Internet users **2 217 per 10 000 people**
International dialling code **1 809**
Time zone **-4**

Economy

Total Gross National Income (GNI) **27 954 US$M**
GNI per capita **4 390 US$**
Debt service ratio **4.5% of GNI**
Total debt service **1 345 913 000 US$**
Aid receipts **0.2% of GNI**
Military spending **0.5% of GDP**

Environment

Forest area **28.4%**
Annual change in forest area **0.0%**
Protected land area **24.4%**
CO_2 emissions **2.0 metric tons per capita**

The state occupies the eastern two-thirds of the Caribbean island of Hispaniola (the western third is Haiti). It has a series of mountain range fertile valleys and a large coastal plain in the eas The climate is hot tropical, with heavy rainfall. Sugar, coffee and cocoa are the main cash crops Nickel (the main export), and gold are mined, and there is some light industry. The USA is the main trading partner. Tourism is the main foreign exchange earner.

East Timor Democratic Republic of Timor-Leste

Area Sq Km **14 874**
Area Sq Miles **5 743**

Population **1 134 000**
Capital **Dili**

Currency **United States dollar**
Languages **Portuguese, Tetun, English**

Religions **Roman Catholic**
Organizations **UN**

Population

Total population **1 134 000**
Population change **3.2%**
Urban population **27.3%**
Total fertility rate **6.5 births per woman**
Population aged 0–14 **45.2%**
Population aged over 65 **2.9%**
2050 projected population **3 265 000**

Social Indicators

Infant mortality rate **77 per 1 000 live births**
Life expectancy **61.3**
Literacy rate **N/A**
Access to safe water **58%**
Doctors **N/A**

Communications

Main telephone lines **0.2 per 100 people**
Cellular mobile subscribers **4.9 per 100 people**
Internet users **12 per 10 000 people**
International dialling code **670**
Time zone **+9**

Economy

Total Gross National Income (GNI) **865 US$M**
GNI per capita **2 460 US$**
Debt service ratio **N/A**
Total debt service **N/A**
Aid receipts **24.7% of GNI**
Military spending **N/A**

Environment

Forest area **53.7%**
Annual change in forest area **-1.3%**
Protected land area **6.3%**
CO_2 emissions **0.2 metric tons per capita**

The island of Timor is part of the Indonesian archipelago, to the north of Western Australia. East Timor occupies the eastern section of the island, and a small coastal enclave (Ocussi) to the west. A referendum in 1999 ended Indonesia's occupation, after which the country was under UN transitional administration until full independence was achieved in 2002. The economy is in a poor state and East Timor is heavily dependent on foreign aid.

Area Sq Km **272 045**
Area Sq Miles **105 037**

Population **13 625 000**
Capital **Quito**

Currency **United States dollar**
Languages **Spanish, Quechua,
and other
Amerindian languages**

Religions **Roman Catholic**

Organizations **OPEC, UN**

Population

Total population **13 625 000**
Population change **1.0%**
Urban population **65.6%**
Total fertility rate **2.6 births per woman**
Population aged 0–14 **31.5%**
Population aged over 65 **6.4%**
2050 projected population **19 214 000**

Communications

Main telephone lines
13.1 per 100 people
Cellular mobile subscribers
63.2 per 100 people
Internet users
1 154 per 10 000 people
International dialling code **593**
Time zone **-5**

Social Indicators

Infant mortality rate
20 per 1 000 live births
Life expectancy **75.0**
Literacy rate **84.2%**
Access to safe water **94%**
Doctors **1.48 per 1 000 people**

Economy

Total Gross National
Income (GNI) **38 481 US$M**
GNI per capita **3 640 US$**
Debt service ratio **10.5% of GNI**
Total debt service **4 157 073 000 US$**
Aid receipts **0.5% of GNI**
Military spending **2.3% of GDP**

Environment

Forest area **39.2%**
Annual change in
forest area **-1.7%**
Protected land area **22.6%**
CO2 emissions **2.2 metric
tons per capita**

Ecuador is in northwest South America,
on the Pacific coast. It consists of a
broad coastal plain, high mountain
ranges in the Andes, and part of the
forested upper Amazon basin to the
east. The climate is tropical, moderated
by altitude. Most people live on the
coast or in the mountain valleys.
Ecuador is one of South America's main
oil producers, and mineral reserves
include gold. Most of the workforce
depends on agriculture. Petroleum,
bananas, shrimps, coffee and cocoa are
exported. The USA is the main trading
partner.

The Equator, Ecuador

52 Egypt Arab Republic of Egypt

Area Sq Km **1 000 250**
Area Sq Miles **386 199**

Population **82 999 000**
Capital **Cairo (Al Qāhirah)**

Currency **Egyptian pound**
Languages **Arabic**

Religions **Sunni Muslim, Coptic Christian**
Organizations **UN**

Population
Total population **82 999 000**
Population change **1.8%**
Urban population **42.7%**
Total fertility rate **2.9 births per woman**
Population aged 0–14 **32.5%**
Population aged over 65 **4.5%**
2050 projected population **125 916 000**

Communications
Main telephone lines **14.3 per 100 people**
Cellular mobile subscribers **23.9 per 100 people**
Internet users **795 per 10 000 people**
International dialling code **20**
Time zone **+2**

Economy
Total Gross National Income (GNI) **100 912 US$M**
GNI per capita **1 800 US$**
Debt service ratio **2.1% of GNI**
Total debt service **2 201 406 000 US$**
Aid receipts **0.8% of GNI**
Military spending **2.7% of GDP**

Environment
Forest area **0.1%**
Annual change in forest area **2.6%**
Protected land area **5.3%**
CO2 emissions **2.2 metric tons per capita**

Social Indicators
Infant mortality rate **30 per 1 000 live births**
Life expectancy **70.2**
Literacy rate **66.4%**
Access to safe water **98%**
Doctors **2.43 per 1 000 people**

The Sphinx, Cairo, Egypt

Egypt, on the eastern Mediterranean coast of north Africa, is low-lying, with areas below sea level in the Qattara depression. It is a land of desert and semi-desert, except for the Nile valley, where ninety-nine per cent of Egyptians live. The Sinai peninsula in the northeast of the country forms the only land bridge between Africa and Asia. The summers are hot, the winters mild and rainfall is negligible. Less than four per cent of land (chiefly around the Nile floodplain and delta) is cultivated. Farming employs about one-third of the workforce; cotton is the main cash crop. Egypt imports over half its food needs. There are oil and natural gas reserves, although nearly a quarter of electricity comes from hydroelectric power. Main exports are oil and oil products, cotton, textiles and clothing.

Area Sq Km **21 041**
Area Sq Miles **8 124**

Population **6 163 000**
Capital **San Salvador**

Currency **El Salvador colón,
United States dollar**
Languages **Spanish**

Religions **Roman Catholic,
Protestant**
Organizations **UN**

Population

Total population **6 163 000**
Population change **0.4%**
Urban population **60.7%**
Total fertility rate **2.3 births per woman**
Population aged 0–14 **33.0%**
Population aged over 65 **7.0%**
2050 projected population **10 823 000**

Communications

Main telephone lines
14.8 per 100 people
Cellular mobile subscribers
55.0 per 100 people
Internet users
1 000 per 10 000 people
International dialling code **503**
Time zone **-6**

Social Indicators

Infant mortality rate
21 per 1 000 live births
Life expectancy **71.4**
Literacy rate **82.0%**
Access to safe water **84%**
Doctors **1.5 per 1 000 people**

Economy

Total Gross National
Income (GNI) **18 096 US$M**
GNI per capita **3 480 US$**
Debt service ratio **6.2% of GNI**
Total debt service **1 133 017 000 US$**
Aid receipts **0.9% of GNI**
Military spending **0.6% of GDP**

Environment

Forest area **14.4%**
Annual change in
forest area **-1.7%**
Protected land area **1.0%**
CO_2 emissions **1.1 metric
tons per capita**

Located on the Pacific coast of central America, El Salvador consists of a coastal plain and volcanic mountain ranges which enclose a densely populated plateau area. The coast is hot, with heavy summer rainfall; the highlands are cooler. Coffee (the chief export), sugar and cotton are the main cash crops. The main trading partners are the USA and Guatemala.

The cathedral, San Salvador, El Salvador

Equatorial Guinea Republic of Equatorial Guinea

Area Sq Km **28 051**
Area Sq Miles **10 831**

Population **676 000**
Capital **Malabo**

Currency **CFA franc**
Languages **Spanish, French, Fang**

Religions **Roman Catholic, traditional beliefs**
Organizations **UN**

Population

Total population **676 000**
Population change **2.6%**
Urban population **39.4%**
Total fertility rate **5.4 births per woman**
Population aged 0–14 **41.2%**
Population aged over 65 **3.0%**
2050 projected population **1 146 000**

Communications

Main telephone lines
2.0 per 100 people
Cellular mobile subscribers
19.3 per 100 people
Internet users
155 per 10 000 people
International dialling code **240**
Time zone **+1**

Social Indicators

Infant mortality rate
124 per 1 000 live births
Life expectancy **50.5**
Literacy rate **N/A**
Access to safe water **43%**
Doctors **0.3 per 1 000 people**

Economy

Total Gross National
Income (GNI) **4 216 US$M**
GNI per capita **14 980 US$**
Debt service ratio **0.1% of GNI**
Total debt service **4 307 000 US$**
Aid receipts **0.5% of GNI**
Military spending **N/A**

Environment

Forest area **58.2%**
Annual change in
forest area **-0.9%**
Protected land area **16.2%**
CO2 emissions **7.1 metric tons per capita**

The state consists of Rio Muni, an enclave on the Atlantic coast of central Africa, and the islands of Bioco, Annobón and the Corisco group. Most of the population lives on the coastal plain and upland plateau of Rio Muni. The capital city, Malabo, is on the fertile volcanic island of Bioco. The climate is hot, humid and wet. Oil production started in 1992, and oil is now the main export, along with timber. The economy depends heavily on foreign aid.

Malabo, Equatorial Guinea

Area Sq Km **117 400**
Area Sq Miles **45 328**

Population **5 073 000**
Capital **Asmara**

Currency **Nakfa**
Languages **Tigrinya, Tigre**

Religions **Sunni Muslim,**
Coptic Christian
Organizations **UN**

Population

Total population **5 073 000**
Population change **3.1%**
Urban population **20.7%**
Total fertility rate **5.0 births per woman**
Population aged 0–14 **41.5%**
Population aged over 65 **2.4%**
2050 projected population **11 229 000**

Communications

Main telephone lines
0.8 per 100 people
Cellular mobile subscribers
1.4 per 100 people
Internet users
219 per 10 000 people
International dialling code **291**
Time zone **+3**

Social Indicators

Infant mortality rate
46 per 1 000 live births
Life expectancy **57.9**
Literacy rate **N/A**
Access to safe water **60%**
Doctors **0.05 per 1 000 people**

Economy

Total Gross National
Income (GNI) **888 US$M**
GNI per capita **300 US$**
Debt service ratio **1.2% of GNI**
Total debt service **12 682 000 US$**
Aid receipts **12.0% of GNI**
Military spending **24.1% of GDP**

Environment

Forest area **15.4%**
Annual change in
forest area **-0.3%**
Protected land area **5.0%**
CO_2 emissions **0.2 metric**
tons per capita

Eritrea, on the Red Sea coast of
northeast Africa, consists of a high
plateau in the north with a coastal
plain which widens to the south. The
coast is hot; inland is cooler. Rainfall
is unreliable. The agriculture-based
economy has suffered from over thirty
years of war and occasional poor rains.
Eritrea is one of the least developed
countries in the world.

Asmara, Eritrea

Estonia Republic of Estonia

Area Sq Km **45 200**
Area Sq Miles **17 452**

Population **1 340 000**
Capital **Tallinn**

Currency **Kroon**
Languages **Estonian, Russian**

Religions **Protestant, Estonian and Russian Orthodox**
Organizations **EU, NATO, UN**

Population
Total population **1 340 000**
Population change **-0.1%**
Urban population **69.5%**
Total fertility rate **1.6 births per woman**
Population aged 0–14 **15.0%**
Population aged over 65 **17.0%**
2050 projected population **1 119 000**

Communications
Main telephone lines **34.1 per 100 people**
Cellular mobile subscribers **125.2 per 100 people**
Internet users **5 736 per 10 000 people**
International dialling code **372**
Time zone **+2**

Economy
Total Gross National Income (GNI) **15 302 US$M**
GNI per capita **14 270 US$**
Debt service ratio **N/A**
Total debt service **N/A**
Aid receipts **N/A**
Military spending **1.4% of GDP**

Environment
Forest area **53.9%**
Annual change in forest area **0.4%**
Protected land area **47.1%**
CO2 emissions **13.5 metric tons per capita**

Social Indicators
Infant mortality rate **4 per 1 000 live births**
Life expectancy **72.9**
Literacy rate **99.8%**
Access to safe water **100%**
Doctors **3.33 per 1 000 people**

Keila-Joa waterfall, Estonia

Estonia is in northern Europe, on the Gulf of Finland and the Baltic Sea. The land, over one-third of which is forested, is generally low-lying with many lakes. Approximately one-third of Estonians live in the capital, Tallinn. Exported goods include machinery, wood products, textiles and food products. The main trading partners are the Russian Federation, Finland and Sweden. Estonia joined the European Union in May 2004.

Area Sq Km **1 133 880**
Area Sq Miles **437 794**

Population **82 825 000**
Capital **Addis Ababa (Ādīs Ābeba)**

Currency **Birr**
Languages **Oromo, Amharic, Tigrinya, local languages**

Religions **Ethiopian Orthodox, Sunni Muslim, trad. beliefs**
Organizations **UN**

Population

Total population **82 825 000**
Population change **2.6%**
Urban population **17.0%**
Total fertility rate **5.4 births per woman**
Population aged 0–14 **43.9%**
Population aged over 65 **3.1%**
2050 projected population **170 190 000**

Communications

Main telephone lines **0.9 per 100 people**
Cellular mobile subscribers **1.1 per 100 people**
Internet users **21 per 10 000 people**
International dialling code **251**
Time zone **+3**

Social Indicators

Infant mortality rate **75 per 1 000 live births**
Life expectancy **55.4**
Literacy rate **35.9%**
Access to safe water **22%**
Doctors **0.03 per 1 000 people**

Economy

Total Gross National Income (GNI) **12 874 US$M**
GNI per capita **280 US$**
Debt service ratio **1.2% of GNI**
Total debt service **163 799 000 US$**
Aid receipts **14.7% of GNI**
Military spending **2.6% of GDP**

Environment

Forest area **13.0%**
Annual change in forest area **-1.1%**
Protected land area **18.6%**
CO2 emissions **0.1 metric tons per capita**

A landlocked country in northeast Africa, Ethiopia comprises a mountainous region in the west which is traversed by the Great Rift Valley. The east is mostly arid plateau land. The highlands are warm with summer rainfall. Most people live in the central–northern area. In recent years civil war, conflict with Eritrea and poor infrastructure have hampered economic development. Subsistence farming is the main activity, although droughts have led to frequent famines. Coffee is the main export and there is some light industry. Ethiopia is one of the least developed countries in the world.

Church of St George, Lalibela, Ethiopia

Falkland Islands United Kingdom Overseas Territory

Area Sq Km **12 170**
Area Sq Miles **4 699**

Currency **Falkland Islands pound**
Languages **English**

Population **2 955**
Capital **Stanley**

Religions **Protestant,
Roman Catholic**

Lying in the southwest Atlantic Ocean, northeast of Cape Horn, two main islands, West Falkland and East Falkland and many smaller islands, form the territory of the Falkland Islands. The economy is based on sheep farming and the sale of fishing licences.

King penguins, Falkland Islands

 Fiji Republic of the Fiji Islands

Area Sq Km **18 330**
Area Sq Miles **7 077**

Population **849 000**
Capital **Suva**

Currency **Fiji dollar**
Languages **English, Fijian, Hindi**

Religions **Christian, Hindu,
Sunni Muslim**
Organizations **Comm., UN**

Population
Total population **849 000**
Population change **0.5%**
Urban population **52.4%**
Total fertility rate **2.8 births per woman**
Population aged 0–14 **31.8%**
Population aged over 65 **4.6%**
2050 projected population **934 000**

Communications
Main telephone lines
13.3 per 100 people
Cellular mobile subscribers
15.9 per 100 people
Internet users
936 per 10 000 people
International dialling code **679**
Time zone **+12**

Social Indicators
Infant mortality rate
16 per 1 000 live births
Life expectancy **68.8**
Literacy rate **N/A**
Access to safe water **47%**
Doctors **0.45 per 1 000 people**

Economy
Total Gross National
Income (GNI) **3 098 US$M**
GNI per capita **3 930 US$**
Debt service ratio **0.5% of GNI**
Total debt service **16 360 000 US$**
Aid receipts **2.0% of GNI**
Military spending **1.2% of GDP**

Environment
Forest area **54.7%**
Annual change in
forest area **0.0%**
Protected land area **0.8%**
CO_2 emissions **2.0 metric
tons per capita**

The southwest Pacific republic of Fiji comprises two mountainous and volcanic islands, Vanua Levu and Viti Levu, and over three hundred smaller islands. The climate is tropical and the economy is based on agriculture (chiefly sugar, the main export), fishing, forestry, gold mining and tourism.

Area Sq Km **338 145**
Area Sq Miles **130 559**

Population **5 326 000**
Capital **Helsinki (Helsingfors)**

Currency **Euro**
Languages **Finnish, Swedish**

Religions **Protestant,**
Greek Orthodox
Organizations **EU, OECD, UN**

Population

Total population **5 326 000**
Population change **0.5%**
Urban population **63.3%**
Total fertility rate **1.8 births per woman**
Population aged 0–14 **16.8%**
Population aged over 65 **16.5%**
2050 projected population **5 329 000**

Communications

Main telephone lines
36.3 per 100 people
Cellular mobile subscribers
107.8 per 100 people
Internet users
5 560 per 10 000 people
International dialling code **358**
Time zone **+2**

Economy

Total Gross National
Income (GNI) **217 803 US$M**
GNI per capita **48 120 US$**
Debt service ratio **N/A**
Total debt service **N/A**
Aid receipts **N/A**
Military spending **1.4% of GDP**

Environment

Forest area **73.9%**
Annual change in
forest area **N/A**
Protected land area **9.7%**
CO2 emissions **10.1 metric
tons per capita**

Social Indicators

Infant mortality rate
3 per 1 000 live births
Life expectancy **79.3**
Literacy rate **N/A**
Access to safe water **100%**
Doctors **3.3 per 1 000 people**

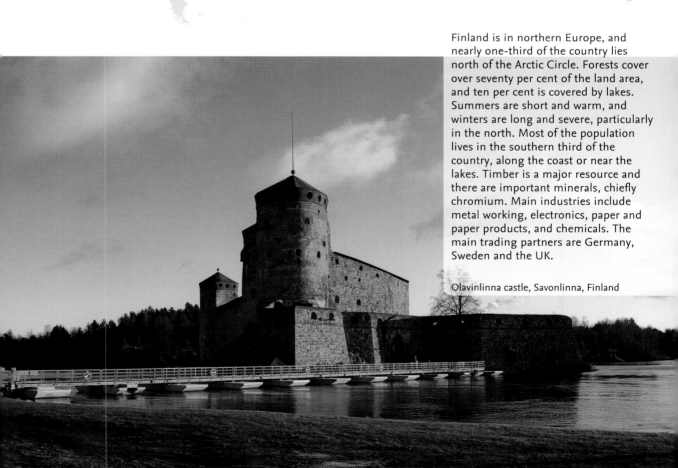

Finland is in northern Europe, and nearly one-third of the country lies north of the Arctic Circle. Forests cover over seventy per cent of the land area, and ten per cent is covered by lakes. Summers are short and warm, and winters are long and severe, particularly in the north. Most of the population lives in the southern third of the country, along the coast or near the lakes. Timber is a major resource and there are important minerals, chiefly chromium. Main industries include metal working, electronics, paper and paper products, and chemicals. The main trading partners are Germany, Sweden and the UK.

Olavinlinna castle, Savonlinna, Finland

France French Republic

Area Sq Km **543 965**
Area Sq Miles **210 026**

Population **62 343 000**
Capital **Paris**

Currency **Euro**
Languages **French, Arabic**

Religions **Roman Catholic, Protestant, Sunni Muslim**
Organizations **EU, NATO, OECD, UN**

Population

Total population **62 343 000**
Population change **0.6%**
Urban population **77.4%**
Total fertility rate **2.0 births per woman**
Population aged 0–14 **18.4%**
Population aged over 65 **16.6%**
2050 projected population **63 116 000**

Communications

Main telephone lines **55.8 per 100 people**
Cellular mobile subscribers **85.1 per 100 people**
Internet users **4 957 per 10 000 people**
International dialling code **33**
Time zone **+1**

Economy

Total Gross National Income (GNI) **2 306 714 US$M**
GNI per capita **42 250 US$**
Debt service ratio **N/A**
Total debt service **N/A**
Aid receipts **N/A**
Military spending **2.4% of GDP**

Environment

Forest area **28.3%**
Annual change in forest area **0.3%**
Protected land area **10.1%**
CO_2 emissions **6.2 metric tons per capita**

Social Indicators

Infant mortality rate **4 per 1 000 live births**
Life expectancy **81.0**
Literacy rate **N/A**
Access to safe water **100%**
Doctors **3.41 per 1 000 people**

Mont St-Michel, France

France lies in western Europe and has coastlines on the Atlantic Ocean and the Mediterranean Sea. It includes the Mediterranean island of Corsica. Northern and western regions consist mostly of flat or rolling countryside, and include the major lowlands of the Paris basin, the Loire valley and the Aquitaine basin, drained by the Seine, Loire and Garonne river systems respectively. The centre-south is dominated by the hill region of the Massif Central. To the east are the Vosges and Jura mountains and the Alps. In the southwest, the Pyrenees form a natural border with Spain. The climate is temperate with warm summers and cool winters, although the Mediterranean coast has hot, dry summers and mild winters. Over seventy per cent of the population lives in towns, with almost a sixth of the population living in the Paris area. The French economy has a substantial and varied agricultural base. It is a major producer of both fresh and processed food. There are relatively few mineral resources; it has coal reserves, and some oil and natural gas, but it relies heavily on nuclear and hydroelectric power and imported fuels. France is one of the world's major industrial countries. Main industries include food processing, iron, steel and aluminium production, chemicals, cars, electronics and oil refining. The main exports are transport equipment, plastics and chemicals. Tourism is a major source of revenue and employment. Trade is predominantly with other European Union countries.

Area Sq Km **90 000**	Currency **Euro**
Area Sq Miles **34 749**	Languages **French, creole**
Population **226 000**	Religions **Roman Catholic**
Capital **Cayenne**	

French Guiana, on the north coast of South America, is densely forested. The climate is tropical, with high rainfall. Most people live in the coastal strip, and agriculture is mostly subsistence farming. Forestry and fishing are important, but mineral resources are largely unexploited and industry is limited. French Guiana depends on French aid. The main trading partners are France and the USA.

Agouti, French Guiana

French Polynesia French Overseas Country

Area Sq Km **3 265**	Currency **CFP franc**
Area Sq Miles **1 261**	Languages **French, Tahitian, Polynesian languages**
Population **269 000**	Religions **Protestant, Roman Catholic**
Capital **Papeete**	

Extending over a vast area of the southeast Pacific Ocean, French Polynesia comprises more than one hundred and thirty islands and coral atolls. The main island groups are the Marquesas Islands, the Tuamotu Archipelago and the Society Islands. The capital, Papeete, is on Tahiti in the Society Islands. The climate is subtropical, and the economy is based on tourism. The main export is cultured pearls.

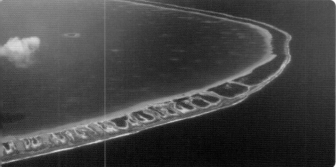

Rangiroa, French Polynesia

French Southern and Antarctic Lands French Overseas Territory

Area Sq Km **439 580**
Area Sq Miles **169 723**

Population **uninhabited**

This territory includes the Crozet Islands, Kerguelen, Amsterdam Island and St Paul Island. All are uninhabited apart from scientific research staff. In accordance with the Antarctic Treaty, French (and all other) territorial claims in Antarctica have been suspended.

Volcan du Diable, Kerguelen, French Southern and Antarctic Lands

 **Gabon** Gabonese Republic

Area Sq Km **267 667**
Area Sq Miles **103 347**

Population **1 475 000**
Capital **Libreville**

Currency **CFA franc**
Languages **French, Fang, local languages**

Religions **Roman Catholic, Protestant, traditional beliefs**
Organizations **UN**

Population

Total population **1 475 000**
Population change **1.8%**
Urban population **85.0%**
Total fertility rate **3.4 births per woman**
Population aged 0–14 **36.7%**
Population aged over 65 **4.3%**
2050 projected population **2 279 000**

Communications

Main telephone lines **2.6 per 100 people**
Cellular mobile subscribers **54.4 per 100 people**
Internet users **576 per 10 000 people**
International dialling code **241**
Time zone **+1**

Social Indicators

Infant mortality rate **60 per 1 000 live births**
Life expectancy **60.7**
Literacy rate **86.2%**
Access to safe water **88%**
Doctors **0.29 per 1 000 people**

Economy

Total Gross National Income (GNI) **7 032 US$M**
GNI per capita **7 240 US$**
Debt service ratio **1.1% of GNI**
Total debt service **84 901 000 US$**
Aid receipts **0.4% of GNI**
Military spending **1.2% of GDP**

Environment

Forest area **84.5%**
Annual change in forest area **N/A**
Protected land area **13.5%**
CO_2 emissions **1.1 metric tons per capita**

Gabon, on the Atlantic coast of central Africa, consists of low plateaus and a coastal plain lined by lagoons and mangrove swamps. The climate is tropical and rainforests cover over three-quarters of the land area. Over seventy per cent of the population lives in towns. The economy is heavily dependent on oil, which accounts for around seventy-five per cent of exports; manganese, uranium and timber are the other main exports. Agriculture is mainly at subsistence level.

Area Sq Km **11 295**
Area Sq Miles **4 361**

Population **1 705 000**
Capital **Banjul**

Currency **Dalasi**
Languages **English, Malinke, Fulani, Wolof**

Religions **Sunni Muslim, Protestant**
Organizations **Comm., UN**

Population

Total population **1 705 000**
Population change **2.7%**
Urban population **56.4%**
Total fertility rate
5.1 births per woman
Population aged 0–14 **42.5%**
Population aged over 65 **2.8%**
2050 projected population **3 106 000**

Communications

Main telephone lines
3.0 per 100 people
Cellular mobile subscribers
26.0 per 100 people
Internet users
529 per 10 000 people
International dialling code **220**
Time zone **GMT**

Social Indicators

Infant mortality rate
82 per 1 000 live births
Life expectancy **56.1**
Literacy rate **N/A**
Access to safe water **82%**
Doctors **0.11 per 1 000 people**

Economy

Total Gross National
Income (GNI) **488 US$M**
GNI per capita **390 US$**
Debt service ratio **6.6% of GNI**
Total debt service **33 137 000 US$**
Aid receipts **14.8% of GNI**
Military spending **0.5% of GDP**

Environment

Forest area **47.1%**
Annual change in
forest area **0.4%**
Protected land area **N/A**
CO_2 emissions **0.2 metric tons per capita**

The Gambia, on the coast of west Africa, occupies a strip of land along the lower Gambia river. Sandy beaches are backed by mangrove swamps, beyond which is savanna. The climate is tropical, with most rainfall in the summer. Over seventy per cent of Gambians are farmers, growing chiefly groundnuts (the main export), cotton, oil palms and food crops. Livestock rearing and fishing are important, while manufacturing is limited. Re-exports, mainly from Senegal, and tourism are major sources of income.

Gaza Semi-autonomous region

Area Sq Km **363**
Area Sq Miles **140**

Currency **Israeli shekel**
Languages **Arabic**

Population **1 486 816**
Capital **Gaza**

Religions **Sunni Muslim, Shi'a Muslim**

aza is a narrow strip of
nd on the southeast corner
f the Mediterranean Sea,
etween Egypt and Israel.
his Palestinian territory has
ternal autonomy, but Israel
xerts full control over its

border with Israel. All Israeli settlers were evacuated in 2005. Hostilities between the two parties continue to restrict its economic development.

Gaza

Georgia Republic of Georgia

Area Sq Km **69 700**
Area Sq Miles **26 911**

Population **4 260 000**
Capital **T'bilisi**

Currency **Lari**
Languages **Georgian, Russian, Armenian, Azeri, Ossetian, Abkhaz**

Religions **Georgian Orthodox, Russian Orthodox, Sunni Muslim**
Organizations **CIS, UN**

Population

Total population **4 260 000**
Population change **-0.8%**
Urban population **52.7%**
Total fertility rate **1.4 births per woman**
Population aged 0–14 **17.1%**
Population aged over 65 **14.5%**
2050 projected population **2 985 000**

Communications

Main telephone lines **12.5 per 100 people**
Cellular mobile subscribers **38.4 per 100 people**
Internet users **749 per 10 000 people**
International dialling code **995**
Time zone **+4**

Economy

Total Gross National Income (GNI) **7 008 US$M**
GNI per capita **2 470 US$**
Debt service ratio **3.6% of GNI**
Total debt service **268 375 000 US$**
Aid receipts **4.9% of GNI**
Military spending **3.1% of GDP**

Environment

Forest area **39.7%**
Annual change in forest area **N/A**
Protected land area **3.9%**
CO_2 emissions **1.1 metric tons per capita**

Social Indicators

Infant mortality rate **27 per 1 000 live births**
Life expectancy **70.8**
Literacy rate **N/A**
Access to safe water **82%**
Doctors **4.65 per 1 000 people**

Georgia is in the northwest Caucasus area of southwest Asia, on the eastern coast of the Black Sea. Mountain ranges in the north and south flank the Kura and Rioni valleys. The climate is generally mild, and along the coast it is subtropical. Agriculture is important, with tea, grapes, and citrus fruits the main crops. Mineral resources include manganese ore and oil, and the main industries are steel, oil refining and machine building. The main trading partners are the Russian Federation and Turkey.

Holy Mountain, T'bilisi, Georgia

Area Sq Km **357 022**
Area Sq Miles **137 849**

Population **82 167 000**
Capital **Berlin**

Currency **Euro**
Languages **German, Turkish**

Religions **Protestant, Roman Catholic**
Organizations **EU, NATO, OECD, UN**

Population

Total population **82 167 000**
Population change **-0.2%**
Urban population **73.6%**
Total fertility rate **1.4 births per woman**
Population aged 0–14 **13.7%**
Population aged over 65 **20.0%**
2050 projected population **78 765 000**

Communications

Main telephone lines
65.9 per 100 people
Cellular mobile subscribers
103.6 per 100 people
Internet users
4 667 per 10 000 people
International dialling code **49**
Time zone **+1**

Economy

Total Gross National
Income (GNI) **3 032 617 US$M**
GNI per capita **42 440 US$**
Debt service ratio **N/A**
Total debt service **N/A**
Aid receipts **N/A**
Military spending **1.3% of GDP**

Environment

Forest area **31.8%**
Annual change in
forest area **0.0%**
Protected land area **21.7%**
CO_2 emissions **9.5 metric tons per capita**

Social Indicators

Infant mortality rate
4 per 1 000 live births
Life expectancy **79.7**
Literacy rate **N/A**
Access to safe water **100%**
Doctors **3.44 per 1 000 people**

The central European state of Germany borders nine countries and has coastlines on the North and Baltic Seas. Behind the indented coastline, and covering about one-third of the country, is the north German plain, a region of fertile farmland and sandy heaths drained by the country's major rivers. The central highlands are a belt of forested hills and plateaus which stretch from the Eifel region in the west to the mountains of the Erzgebirge along the border with the Czech Republic. Farther south the land rises to the Swabian Alps (Schwäbische Alb), with the high rugged and forested Black Forest (Schwarzwald) in the southwest. In the far south the Bavarian Alps form the border with Austria. The climate is temperate, with continental conditions in eastern areas. The population is highly urbanized, with over eighty-five per cent living in cities and towns. With the exception of coal, lignite, potash and baryte, Germany lacks minerals and other industrial raw materials. It has a small agricultural base, although a few products (chiefly wines and beers) enjoy an international reputation. Germany is the world's third ranking economy after the USA and Japan. Its industries are amongst the world's most technologically advanced.

Exports include machinery, vehicles and chemicals. The majority of trade is with other countries in the European Union, the USA and Japan.

Neuschwanstein Castle, Germany

Ghana Republic of Ghana

Area Sq Km **238 537**
Area Sq Miles **92 100**

Population **23 837 000**
Capital **Accra**

Currency **Cedi**
Languages **English, Hausa, Akan, local languages**

Religions **Christian, Sunni Muslim, traditional beliefs**
Organizations **Comm., UN**

Population

Total population **23 837 000**
Population change **2.1%**
Urban population **50.0%**
Total fertility rate **4.3 births per woman**
Population aged 0–14 **38.7%**
Population aged over 65 **3.6%**
2050 projected population **40 573 000**

Communications

Main telephone lines **1.6 per 100 people**
Cellular mobile subscribers **23.1 per 100 people**
Internet users **270 per 10 000 people**
International dialling code **233**
Time zone **GMT**

Social Indicators

Infant mortality rate **73 per 1 000 live births**
Life expectancy **56.8**
Literacy rate **65.0%**
Access to safe water **75%**
Doctors **0.15 per 1 000 people**

Economy

Total Gross National Income (GNI) **11 778 US$M**
GNI per capita **670 US$**
Debt service ratio **2.0% of GNI**
Total debt service **261 043 000 US$**
Aid receipts **9.2% of GNI**
Military spending **0.7% of GDP**

Environment

Forest area **24.2%**
Annual change in forest area **-2.0%**
Protected land area **15.9%**
CO2 emissions **0.3 metric tons per capita**

A west African state on the Gulf of Guinea, Ghana is a land of plains and low plateaus covered with savanna and rainforest. In the east is the Volta basin and Lake Volta. The climate is tropical, with the highest rainfall in the south, where most of the population lives. Agriculture employs around sixty per cent of the workforce. Main exports are gold, timber, cocoa, bauxite and manganese ore.

Gibraltar United Kingdom Overseas Territory

Area Sq Km **7**
Area Sq Miles **3**

Currency **Gibraltar pound**
Languages **English, Spanish**

Population **31 000**
Capital **Gibraltar**

Religions **Roman Catholic, Protestant, Sunni Muslim**

Gibraltar lies on the south coast of Spain at the western entrance to the Mediterranean Sea. The economy depends on tourism, offshore banking and shipping services.

Barbary macaques, Gibraltar

Area Sq Km **131 957**
Area Sq Miles **50 949**

Population **11 161 000**
Capital **Athens (Athina)**

Currency **Euro**
Languages **Greek**

Religions **Greek Orthodox, Sunni Muslim**
Organizations **EU, NATO, OECD, UN**

Population

Total population **11 161 000**
Population change **0.4%**
Urban population **61.0%**
Total fertility rate **1.4 births per woman**
Population aged 0–14 **14.2%**
Population aged over 65 **18.2%**
2050 projected population **10 742 000**

Communications

Main telephone lines **55.4 per 100 people**
Cellular mobile subscribers **98.6 per 100 people**
Internet users **1 838 per 10 000 people**
International dialling code **30**
Time zone **+2**

Economy

Total Gross National Income (GNI) **305 308 US$M**
GNI per capita **28 650 US$**
Debt service ratio **N/A**
Total debt service **N/A**
Aid receipts **N/A**
Military spending **3.2% of GDP**

Environment

Forest area **29.1%**
Annual change in forest area **0.8%**
Protected land area **3.1%**
CO_2 emissions **8.6 metric tons per capita**

Social Indicators

Infant mortality rate **4 per 1 000 live births**
Life expectancy **79.7**
Literacy rate **97.1%**
Access to safe water **N/A**
Doctors **5 per 1 000 people**

Greece comprises a mountainous peninsula in the Balkan region of southeastern Europe and many islands in the Ionian, Aegean and Mediterranean Seas. The islands make up over one-fifth of its area. Mountains and hills cover much of the country. The main lowland areas are the plains of Thessaly in the centre and around Thessaloniki in the northeast. Summers are hot and dry while winters are mild and wet, but colder in the north with heavy snowfalls in the mountains. One-third of Greeks live in the Athens area. Employment in agriculture accounts for approximately twenty per cent of the workforce, and exports include citrus fruits, raisins, wine, olives and olive oil. Aluminium and nickel are mined and a wide range of manufactures are produced, including food products and tobacco, textiles, clothing, and chemicals. Tourism is an important industry and there is a large services sector. Most trade is with other European Union countries.

Tholos, Delphi, Greece

Greenland Self-governing Danish Territory

Area Sq Km **2 175 600**
Area Sq Miles **840 004**

Population **57 000**
Capital **Nuuk (Godthåb)**

Currency **Danish krone**
Languages **Greenlandic, Danish**

Religions **Protestant**

Social Indicators

Infant mortality rate **N/A**
Life expectancy **N/A**
Literacy rate **N/A**
Access to safe water **N/A**
Doctors **N/A**

Population

Total population **57 000**
Population change **0.0%**
Urban population **83.5%**
Total fertility rate **N/A**
Population aged 0–14 **N/A**
Population aged over 65 **N/A**
2050 projected population **N/A**

Communications

Main telephone lines **N/A**
Cellular mobile subscribers **N/A**
Internet users **N/A**
International dialling code **N/A**
Time zone **N/A**

Economy

Total Gross National Income (GNI) **N/A**
GNI per capita **N/A**
Debt service ratio **N/A**
Total debt service **N/A**
Aid receipts **N/A**
Military spending **N/A**

Environment

Forest area **0.0%**
Annual change in forest area **N/A**
Protected land area **0.0%**
CO_2 emissions **9.8 metric tons per capita**

Situated to the northeast of North America between the Atlantic and Arctic Oceans, Greenland is the largest island in the world. It has a polar climate and over eighty per cent of the land area is covered by permanent ice cap. The economy is based on fishing and fish processing.

Grenada

Area Sq Km **378**
Area Sq Miles **146**

Population **104 000**
Capital **St George's**

Currency **East Caribbean dollar**
Languages **English, creole**

Religions **Roman Catholic, Protestant**
Organizations **CARICOM, Comm., UN**

Social Indicators

Infant mortality rate **15 per 1 000 live births**
Life expectancy **68.6**
Literacy rate **N/A**
Access to safe water **95%**
Doctors **N/A**

Population

Total population **104 000**
Population change **-0.1%**
Urban population **30.8%**
Total fertility rate **2.3 births per woman**
Population aged 0–14 **28.2%**
Population aged over 65 **7.2%**
2050 projected population **157 000**

Communications

Main telephone lines **26.7 per 100 people**
Cellular mobile subscribers **44.6 per 100 people**
Internet users **1 864 per 10 000 people**
International dialling code **1 473**
Time zone **-4**

Economy

Total Gross National Income (GNI) **495 US$M**
GNI per capita **5 710 US$**
Debt service ratio **2.2% of GNI**
Total debt service **15 321 000 US$**
Aid receipts **5.6% of GNI**
Military spending **N/A**

Environment

Forest area **12.1%**
Annual change in forest area **0.0%**
Protected land area **1.8%**
CO_2 emissions **2.2 metric tons per capita**

The Caribbean state comprises Grenada, the most southerly of the Windward Islands, and the southern islands of the Grenadines. Grenada has wooded hills, with beaches in the southwest. The climate is warm and wet. Agriculture is the main activity, with bananas, nutmeg and cocoa the main exports. Tourism is the main foreign exchange earner.

Area Sq Km **1 780**
Area Sq Miles **687**

Currency **Euro**
Languages **French, creole**

Population **465 000**
Capital **Basse-Terre**

Religions **Roman Catholic**

Guadeloupe, in the Leeward islands in the Caribbean, consists of two main islands (Basse-Terre and Grande-Terre, connected by a bridge), Marie-Galante, and a few outer islands. The climate is tropical, but moderated by trade winds. Bananas, sugar and rum are the main exports and tourism is a major source of income.

Pointe de la Vigie, Guadeloupe

Guam United States Unincorporated Territory

Area Sq Km **541**
Area Sq Miles **209**

Currency **United States dollar**
Languages **Chamorro, English, Tagalog**

Population **178 000**
Capital **Hagåtña (Agana)**

Religions **Roman Catholic**

Lying at the south end of the Northern Mariana Islands in the western Pacific Ocean, Guam has a humid tropical climate. The island has a large US military base and the economy relies on that and on tourism, which has grown rapidly.

Talofofo Falls, Guam

Guatemala Republic of Guatemala

Area Sq Km **108 890**
Area Sq Miles **42 043**

Population **14 027 000**
Capital **Guatemala City**

Currency **Quetzal, United States dollar**
Languages **Spanish, Mayan languages**

Religions **Roman Catholic, Protestant**
Organizations **UN**

Social Indicators

Infant mortality rate **29 per 1 000 live births**
Life expectancy **70.2**
Literacy rate **73.2**
Access to safe water **95%**
Doctors **N/A**

Population

Total population **14 027 000**
Population change **2.4%**
Urban population **48.6%**
Total fertility rate **4.2 births per woman**
Population aged 0–14 **42.2%**
Population aged over 65 **4.4%**
2050 projected population **25 612 000**

Communications

Main telephone lines **10.5 per 100 people**
Cellular mobile subscribers **55.6 per 100 people**
Internet users **1 022 per 10 000 people**
International dialling code **502**
Time zone **-6**

Economy

Total Gross National Income (GNI) **33 725 US$M**
GNI per capita **2 680 US$**
Debt service ratio **1.6% of GNI**
Total debt service **550 958 000 US$**
Aid receipts **1.4% of GNI**
Military spending **0.4% of GDP**

Environment

Forest area **36.3%**
Annual change in forest area **-1.3%**
Protected land area **32.6%**
CO_2 emissions **0.9 metric tons per capita**

The most populous country in Central America after Mexico, Guatemala has long Pacific and short Caribbean coasts separated by a mountain chain which includes several active volcanoes. The climate is hot tropical in the lowlands and cooler in the highlands, where most of the population lives. Farming is the main activity and coffee, sugar and bananas are the main exports. There is some manufacturing of clothing and textiles. The main trading partner is the USA.

Guernsey United Kingdom Crown Dependency

Area Sq Km **78**
Area Sq Miles **30**

Currency **Pound sterling**
Languages **English, French**

Population **64 801**
Capital **St Peter Port**

Religions **Protestant, Roman Catholic**

Guernsey is one of the Channel Islands, lying off northern France. The dependency also includes the nearby islands of Alderney, Sark and Herm. Financial services are an important part of the island's economy.

Martello tower, Guernsey

Area Sq Km **245 857**
Area Sq Miles **94 926**

Population **10 069 000**
Capital **Conakry**

Currency **Guinea franc**
Languages **French, Fulani, Malinke, local languages**

Religions **Sunni Muslim, traditional beliefs, Christian**
Organizations **UN**

Social Indicators

Infant mortality rate
93 per 1 000 live births
Life expectancy **58.1**
Literacy rate **N/A**
Access to safe water **50%**
Doctors **0.11 per 1 000 people**

Population

Total population **10 069 000**
Population change **2.2%**
Urban population **34.4%**
Total fertility rate **5.5 births per woman**
Population aged 0–14 **42.9%**
Population aged over 65 **3.2%**
2050 projected population **22 987 000**

Communications

Main telephone lines
0.3 per 100 people
Cellular mobile subscribers
2.4 per 100 people
Internet users
52 per 10 000 people
International dialling code **224**
Time zone **GMT**

Economy

Total Gross National Income (GNI) **3 713 US$M**
GNI per capita **390 US$**
Debt service ratio **5.0% of GNI**
Total debt service **164 764 000 US$**
Aid receipts **5.0% of GNI**
Military spending **2.0% of GDP**

Environment

Forest area **27.4%**
Annual change in forest area **-0.5%**
Protected land area **6.1%**
CO2 emissions **0.1 metric tons per capita**

Guinea is in west Africa, on the Atlantic Ocean. There are mangrove swamps along the coast, while inland are lowlands and the Fouta Djallon mountains and plateaus. To the east are savanna plains drained by the upper Niger river system. The southeast is hilly. The climate is tropical, with high coastal rainfall. Agriculture is the main activity, employing nearly eighty per cent of the workforce, with coffee, bananas and pineapples the chief cash crops. There are huge reserves of bauxite, which accounts for more than seventy per cent of exports. Other exports include aluminium oxide, gold, coffee and diamonds.

Guinea-Bissau Republic of Guinea-Bissau

Area Sq Km **36 125**
Area Sq Miles **13 948**

Population **1 611 000**
Capital **Bissau**

Currency **CFA franc**
Languages **Portuguese, crioulo, local languages**

Religions **Traditional beliefs, Sunni Muslim, Christian**
Organizations **UN**

Social Indicators

Infant mortality rate
118 per 1 000 live births
Life expectancy **48.0**
Literacy rate **N/A**
Access to safe water **59%**
Doctors
0.12 per 1 000 people

Population

Total population **1 611 000**
Population change **2.2%**
Urban population **29.8%**
Total fertility rate **5.7 births per woman**
Population aged 0–14 **42.7%**
Population aged over 65 **3.4%**
2050 projected population **5 312 000**

Communications

Main telephone lines
0.4 per 100 people
Cellular mobile subscribers
9.2 per 100 people
Internet users
226 per 10 000 people
International dialling code **245**
Time zone **GMT**

Economy

Total Gross National Income (GNI) **307 US$M**
GNI per capita **250 US$**
Debt service ratio **11.5% of GNI**
Total debt service **33 831 000 US$**
Aid receipts **27.9% of GNI**
Military spending **4.0% of GDP**

Environment

Forest area **73.7%**
Annual change in forest area **-0.5%**
Protected land area **10.2%**
CO2 emissions **0.2 metric tons per capita**

Guinea-Bissau is on the Atlantic coast of west Africa. The mainland coast is swampy and contains many estuaries. Inland are forested plains, and to the east are savanna plateaus. The climate is tropical. The economy is based mainly on subsistence farming. There is little industry, and timber and mineral resources are largely unexploited. Cashews account for seventy per cent of exports. Guinea-Bissau is one of the least developed countries in the world.

Area Sq Km **214 969**
Area Sq Miles **83 000**

Population **762 000**
Capital **Georgetown**

Currency **Guyana dollar**
Languages **English, creole, Amerindian languages**

Religions **Protestant, Hindu, Roman Catholic, Sunni Muslim**
Organizations **CARICOM, Comm., UN**

Population

Total population **762 000**
Population change **-0.1%**
Urban population **28.4%**
Total fertility rate **2.3 births per woman**
Population aged 0–14 **30.2%**
Population aged over 65 **5.9%**
2050 projected population **488 000**

Communications

Main telephone lines
14.7 per 100 people
Cellular mobile subscribers
37.5 per 100 people
Internet users
2 130 per 10 000 people
International dialling code **592**
Time zone **-4**

Social Indicators

Infant mortality rate
45 per 1 000 live births
Life expectancy **67.3**
Literacy rate **N/A**
Access to safe water **83%**
Doctors **0.48 per 1 000 people**

Economy

Total Gross National
Income (GNI) **849 US$M**
GNI per capita **1 420 US$**
Debt service ratio **3.8% of GNI**
Total debt service **32 940 000 US$**
Aid receipts **20.1% of GNI**
Military spending **N/A**

Environment

Forest area **76.7%**
Annual change in
forest area **0.0%**
Protected land area **2.5%**
CO2 emissions **2.0 metric tons per capita**

Guyana, on the northeast coast of South America, consists of highlands in the west and savanna uplands in the southwest. Most of the country is densely forested. A lowland coastal belt supports crops and most of the population. The generally hot, humid and wet conditions are modified along the coast by sea breezes. The economy is based on agriculture, bauxite, and forestry. Sugar, bauxite, gold, rice and timber are the main exports.

Scarlet macaw, Guyana

Area Sq Km **27 750**
Area Sq Miles **10 714**

Population **10 033 000**
Capital **Port-au-Prince**

Currency **Gourde**
Languages **French, creole**

Religions **Roman Catholic, Protestant, Voodoo**
Organizations **CARICOM, UN**

Social Indicators

Infant mortality rate
57 per 1 000 live births
Life expectancy **60.9**
Literacy rate
N/A
Access to
safe water **54%**
Doctors **N/A**

Population

Total population **10 033 000**
Population change **1.7%**
Urban population **46.8%**
Total fertility rate **3.8 births per woman**
Population aged 0–14 **36.7%**
Population aged over 65 **4.3%**
2050 projected population **12 996 000**

Communications

Main telephone lines
1.7 per 100 people
Cellular mobile subscribers
13.9 per 100 people
Internet users
751 per 10 000 people
International dialling code **509**
Time zone **-5**

Economy

Total Gross National
Income (GNI) **4 044 US$M**
GNI per capita **660 US$**
Debt service ratio **1.3% of GNI**
Total debt service **56 732 000 US$**
Aid receipts **13.4% of GNI**
Military spending **N/A**

Environment

Forest area **3.8%**
Annual change in
forest area **-0.7%**
Protected land area **0.3%**
CO_2 emissions **0.2 metric tons per capita**

Haiti, occupying the western third of the Caribbean island of Hispaniola, is a mountainous state with small coastal plains and a central valley. The Dominican Republic occupies the rest of the island. The climate is tropical, and is hottest in coastal areas. Haiti has few natural resources, is densely populated and relies on exports of local crafts and coffee, and remittances from workers abroad.

Honduras Republic of Honduras

Area Sq Km **112 088**
Area Sq Miles **43 277**

Population **7 466 000**
Capital **Tegucigalpa**

Currency **Lempira**
Languages **Spanish, Amerindian languages**

Religions **Roman Catholic, Protestant**
Organizations **UN**

Social Indicators

Infant mortality rate
20 per 1 000 live births
Life expectancy **70.2**
Literacy rate
83.6%
Access to
safe water **87%**
Doctors **0.57 per 1 000 people**

Population

Total population **7 466 000**
Population change **1.9%**
Urban population **47.9%**
Total fertility rate **3.3 births per woman**
Population aged 0–14 **38.0%**
Population aged over 65 **4.2%**
2050 projected population **12 776 000**

Communications

Main telephone lines
9.7 per 100 people
Cellular mobile subscribers
30.4 per 100 people
Internet users
467 per 10 000 people
International dialling code **504**
Time zone **-6**

Economy

Total Gross National
Income (GNI) **8 844 US$M**
GNI per capita **1 800 US$**
Debt service ratio **3.6% of GNI**
Total debt service **325 235 000 US$**
Aid receipts **6.6% of GNI**
Military spending **0.6% of GDP**

Environment

Forest area **41.5%**
Annual change in
forest area **-3.1%**
Protected land area **19.6%**
CO_2 emissions **1.1 metric tons per capita**

Honduras, in central America, is a mountainous and forested country with lowland areas along its long Caribbean and short Pacific coasts. Coastal areas are hot and humid with heavy summer rainfall; inland is cooler and drier. Most of the population lives in the central valleys. Coffee and bananas are the main exports, along with shellfish and zinc. Industry involves mainly agricultural processing.

Hungary Republic of Hungary

Area Sq Km **93 030**
Area Sq Miles **35 919**

Population **9 993 000**
Capital **Budapest**

Currency **Forint**
Languages **Hungarian**

Religions **Roman Catholic, Protestant**
Organizations **EU, NATO, OECD, UN**

Population

Total population **9 993 000**
Population change **-0.2%**
Urban population **67.5%**
Total fertility rate **1.3 births per woman**
Population aged 0–14 **15.0%**
Population aged over 65 **16.1%**
2050 projected population **8 262 000**

Communications

Main telephone lines **33.4 per 100 people**
Cellular mobile subscribers **99.0 per 100 people**
Internet users **3 475 per 10 000 people**
International dialling code **36**
Time zone **+1**

Economy

Total Gross National Income (GNI) **109 461 US$M**
GNI per capita **12 810 US$**
Debt service ratio **29.4% of GNI**
Total debt service **30 827 896 000 US$**
Aid receipts **N/A**
Military spending **1.2% of GDP**

Environment

Forest area **22.1%**
Annual change in forest area **0.7%**
Protected land area **5.8%**
CO2 emissions **5.6 metric tons per capita**

Social Indicators

Infant mortality rate **6 per 1 000 live births**
Life expectancy **73.1**
Literacy rate **98.9%**
Access to safe water **99%**
Doctors **3.04 per 1 000 people**

The Danube river flows north-south through central Hungary, a landlocked country in eastern Europe. In the east lies a great plain, flanked by highlands in the north. In the west low mountains and Lake Balaton separate a smaller plain and southern uplands. The climate is continental. Sixty per cent of the population lives in urban areas, and one-fifth lives in the capital, Budapest.

Some minerals and energy resources are exploited, chiefly bauxite, coal and natural gas. Hungary has an industrial economy based on metals, machinery, transport equipment, chemicals and food products. The main trading partners are Germany and Austria. Hungary joined the European Union in May 2004.

Széchenyi Bath, Budapest, Hungary

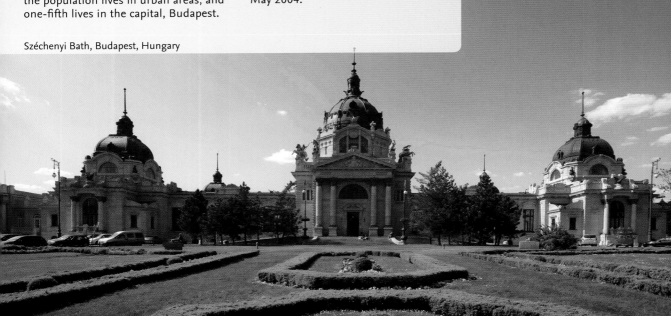

Area Sq Km **102 820**
Area Sq Miles **39 699**

Population **323 000**
Capital **Reykjavík**

Currency **Icelandic króna**
Languages **Icelandic**

Religions **Protestant**
Organizations **NATO, OECD, UN**

Population

Total population **323 000**
Population change **1.9%**
Urban population **92.3%**
Total fertility rate **2.5 births per woman**
Population aged 0–14 **20.9%**
Population aged over 65 **11.7%**
2050 projected population **370 000**

Communications

Main telephone lines
63.5 per 100 people
Cellular mobile subscribers
108.7 per 100 people
Internet users
6 530 per 10 000 people
International dialling code **354**
Time zone **GMT**

Economy

Total Gross National
Income (GNI) **15 078 US$M**
GNI per capita **40 070 US$**
Debt service ratio **N/A**
Total debt service **N/A**
Aid receipts **N/A**
Military spending **0.0% of GDP**

Environment

Forest area **0.5%**
Annual change in
forest area **3.9%**
Protected land area **3.9%**
CO_2 emissions **7.4 metric
tons per capita**

Social Indicators

Infant mortality rate
2 per 1 000 live births
Life expectancy **81.2**
Literacy rate **N/A**
Access to safe water **100%**
Doctors **3.77 per 1 000 people**

Iceland lies in the north Atlantic Ocean near the Arctic Circle, to the northwest of Scandinavia. The landscape is volcanic, with numerous hot springs, geysers, and approximately two hundred volcanoes. One-tenth of the country is covered by ice caps. Only coastal lowlands are cultivated and settled, and over half the population lives in the Reykjavik area. The climate is mild, moderated by the North Atlantic Drift ocean current and by southwesterly winds. The mainstays of the economy are fishing and fish processing, which account for seventy per cent of exports. Agriculture involves mainly sheep and dairy farming. Hydroelectric and geothermal energy resources are considerable. The main industries produce aluminium, ferro-silicon and fertilizers. Tourism, including ecotourism, is growing in importance.

Blue lagoon geothermal resort, Iceland

India Republic of India

Area Sq Km **3 287 134**
Area Sq Miles **1 269 170**

Population **1 211 003 000**
Capital **New Delhi**

Currency **Indian rupee**
Languages **Hindi, English, many regional languages**

Religions **Hindu, Sunni Muslim, Shi'a Muslim, Sikh, Christian**
Organizations **Comm., UN**

Population

Total population **1 211 003 000**
Population change **1.3%**
Urban population **29.5%**
Total fertility rate **2.7 births per woman**
Population aged 0–14 **31.7%**
Population aged over 65 **4.8%**
2050 projected population **1 592 704 000**

Communications

Main telephone lines **3.6 per 100 people**
Cellular mobile subscribers **14.8 per 100 people**
Internet users **1 072 per 10 000 people**
International dialling code **91**
Time zone **+5.5**

Economy

Total Gross National Income (GNI) **909 138 US$M**
GNI per capita **1 070 US$**
Debt service ratio **2.0% of GNI**
Total debt service **17 878 568 000 US$**
Aid receipts **0.2% of GNI**
Military spending **2.7% of GDP**

Environment

Forest area **22.8%**
Annual change in forest area **N/A**
Protected land area **5.1%**
CO_2 emissions **1.3 metric tons per capita**

Social Indicators

Infant mortality rate **54 per 1 000 live births**
Life expectancy **64.7**
Literacy rate **66.0%**
Access to safe water **86%**
Doctors **0.6 per 1 000 people**

The south Asian country of India occupies a peninsula that juts out into the Indian Ocean between the Arabian Sea and Bay of Bengal. The heart of the peninsula is the Deccan plateau, bordered on either side by ranges of hills, the Western Ghats and the lower Eastern Ghats, which fall away to narrow coastal plains. To the north is a broad plain, drained by the Indus, Ganges and Brahmaputra rivers and their tributaries. The plain is intensively farmed and is the most populous region. In the west is the Thar Desert. The mountains of the Himalaya form India's northern border, together with parts of the Karakoram and Hindu Kush ranges in the northwest. The climate shows marked seasonal variation: a hot season from March to June; a monsoon season from June to October; and a cold season from November to February. Rainfall ranges between very high in the northeast Assam region to negligible in the Thar Desert.

Temperatures range from very cold in the Himalaya to tropical heat over much of the south. Over seventy per cent of the huge population – the second largest in the world – is rural, although Delhi, Mumbai (Bombay) and Kolkata (Calcutta) all rank among the ten largest cities in the world. Agriculture, forestry and fishing account for a quarter of national output and two-thirds of employment. Much of the farming is on a subsistence basis and involves mainly rice and wheat. India is a major world producer of tea, sugar, jute, cotton and tobacco. Livestock is reared mainly for dairy products and hides. There are major reserves of coal, reserves of oil and natural gas, and many minerals, including iron, manganese, bauxite, diamonds and gold. The manufacturing sector is large and diverse – mainly chemicals and chemical products, textiles, iron and steel, food products, electrical goods and transport equipment; software and pharmaceuticals are also important. All the main manufactured products are exported, together with diamonds and jewellery. The USA, Germany, Japan and the UK are the main trading partners.

Taj Mahal, Agra, India

Area Sq Km **1 919 445**	Population **229 965 000**
Area Sq Miles **741 102**	Capital **Jakarta**

Currency **Rupiah**
Languages **Indonesian, local languages**

Religions **Sunni Muslim, Protestant, Roman Catholic, Hindu, Buddhist**
Organizations **APEC, ASEAN, OPEC, UN**

Population

Total population **229 965 000**
Population change **1.2%**
Urban population **51.5%**
Total fertility rate **2.2 births per woman**
Population aged 0–14 **27.4%**
Population aged over 65 **5.9%**
2050 projected population **284 640 000**

Communications

Main telephone lines
6.6 per 100 people
Cellular mobile subscribers
28.3 per 100 people
Internet users
469 per 10 000 people
International dialling code **62**
Time zone **+7 to +9**

Social Indicators

Infant mortality rate
25 per 1 000 live births
Life expectancy **70.6**
Literacy rate **92.0%**
Access to safe water **77%**
Doctors **0.13 per 1 000 people**

Economy

Total Gross National
Income (GNI) **315 845 US$M**
GNI per capita **2 010 US$**
Debt service ratio **5.9% of GNI**
Total debt service **20 434 246 000 US$**
Aid receipts **0.4% of GNI**
Military spending **1.2% of GDP**

Environment

Forest area **48.8%**
Annual change in
forest area **-2.0%**
Protected land area **11.2%**
CO2 emissions **1.9 metric tons per capita**

Indonesia, the largest and most populous country in southeast Asia, consists of over thirteen thousand islands extending between the Pacific and Indian Oceans. Sumatra, Java, Sulawesi, Kalimantan (two-thirds of Borneo) and Papua (formerly Irian Jaya, western New Guinea) make up ninety per cent of the land area. Most of Indonesia is mountainous and covered with rainforest or mangrove swamps, and there are over three hundred volcanoes, many active. Two-thirds of the population lives in the lowland areas of the islands of Java and Madura. The climate is tropical monsoon. Agriculture is the largest sector of the economy and Indonesia is among the world's top producers of rice, palm oil, tea, coffee, rubber and tobacco. Many goods are produced, including textiles, clothing, cement, tin, fertilizers and vehicles. Main exports are oil, natural gas, timber products and clothing. Main trading partners are Japan, the USA and Singapore. Indonesia is a relatively poor country, and ethnic tensions and civil unrest often hinder economic development.

Balinese temple, Bali, Indonesia

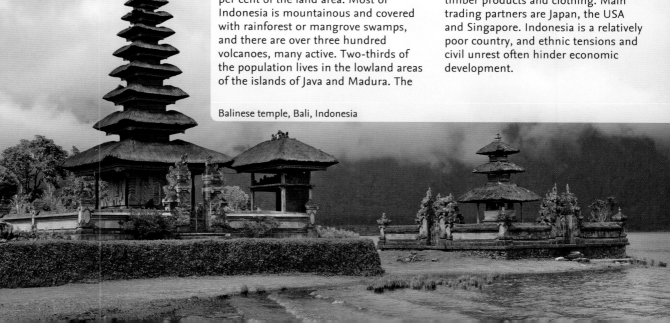

Area Sq Km **1 648 000**
Area Sq Miles **636 296**

Population **74 196 000**
Capital **Tehrān**

Currency **Iranian rial**
Languages **Farsi, Azeri, Kurdish, regional languages**

Religions **Shi'a Muslim, Sunni Muslim**
Organizations **OPEC, UN**

Population

Total population **74 196 000**
Population change **1.3%**
Urban population **68.5%**
Total fertility rate **2.0 births per woman**
Population aged 0–14 **24.4%**
Population aged over 65 **4.9%**
2050 projected population **101 944 000**

Communications

Main telephone lines **31.2 per 100 people**
Cellular mobile subscribers **21.8 per 100 people**
Internet users **2 554 per 10 000 people**
International dialling code **98**
Time zone **+3.5**

Economy

Total Gross National Income (GNI) **205 040 US$M**
GNI per capita **3 540 US$**
Debt service ratio **1.2% of GNI**
Total debt service **2 555 530 000 US$**
Aid receipts **0.1% of GNI**
Military spending **4.8% of GDP**

Environment

Forest area **6.8%**
Annual change in forest area **0.0%**
Protected land area **6.4%**
CO_2 emissions **6.5 metric tons per capita**

Social Indicators

Infant mortality rate **29 per 1 000 live births**
Life expectancy **71.0**
Literacy rate **82.3%**
Access to safe water **94%**
Doctors **0.89 per 1 000 people**

Persepolis, Iran

Iran is in southwest Asia, and has coasts on The Gulf, the Caspian Sea and the Gulf of Oman. In the east is a high plateau, with large salt pans and a vast sand desert. In the west the Zagros Mountains form a series of ridges, and to the north lie the Elburz Mountains. Most farming and settlement is on the narrow plain along the Caspian Sea and in the foothills of the north and west. The climate is one of extremes, with hot summers and very cold winters. Most of the light rainfall is in the winter months. Agriculture involves approximately one-third of the workforce. Wheat is the main crop, but fruit (especially dates) and pistachio nuts are grown for export. Petroleum (the main export) and natural gas are Iran's leading natural resources. Manufactured goods include carpets, clothing, food products and construction materials.

Area Sq Km **438 317**
Area Sq Miles **169 235**

Population **30 747 000**
Capital **Baghdād**

Currency **Iraqi dinar**
Languages **Arabic, Kurdish, Turkmen**

Religions **Shi'a Muslim, Sunni Muslim, Christian**
Organizations **OPEC, UN**

Population

Total population **30 747 000**
Population change **N/A**
Urban population **N/A**
Total fertility rate **4.1 births per woman**
Population aged 0–14 **N/A**
Population aged over 65 **N/A**
2050 projected population **63 693 000**

Communications

Main telephone lines
4.0 per 100 people
Cellular mobile subscribers
15.5 per 100 people
Internet users
16 per 10 000 people
International dialling code **964**
Time zone **+3**

Economy

Total Gross National Income (GNI) **N/A**
GNI per capita **N/A**
Debt service ratio **N/A**
Total debt service **N/A**
Aid receipts **N/A**
Military spending **N/A**

Environment

Forest area **1.9%**
Annual change in forest area **0.1%**
Protected land area **N/A**
CO2 emissions **N/A**

Social Indicators

Infant mortality rate
36 per 1 000 live births
Life expectancy **68.0**
Literacy rate **N/A**
Access to safe water **81%**
Doctors **0.66 per 1 000 people**

Iraq, in southwest Asia, has at its heart the lowland valley of the Tigris and Euphrates rivers. In the southeast, where the two rivers join, are the Mesopotamian marshes and the Shaṭṭ al 'Arab waterway. Northern Iraq is hilly, while western Iraq is desert. Summers are hot and dry, while winters are mild with light, unreliable rainfall. One in five of the population lives in the capital, Baghdād. The economy has suffered following the 1991 Gulf War and the invasion of US-led coalition forces in 2005. The latter resulted in the overthrow of the dictator Saddam Hussein, but there is continuing internal instability. Oil is normally the main export.

Arbil Castle, Arbil, Iraq

Ireland Republic of Ireland

Area Sq Km **70 282**
Area Sq Miles **27 136**

Population **4 515 000**
Capital **Dublin**
(Baile Átha Cliath)

Currency **Euro**
Languages **English, Irish**

Religions **Roman Catholic, Protestant**
Organizations **EU, OECD, UN**

Population

Total population **4 515 000**
Population change **2.1%**
Urban population **61.3%**
Total fertility rate **1.9 births per woman**
Population aged 0–14 **20.6%**
Population aged over 65 **11.1%**
2050 projected population **5 762 000**

Communications

Main telephone lines **49.9 per 100 people**
Cellular mobile subscribers **112.6 per 100 people**
Internet users **3 423 per 10 000 people**
International dialling code **353**
Time zone **GMT**

Economy

Total Gross National Income (GNI) **191 315 US$M**
GNI per capita **49 590 US$**
Debt service ratio **N/A**
Total debt service **N/A**
Aid receipts **N/A**
Military spending **0.5% of GDP**

Environment

Forest area **9.7%**
Annual change in forest area **1.9%**
Protected land area **1.1%**
CO2 emissions **10.2 metric tons per capita**

Social Indicators

Infant mortality rate **4 per 1 000 live births**
Life expectancy **79.4**
Literacy rate **N/A**
Access to safe water **N/A**
Doctors **2.94 per 1 000 people**

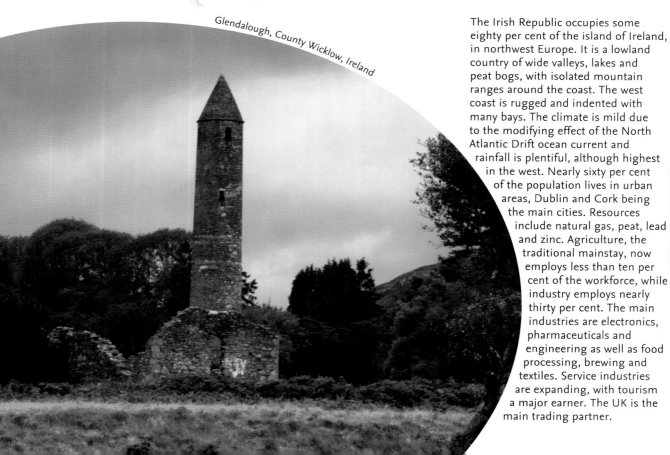

Glendalough, County Wicklow, Ireland

The Irish Republic occupies some eighty per cent of the island of Ireland, in northwest Europe. It is a lowland country of wide valleys, lakes and peat bogs, with isolated mountain ranges around the coast. The west coast is rugged and indented with many bays. The climate is mild due to the modifying effect of the North Atlantic Drift ocean current and rainfall is plentiful, although highest in the west. Nearly sixty per cent of the population lives in urban areas, Dublin and Cork being the main cities. Resources include natural gas, peat, lead and zinc. Agriculture, the traditional mainstay, now employs less than ten per cent of the workforce, while industry employs nearly thirty per cent. The main industries are electronics, pharmaceuticals and engineering as well as food processing, brewing and textiles. Service industries are expanding, with tourism a major earner. The UK is the main trading partner.

Area Sq Km **572**
Area Sq Miles **221**

Currency **Pound sterling**
Languages **English**

Population **80 000**
Capital **Douglas**

Religions **Protestant, Roman Catholic**

he Isle of Man lies in the
ish Sea between England and
orthern Ireland. The island
self-governing, although
e UK is responsible for its
efence and foreign affairs.
is not part of the European

Union, but has a special
relationship with the EU which
allows for free trade. Eighty
per cent of the economy is
based on the service sector,
particularly financial services.

Laxey Water Wheel, Isle of Man

Israel State of Israel

Area Sq Km **20 770**
Area Sq Miles **8 019**

Population **7 170 000**
Capital **Jerusalem (Yerushalayim) (El Quds)** *De facto capital. Disputed*

Currency **Shekel**
Languages **Hebrew, Arabic**

Religions **Jewish, Sunni Muslim, Christian, Druze**
Organizations **UN**

Population

Total population **7 170 000**
Population change **1.8%**
Urban population **91.7%**
Total fertility rate **2.9 births per woman**
Population aged 0–14 **27.8%**
Population aged over 65 **10.0%**
2050 projected population **10 403 000**

Communications

Main telephone lines **43.9 per 100 people**
Cellular mobile subscribers **122.7 per 100 people**
Internet users **2 774 per 10 000 people**
International dialling code **972**
Time zone **+2**

Social Indicators

Infant mortality rate **4 per 1 000 live births**
Life expectancy **80.6**
Literacy rate **N/A**
Access to safe water **100%**
Doctors **3.67 per 1 000 people**

Economy

Total Gross National Income (GNI) **142 199 US$M**
GNI per capita **24 700 US$**
Debt service ratio **N/A**
Total debt service **N/A**
Aid receipts **N/A**
Military spending **8.4% of GDP**

Environment

Forest area **7.9%**
Annual change in forest area **0.8%**
Protected land area **15.6%**
CO2 emissions **9.2 metric tons per capita**

Israel lies on the Mediterranean coast of southwest
Asia. Most of the population lives on the coastal plain
or in northern and central areas. Much of Israel has
warm summers and mild, wet winters. The south is hot
and dry. Agricultural production was boosted by the
occupation of the West Bank in 1967. Manufacturing
makes the largest contribution to the economy,
and tourism is also important. Israel's main exports
are machinery and transport equipment, software,
diamonds, clothing, fruit and vegetables. The country
relies heavily on foreign aid. Security issues relating to
the West Bank and Gaza have still to be resolved.

Italy Italian Republic

Area Sq Km **301 245**
Area Sq Miles **116 311**

Population **59 870 000**
Capital **Rome (Roma)**

Currency **Euro**
Languages **Italian**

Religions **Roman Catholic**
Organizations **EU, NATO, OECD, UN**

Population

Total population **59 870 000**
Population change **0.8%**
Urban population **68.1%**
Total fertility rate **1.3 births per woman**
Population aged 0–14 **14.2%**
Population aged over 65 **20.1%**
2050 projected population **50 912 000**

Communications

Main telephone lines **46.3 per 100 people**
Cellular mobile subscribers **135.1 per 100 people**
Internet users **5 291 per 10 000 people**
International dialling code **39**
Time zone **+1**

Economy

Total Gross National Income (GNI) **1 882 544 US$M**
GNI per capita **35 240 US$**
Debt service ratio **N/A**
Total debt service **N/A**
Aid receipts **N/A**
Military spending **1.7% of GDP**

Environment

Forest area **33.9%**
Annual change in forest area **1.1%**
Protected land area **6.6%**
CO_2 emissions **7.7 metric tons per capita**

Social Indicators

Infant mortality rate **3 per 1 000 live births**
Life expectancy **81.3**
Literacy rate **98.9%**
Access to safe water **N/A**
Doctors **3.7 per 1 000 people**

Most of the southern European state of Italy occupies a peninsula that juts out into the Mediterranean Sea. It includes the islands of Sicily and Sardinia and approximately seventy much smaller islands in the surrounding seas. Italy is mountainous, dominated by the Alps, which form its northern border, and the various ranges of the Apennines, which run almost the full length of the peninsula. Many of Italy's mountains are of volcanic origin, and its active volcanoes are Vesuvius, near Naples, Etna and Stromboli. The main lowland area, the Po river valley in the northeast, is the main agricultural and industrial area and is the most populous region. Italy has a Mediterranean climate, although the north experiences colder, wetter winters, with heavy snow in the Alps. Natural resources are limited, and only about twenty per cent of the land is suitable for cultivation. The economy is fairly diversified. Some oil, natural gas and coal are produced, but most fuels and minerals used by industry are imported. Agriculture is important, with cereals, vines, fruit and vegetables the main crops. Italy is the world's largest wine producer. The north is the centre of Italian industry, especially around Turin, Milan and Genoa. Leading manufactures include industrial and office equipment, domestic appliances, cars, textiles, clothing, leather goods, chemicals and metal products. There is a strong service sector, and with over twenty-five million visitors a year, tourism is a major employer and accounts for five per cent of the national income. Finance and banking are also important. Most trade is with other European Union countries.

Venice, Italy

Area Sq Km **10 991**
Area Sq Miles **4 244**

Population **2 719 000**
Capital **Kingston**

Currency **Jamaican dollar**
Languages **English, creole**

Religions **Protestant, Roman Catholic**
Organizations **CARICOM, Comm., UN**

Social Indicators

Infant mortality rate
26 per 1 000 live births

Life expectancy **72.5**

Literacy rate
86.0%

Access to
safe water **93%**

Doctors **0.85 per 1 000 people**

Population

Total population **2 719 000**

Population change **0.5%**

Urban population **53.3%**

Total fertility rate **2.4 births per woman**

Population aged 0–14 **30.0%**

Population aged over 65 **7.7%**

2050 projected population **2 586 000**

Communications

Main telephone lines
12.9 per 100 people

Cellular mobile subscribers
93.7 per 100 people

Internet users
2 942 per 10 000 people

International dialling code **1 876**

Time zone **-5**

Economy

Total Gross National
Income (GNI) **9 504 US$M**

GNI per capita **4 870 US$**

Debt service ratio **8.8% of GNI**

Total debt service **824 547 000 US$**

Aid receipts **0.4% of GNI**

Military spending **0.6% of GDP**

Environment

Forest area **31.3%**

Annual change in
forest area **-0.1%**

Protected land area **15.0%**

CO2 emissions **3.8 metric tons per capita**

Jamaica, the third largest Caribbean island, has beaches and densely populated coastal plains traversed by hills and plateaus rising to the forested Blue Mountains in the east. The climate is tropical, but cooler and wetter on high ground. The economy is based on tourism, agriculture, mining and light manufacturing. Bauxite, aluminium oxide, sugar and bananas are the main exports. The USA is the main trading partner. Foreign aid is also significant.

Ocho Rios, Jamaica

Japan

Area Sq Km **377 727**
Area Sq Miles **145 841**

Population **127 156 000**
Capital **Tōkyō**

Currency **Yen**
Languages **Japanese**

Religions **Shintoist, Buddhist, Christian**
Organizations **APEC, OECD, UN**

Population

Total population **127 156 000**
Population change **-0.1%**
Urban population **66.5%**
Total fertility rate **1.3 births per woman**
Population aged 0–14 **13.4%**
Population aged over 65 **21.4%**
2050 projected population **112 198 000**

Communications

Main telephone lines
43.0 per 100 people
Cellular mobile subscribers
79.3 per 100 people
Internet users
6 827 per 10 000 people
International dialling code **81**
Time zone **+9**

Economy

Total Gross National
Income (GNI) **4 934 676 US$M**
GNI per capita **38 210 US$**
Debt service ratio **N/A**
Total debt service **N/A**
Aid receipts **N/A**
Military spending **0.9% of GDP**

Environment

Forest area **68.2%**
Annual change in
forest area **N/A**
Protected land area **9.5%**
CO_2 emissions **9.6 metric tons per capita**

Social Indicators

Infant mortality rate
3 per 1 000 live births
Life expectancy **82.5**
Literacy rate **N/A**
Access to safe water **100%**
Doctors **2.12 per 1 000 people**

Japan lies in the Pacific Ocean off the coast of eastern Asia and consists of four main islands – Hokkaidō, Honshū, Shikoku and Kyūshū – and more than three thousand smaller islands in the surrounding Sea of Japan, East China Sea and Pacific Ocean. The central island of Honshū accounts for sixty per cent of the total land area and contains eighty per cent of the population.

Behind the long and deeply indented coastline, nearly three-quarters of the country is mountainous and heavily forested. Japan has over sixty active volcanoes, and is subject to frequent earthquakes and typhoons. The climate is generally temperate maritime, with warm summers and mild winters, except in western Hokkaidō and northwest Honshū, where the winters are very cold with heavy snow. Only fourteen per cent of the land area is suitable for cultivation, and its few raw materials (coal, oil, natural gas, lead, zinc and copper) are insufficient for its industry. Most materials must

be imported, including about ninety per cent of energy requirements. Yet Japan has the world's second largest industrial economy, with a range of modern heavy and light industries centred mainly around the major ports of Yokohama, Ōsaka and Tōkyō. It is the world's largest manufacturer of cars, motorcycles and merchant ships, and a major producer of steel, textiles, chemicals and cement. It is also a leading producer of many consumer durables, such as washing machines, and electronic equipment, chiefly office equipment and computers. Japan has a strong service sector, banking and finance being particularly important, and Tōkyō has one of the world's major stock exchanges. Owing to intensive agricultural production, Japan is seventy per cent self-sufficient in food. The main food crops are rice, barley, fruit, wheat and soya beans. Livestock rearing (chiefly cattle, pigs and chickens) and fishing are also important, and Japan has one of the largest fishing fleets in the world. A major trading nation, Japan has trade links with many countries in southeast Asia and in Europe, although its main trading partner is the USA.

Mount Fuji, Japan

Area Sq Km **116**
Area Sq Miles **45**

Currency **Pound sterling**
Languages **English, French**

Population **90 800**
Capital **St Helier**

Religions **Protestant, Roman Catholic**

One of the Channel Islands lying off the west coast of the Cherbourg peninsula in northern France. Financial services are the most important part of the economy.

German observation post, Jersey

Jordan Hashemite Kingdom of Jordan

Area Sq Km **89 206**
Area Sq Miles **34 443**

Population **6 316 000**
Capital **ʿAmmān**

Currency **Jordanian dinar**
Languages **Arabic**

Religions **Sunni Muslim, Christian**
Organizations **UN**

Population

Total population **6 316 000**
Population change **3.2%**
Urban population **78.4%**
Total fertility rate **3.6 births per woman**
Population aged 0–14 **35.1%**
Population aged over 65 **3.6%**
2050 projected population **10 225 000**

Communications

Main telephone lines **10.5 per 100 people**
Cellular mobile subscribers **74.4 per 100 people**
Internet users **1 365 per 10 000 people**
International dialling code **962**
Time zone **+2**

Social Indicators

Infant mortality rate **21 per 1 000 live births**
Life expectancy **72.6**
Literacy rate **91.1%**
Access to safe water **97%**
Doctors **2.36 per 1 000 people**

Economy

Total Gross National Income (GNI) **14 653 US$M**
GNI per capita **3 310 US$**
Debt service ratio **4.7% of GNI**
Total debt service **688 206 000 US$**
Aid receipts **3.9% of GNI**
Military spending **4.9% of GDP**

Environment

Forest area **0.9%**
Annual change in forest area **0.0%**
Protected land area **10.6%**
CO2 emissions **3.8 metric tons per capita**

Jordan, in southwest Asia, is landlocked apart from a short coastline on the Gulf of Aqaba. Much of the country is rocky desert plateau. To the west of the mountains, the land falls below sea level to the Dead Sea and the Jordan river. The climate is hot and dry. Most people live in the northwest. Phosphates, potash, pharmaceuticals, fruit and vegetables are the main exports. The tourist industry is important, and the economy relies on workers' remittances from abroad and foreign aid.

Kazakhstan Republic of Kazakhstan

Area Sq Km **2 717 300**
Area Sq Miles **1 049 155**

Population **15 637 000**
Capital **Astana (Akmola)**

Currency **Tenge**
Languages **Kazakh, Russian, Ukrainian, German, Uzbek, Tatar**

Religions **Sunni Muslim, Russian Orthodox, Protestant**
Organizations **CIS, UN**

Population

Total population **15 637 000**
Population change **1.2%**
Urban population **57.9%**
Total fertility rate **2.4 births per woman**
Population aged 0–14 **23.7%**
Population aged over 65 **7.4%**
2050 projected population **13 086 000**

Communications

Main telephone lines **19.8 per 100 people**
Cellular mobile subscribers **52.9 per 100 people**
Internet users **842 per 10 000 people**
International dialling code **7**
Time zone **+5 to +6**

Economy

Total Gross National Income (GNI) **59 175 US$M**
GNI per capita **6 140 US$**
Debt service ratio **20.3% of GNI**
Total debt service **14 531 967 000 US$**
Aid receipts **0.3% of GNI**
Military spending **0.9% of GDP**

Environment

Forest area **1.2%**
Annual change in forest area **-0.2%**
Protected land area **2.9%**
CO_2 emissions **11.9 metric tons per capita**

Social Indicators

Infant mortality rate **28 per 1 000 live births**
Life expectancy **66.4**
Literacy rate **99.6%**
Access to safe water **86%**
Doctors **3.88 per 1 000 people**

Stretching across central Asia, Kazakhstan covers a vast area of steppe land and semi-desert. The land is flat in the west, with large lowlands around the Caspian Sea, rising to mountains in the southeast. The climate is continental. Agriculture and livestock rearing are important, and cotton and tobacco are the main cash crops. Kazakhstan is very rich in minerals, including coal, chromium, gold, molybdenum, lead and zinc, and has substantial reserves of oil and gas. Mining, metallurgy, machine building and food processing are major industries. Oil, gas and minerals are the main exports, and the Russian Federation is the dominant trading partner.

Petroglyphs, Tamgaly, Kazakhstan

Area Sq Km **582 646**
Area Sq Miles **224 961**

Population **39 802 000**
Capital **Nairobi**

Currency **Kenyan shilling**
Languages **Swahili, English, local languages**

Religions **Christian, traditional beliefs**
Organizations **Comm., UN**

Population

Total population **39 802 000**
Population change **2.6%**
Urban population **21.6%**
Total fertility rate **5.0 births per woman**
Population aged 0–14 **42.8%**
Population aged over 65 **2.7%**
2050 projected population **83 073 000**

Communications

Main telephone lines
0.8 per 100 people
Cellular mobile subscribers
20.9 per 100 people
Internet users
789 per 10 000 people
International dialling code **254**
Time zone **+3**

Environment

Forest area **6.2%**
Annual change in forest area **-0.3%**
Protected land area **12.1%**
CO_2 emissions **0.3 metric tons per capita**

Economy

Total Gross National Income (GNI) **21 335 US$M**
GNI per capita **770 US$**
Debt service ratio **1.9% of GNI**
Total debt service **432 974 000 US$**
Aid receipts **4.5% of GNI**
Military spending **1.6% of GDP**

Social Indicators

Infant mortality rate
80 per 1 000 live births
Life expectancy **54.1**
Literacy rate **N/A**
Access to safe water **61%**
Doctors **0.139 per 1 000 people**

Kenya is in east Africa, on the Indian Ocean. Inland beyond the coastal plains the land rises to plateaus interrupted by volcanic mountains. The Great Rift Valley runs north-south to the west of the capital, Nairobi. Most of the population lives in the central area. Conditions are tropical on the coast, semi-desert in the north and savanna in the south. Hydroelectric power from the Upper Tana river provides most of the country's electricity. Agricultural products, mainly tea, coffee, fruit and vegetables, are the main exports. Light industry is important, and tourism, oil refining and re-exports for landlocked neighbours are major foreign exchange earners.

Giraffe, Masai Mara, Kenya

Kiribati Republic of Kiribati

Area Sq Km **717**
Area Sq Miles **277**

Population **98 000**
Capital **Bairiki**

Currency **Australian dollar**
Languages **Gilbertese, English**

Religions **Roman Catholic, Protestant**
Organizations **Comm., UN**

Population
Total population **98 000**
Population change **1.6%**
Urban population **43.8%**
Total fertility rate **3.4 births per woman**
Population aged 0–14 **N/A**
Population aged over 65 **N/A**
2050 projected population **177 000**

Communications
Main telephone lines **5.1 per 100 people**
Cellular mobile subscribers **0.7 per 100 people**
Internet users **215 per 10 000 people**
International dialling code **686**
Time zone **+12 to +14**

Social Indicators
Infant mortality rate **46 per 1 000 live births**
Life expectancy **61**
Literacy rate **N/A**
Access to safe water **65%**
Doctors **0.23 per 1 000 people**

Economy
Total Gross National Income (GNI) **124 US$M**
GNI per capita **2 000 US$**
Debt service ratio **N/A**
Total debt service **N/A**
Aid receipts **-37.6% of GNI**
Military spending **N/A**

Environment
Forest area **2.7%**
Annual change in forest area **0.0%**
Protected land area **N/A**
CO_2 emissions **0.3 metric tons per capita**

Kiribati, in the Pacific Ocean, straddles the Equator and comprises coral islands in the Gilbert, Phoenix and Line Island groups and the volcanic island of Banaba. Most people live on the Gilbert Islands, and the capital, Bairiki, is on Tarawa island in this group. The climate is hot, and wetter in the north. Copra and fish are exported. Kiribati relies on remittances from workers abroad and foreign aid.

 Kosovo Republic of Kosovo

Area Sq Km **10 908**
Area Sq Miles **4 212**

Population **2 153 139**
Capital **Prishtinë (Priština)**

Currency **Euro**
Languages **Albanian, Serbian**

Religions **Sunni Muslim, Serbian Orthodox,**

Kosovo, traditionally an autonomous southern province of Serbia, was the focus of ethnic conflict between Serbs and the majority ethnic Albanians in the 1990s until international intervention in 1999, after which it was administered by the UN. Kosovo declared its independence from Serbia in February 2008. The landscape is largely hilly or mountainous, especially along the southern and western borders.

Prishtinë, capital of Kosovo

Area Sq Km **17 818**
Area Sq Miles **6 880**

Population **2 985 000**
Capital **Kuwait (Al Kuwayt)**

Currency **Kuwaiti dinar**
Languages **Arabic**

Religions **Sunni Muslim,**
Shi'a Muslim,
Christian, Hindu
Organizations **OPEC, UN**

Population

Total population **2 985 000**
Population change **2.4%**
Urban population **98.4%**
Total fertility rate **2.2 births per woman**
Population aged 0–14 **23.4%**
Population aged over 65 **2.1%**
2050 projected population **5 279 000**

Communications

Main telephone lines
18.7 per 100 people
Cellular mobile subscribers
91.5 per 100 people
Internet users
2 953 per 10 000 people
International dialling code **965**
Time zone **+3**

Economy

Total Gross National
Income (GNI) **77 660 US$M**
GNI per capita **38 420 US$**
Debt service ratio **N/A**
Total debt service **N/A**
Aid receipts **N/A**
Military spending **4.8% of GDP**

Environment

Forest area **0.3%**
Annual change in
forest area **2.7%**
Protected land area **0.0%**
CO2 emissions **36.9 metric
tons per capita**

Social Indicators

Infant mortality rate
9 per 1 000 live births
Life expectancy **77.9**
Literacy rate **94.5%**
Access to safe water **N/A**
Doctors **1.8 per 1 000 people**

Kuwait lies on the northwest shores of
The Gulf in southwest Asia. It is mainly
low-lying desert, with irrigated areas
along the bay, Kuwait Jun, where most
people live. Summers are hot and dry,
and winters are cool with some rainfall.
The oil industry, which accounts for
eighty per cent of exports, has largely
recovered from the damage caused
by the Gulf War in 1991. Income is
also derived from extensive overseas
investments. Japan and the USA are
the main trading partners.

Kuwait Towers, Kuwait

Kyrgyzstan Kyrgyz Republic

Area Sq Km **198 500**
Area Sq Miles **76 641**

Population **5 482 000**
Capital **Bishkek (Frunze)**

Currency **Kyrgyz som**
Languages **Kyrgyz, Russian, Uzbek**

Religions **Sunni Muslim, Russian Orthodox**
Organizations **CIS, UN**

Population

Total population **5 482 000**
Population change **0.8%**
Urban population **36.3%**
Total fertility rate **2.7 births per woman**
Population aged 0–14 **29.7%**
Population aged over 65 **5.4%**
2050 projected population **6 664 000**

Communications

Main telephone lines
8.6 per 100 people
Cellular mobile subscribers
23.7 per 100 people
Internet users
560 per 10 000 people
International dialling code **996**
Time zone **+6**

Economy

Total Gross National
Income (GNI) **2 609 US$M**
GNI per capita **740 US$**
Debt service ratio **3.5% of GNI**
Total debt service **96 608 000 US$**
Aid receipts **11.8% of GNI**
Military spending **3.1% of GDP**

Environment

Forest area **4.5%**
Annual change in
forest area **0.3%**
Protected land area **3.2%**
CO_2 emissions **1.1 metric tons per capita**

Social Indicators

Infant mortality rate
34 per 1 000 live births
Life expectancy **67.7**
Literacy rate **99.3%**
Access to safe water **77%**
Doctors **2.39 per 1 000 people**

A landlocked central Asian state, Kyrgyzstan is rugged and mountainous, lying to the west of the Tien Shan mountain range. Most of the population lives in the valleys of the north and west. Summers are hot and winters cold. Agriculture (chiefly livestock farming) is the main activity. Some oil and gas, coal, gold, antimony and mercury are produced. Manufactured goods include machinery, metals and metal products, which are the main exports. Most trade is with Germany, the Russian Federation, Kazakhstan and Uzbekistan.

Tien Shan mountains, Kyrgyzstan

Area Sq Km **236 800**
Area Sq Miles **91 429**

Population **6 320 000**
Capital **Vientiane (Viangchan)**

Currency **Kip**
Languages **Lao, local languages**

Religions **Buddhist, traditional beliefs**
Organizations **ASEAN, UN**

Population

Total population **6 320 000**
Population change **1.8%**
Urban population **30.9%**
Total fertility rate **3.5 births per woman**
Population aged 0–14 **38.2%**
Population aged over 65 **3.6%**
2050 projected population **11 586 000**

Communications

Main telephone lines **1.5 per 100 people**
Cellular mobile subscribers **16.7 per 100 people**
Internet users **116 per 10 000 people**
International dialling code **856**
Time zone **+7**

Social Indicators

Infant mortality rate **56 per 1 000 live births**
Life expectancy **65.2**
Literacy rate **72.7%**
Access to safe water **51%**
Doctors **0.35 per 1 000 people**

Economy

Total Gross National Income (GNI) **2 890 US$M**
GNI per capita **740 US$**
Debt service ratio **5.6% of GNI**
Total debt service **169 326 000 US$**
Aid receipts **12.1% of GNI**
Military spending **N/A**

Environment

Forest area **69.9%**
Annual change in forest area **-0.5%**
Protected land area **16.3%**
CO_2 emissions **0.2 metric tons per capita**

A landlocked country in southeast Asia, Laos is a land of mostly forested mountains and plateaus. The climate is tropical monsoon. Most of the population lives in the Mekong valley and the low plateau in the south, where food crops, chiefly rice, are grown. Hydroelectricity from a plant on the Mekong river, timber, coffee and tin are exported. Laos relies heavily on foreign aid.

Buddha Park, Vientiane, Laos

Latvia Republic of Latvia

Area Sq Km **64 589**
Area Sq Miles **24 938**

Population **2 249 000**
Capital **Rīga**

Currency **Lats**
Languages **Latvian, Russian**

Religions **Protestant, Roman Catholic, Russian Orthodox**
Organizations **EU, NATO, UN**

Population

Total population **2 249 000**
Population change **-0.4%**
Urban population **68.1%**
Total fertility rate **1.4 births per woman**
Population aged 0–14 **13.8%**
Population aged over 65 **17.2%**
2050 projected population **1 678 000**

Communications

Main telephone lines **28.6 per 100 people**
Cellular mobile subscribers **95.1 per 100 people**
Internet users **4 665 per 10 000 people**
International dialling code **371**
Time zone **+2**

Economy

Total Gross National Income (GNI) **18 525 US$M**
GNI per capita **11 860 US$**
Debt service ratio **16.9% of GNI**
Total debt service **3 279 260 000 US$**
Aid receipts **N/A**
Military spending **1.6% of GDP**

Environment

Forest area **47.2%**
Annual change in forest area **0.4%**
Protected land area **16.7%**
CO_2 emissions **2.8 metric tons per capita**

Social Indicators

Infant mortality rate **7 per 1 000 live births**
Life expectancy **71.2**
Literacy rate **99.8%**
Access to safe water **99%**
Doctors **3.14 per 1 000 people**

Rīga, Latvia

Latvia is in northern Europe, on the Baltic Sea and the Gulf of Riga. The land is flat near the coast but hilly with woods and lakes inland. The country has a modified continental climate. One-third of the people live in the capital, Rīga. Crop and livestock farming are important. There are few natural resources. Industries and main exports include food products, transport equipment, wood and wood products and textiles. The main trading partners are the Russian Federation and Germany. Latvia joined the European Union in May 2004.

Area Sq Km **10 452**
Area Sq Miles **4 036**

Population **4 224 000**
Capital **Beirut (Beyrouth)**

Currency **Lebanese pound**
Languages **Arabic, Armenian, French**

Religions **Shi'a Muslim, Sunni Muslim, Christian**
Organizations **UN**

Population

Total population **4 224 000**
Population change **1.0%**
Urban population **87.0%**
Total fertility rate **2.2 births per woman**
Population aged 0–14 **25.8%**
Population aged over 65 **7.3%**
2050 projected population **4 702 000**

Communications

Main telephone lines
18.9 per 100 people
Cellular mobile subscribers
30.6 per 100 people
Internet users
2 628 per 10 000 people
International dialling code **961**
Time zone **+2**

Economy

Total Gross National
Income (GNI) **22 640 US$M**
GNI per capita **6 350 US$**
Debt service ratio **19.8% of GNI**
Total debt service **4 433 178 000 US$**
Aid receipts **3.2% of GNI**
Military spending **4.1% of GDP**

Environment

Forest area **13.3%**
Annual change in
forest area **0.8%**
Protected land area **0.4%**
CO_2 emissions **4.2 metric tons per capita**

Social Indicators

Infant mortality rate
26 per 1 000 live births
Life expectancy **72.0**
Literacy rate **89.6%**
Access to safe water **100%**
Doctors **2.36 per 1 000 people**

Lebanon lies on the Mediterranean coast of southwest Asia. Beyond the coastal strip, where most of the population lives, are two parallel mountain ranges, separated by the Bekaa Valley (El Beq'a). The economy and infrastructure have been recovering since the 1975-1991 civil war crippled the traditional sectors of financial services and tourism. Italy, France and the UAE are the main trading partners.

Pigeon Rocks, Beirut, Lebanon

 **Lesotho** Kingdom of Lesotho

Area Sq Km **30 355**
Area Sq Miles **11 720**

Population **2 067 000**
Capital **Maseru**

Currency **Loti, South African rand**
Languages **Sesotho, English, Zulu**

Religions **Christian, traditional beliefs**
Organizations **Comm., SADC, UN**

Population

Total population **2 067 000**
Population change **0.5%**
Urban population **25.5%**
Total fertility rate **3.4 births per woman**
Population aged 0–14 **39.2%**
Population aged over 65 **4.7%**
2050 projected population **1 601 000**

Communications

Main telephone lines **3.0 per 100 people**
Cellular mobile subscribers **20.0 per 100 people**
Internet users **287 per 10 000 people**
International dialling code **266**
Time zone **+2**

Environment

Forest area **0.3%**
Annual change in forest area **2.7%**
Protected land area **0.2%**
CO2 emissions **N/A**

Economy

Total Gross National Income (GNI) **1 957 US$M**
GNI per capita **1 080 US$**
Debt service ratio **2.5% of GNI**
Total debt service **47 040 000 US$**
Aid receipts **4.0% of GNI**
Military spending **2.4% of GDP**

Social Indicators

Infant mortality rate **68 per 1 000 live births**
Life expectancy **42.6**
Literacy rate **N/A**
Access to safe water **79%**
Doctors **0.05 per 1 000 people**

Lesotho is a landlocked state surrounded by the Republic of South Africa. It is a mountainous country lying within the Drakensberg mountain range. Farming and herding are the main activities. The economy depends heavily on South Africa for transport links and employment. A major hydroelectric plant completed in 1998 allows the sale of water to South Africa. Exports include manufactured goods (mainly clothing and road vehicles), food, live animals, wool and mohair.

Maletsunyane Falls, Lesotho

Area Sq Km **111 369**
Area Sq Miles **43 000**

Population **3 955 000**
Capital **Monrovia**

Currency **Liberian dollar**
Languages **English, creole, local languages**

Religions **Traditional beliefs, Christian, Sunni Muslim**
Organizations **UN**

Population

Total population **3 955 000**
Population change **4.5%**
Urban population **60.1%**
Total fertility rate **5.1 births per woman**
Population aged 0–14 **42.9%**
Population aged over 65 **3.1%**
2050 projected population **10 653 000**

Communications

Main telephone lines
0.2 per 100 people
Cellular mobile subscribers
4.9 per 100 people
Internet users **N/A**
International dialling code **231**
Time zone **GMT**

Environment

Forest area **32.7%**
Annual change in forest area **-1.8%**
Protected land area **15.8%**
CO_2 emissions **0.1 metric tons per capita**

Economy

Total Gross National Income (GNI) **469 US$M**
GNI per capita **170 US$**
Debt service ratio **0.2% of GNI**
Total debt service **809 000 US$**
Aid receipts **54.4% of GNI**
Military spending **N/A**

Social Indicators

Infant mortality rate
93 per 1 000 live births
Life expectancy **58.4**
Literacy rate **55.5%**
Access to safe water **61%**
Doctors **0.03 per 1 000 people**

Liberia is on the Atlantic coast of west Africa. Beyond the coastal belt of sandy beaches and mangrove swamps the land rises to a forested plateau and highlands along the Guinea border. A quarter of the population lives along the coast. The climate is hot with heavy rainfall. Liberia is rich in mineral resources and forests. The economy is based on the production and export of basic products. Exports include diamonds, iron ore, rubber and timber. Liberia has a huge international debt and relies heavily on foreign aid.

Bomi Lake, Liberia

Libya Great Socialist People's Libyan Arab Jamahiriya

Area Sq Km **1 759 540**
Area Sq Miles **679 362**

Population **6 420 000**
Capital **Tripoli (Ṭarābulus)**

Currency **Libyan dinar**
Languages **Arabic, Berber**

Religions **Sunni Muslim**
Organizations **OPEC, UN**

Population

Total population **6 420 000**
Population change **1.9%**
Urban population **77.5%**
Total fertility rate **2.7 births per woman**
Population aged 0–14 **30.2%**
Population aged over 65 **4.1%**
2050 projected population **9 553 000**

Communications

Main telephone lines
8.1 per 100 people
Cellular mobile subscribers
65.8 per 100 people
Internet users
436 per 10 000 people
International dialling code **218**
Time zone **+2**

Economy

Total Gross National
Income (GNI) **44 011 US$M**
GNI per capita **11 590 US$**
Debt service ratio **N/A**
Total debt service **N/A**
Aid receipts **0.1% of GNI**
Military spending **1.5% of GDP**

Environment

Forest area **0.1%**
Annual change in
forest area **0.0%**
Protected land area **0.1%**
CO_2 emissions **9.5 metric
tons per capita**

Social Indicators

Infant mortality rate
17 per 1 000 live births
Life expectancy **74.2**
Literacy rate **86.8%**
Access to safe water **N/A**
Doctors **1.25 per 1 000 people**

Libya lies on the Mediterranean coast of north Africa. The desert plains and hills of the Sahara dominate the landscape and the climate is hot and dry. Most of the population lives in cities near the coast, where the climate is cooler with moderate rainfall. Farming and herding, chiefly in the northwest, are important but the main industry is oil. Libya is a major producer, and oil accounts for virtually all of its export earnings. Italy and Germany are the main trading partners.

Ancient Leptis Magna, Libya

Area Sq Km **160**
Area Sq Miles **62**

Population **36 000**
Capital **Vaduz**

Currency **Swiss franc**
Languages **German**

Religions **Roman Catholic,**
Protestant
Organizations **UN**

Population

Total population **36 000**
Population change **0.7%**
Urban population **14.3%**
Total fertility rate **N/A**
Population aged 0–14 **N/A**
Population aged over 65 **N/A**
2050 projected population **44 000**

Communications

Main telephone lines
57.2 per 100 people
Cellular mobile subscribers
81.8 per 100 people
Internet users
6 398 per 10 000 people
International dialling code **423**
Time zone **+1**

Economy

Total Gross National
Income (GNI) **N/A**
GNI per capita **N/A**
Debt service ratio **N/A**
Total debt service **N/A**
Aid receipts **N/A**
Military spending **N/A**

Environment

Forest area **43.1%**
Annual change in
forest area **0.0%**
Protected land area **40.0%**
CO2 emissions **N/A**

Social Indicators

Infant mortality rate
2 per 1 000 live births
Life expectancy **N/A**
Literacy rate **N/A**
Access to safe water **N/A**
Doctors **N/A**

A landlocked state between Switzerland
and Austria, Liechtenstein has an
industrialized, free-enterprise economy.
Low business taxes have attracted
companies to establish offices which
provide approximately one-third of state
revenues. Banking is also important.
Major products include precision
instruments, ceramics and textiles.

Gutenberg Castle, Balzers, Liechtenstein

Lithuania Republic of Lithuania

Area Sq Km **65 200**
Area Sq Miles **25 174**

Population **3 287 000**
Capital **Vilnius**

Currency **Litas**
Languages **Lithuanian, Russian, Polish**

Religions **Roman Catholic, Protestant, Russian Orthodox**
Organizations **EU, NATO, UN**

Population

Total population **3 287 000**
Population change **-0.5%**
Urban population **67.0%**
Total fertility rate **1.4 births per woman**
Population aged 0–14 **15.3%**
Population aged over 65 **16.0%**
2050 projected population **2 565 000**

Communications

Main telephone lines **23.2 per 100 people**
Cellular mobile subscribers **138.1 per 100 people**
Internet users **3 169 per 10 000 people**
International dialling code **370**
Time zone **+2**

Economy

Total Gross National Income (GNI) **26 917 US$M**
GNI per capita **11 870 US$**
Debt service ratio **15.3% of GNI**
Total debt service **4 215 870 000 US$**
Aid receipts **N/A**
Military spending **1.2% of GDP**

Environment

Forest area **33.5%**
Annual change in forest area **0.8%**
Protected land area **5.7%**
CO2 emissions **4.1 metric tons per capita**

Social Indicators

Infant mortality rate **7 per 1 000 live births**
Life expectancy **70.9**
Literacy rate **99.7%**
Access to safe water **N/A**
Doctors **3.95 per 1 000 people**

Lithuania is in northern Europe on the eastern shores of the Baltic Sea. It is mainly lowland with many lakes, rivers and marshes. Agriculture, fishing and forestry are important, but manufacturing dominates the economy. The main exports are machinery, mineral products and chemicals. The Russian Federation and Germany are the main trading partners. Lithuania joined the European Union in May 2004.

Trakai, Lithuania

Area Sq Km **2 586**
Area Sq Miles **998**

Population **486 000**
Capital **Luxembourg**

Currency **Euro**
Languages **Letzeburgish,
German, French**

Religions **Roman Catholic**
Organizations **EU, NATO,
OECD, UN**

Population

Total population **486 000**
Population change **1.6%**
Urban population **82.4%**
Total fertility rate **1.6 births per woman**
Population aged 0–14 **18.0%**
Population aged over 65 **14.0%**
2050 projected population **721 000**

Communications

Main telephone lines
52.4 per 100 people
Cellular mobile subscribers
116.8 per 100 people
Internet users
7 201 per 10 000 people
International dialling code **352**
Time zone **+1**

Economy

Total Gross National
Income (GNI) **32 904 US$M**
GNI per capita **84 890 US$**
Debt service ratio **N/A**
Total debt service **N/A**
Aid receipts **N/A**
Military spending **0.8% of GDP**

Environment

Forest area **33.5%**
Annual change in
forest area **0.0%**
Protected land area **16.6%**
CO2 emissions **24.3 metric
tons per capita**

Social Indicators

Infant mortality rate
2 per 1 000 live births
Life expectancy **79.2**
Literacy rate **N/A**
Access to safe water **100%**
Doctors **2.73 per 1 000 people**

Luxembourg, a small landlocked
country in western Europe, borders
Belgium, France and Germany. The hills
and forests of the Ardennes dominate
the north, with rolling pasture to the
south, where the main towns, farms
and industries are found. The iron and
steel industry is still important, but
light industries (including textiles,
chemicals and food products)
are growing. Luxembourg
is a major banking centre.
Main trading partners are
Belgium, Germany and
France.

Luxembourg city, Luxembourg

Macedonia (F.Y.R.O.M.) Republic of Macedonia

Area Sq Km **25 713**
Area Sq Miles **9 928**

Population **2 042 000**
Capital **Skopje**

Currency **Macedonian denar**
Languages **Macedonian, Albanian, Turkish**

Religions **Macedonian Orthodox, Sunni Muslim**
Organizations **UN**

Population

Total population **2 042 000**
Population change **0.0%**
Urban population **66.9%**
Total fertility rate **1.4 births per woman**
Population aged 0–14 **18.4%**
Population aged over 65 **11.6%**
2050 projected population **1 884 000**

Communications

Main telephone lines **24.1 per 100 people**
Cellular mobile subscribers **69.6 per 100 people**
Internet users **1 315 per 10 000 people**
International dialling code **389**
Time zone **+1**

Economy

Total Gross National Income (GNI) **6 260 US$M**
GNI per capita **4 140 US$**
Debt service ratio **8.4% of GNI**
Total debt service **522 292 000 US$**
Aid receipts **3.2% of GNI**
Military spending **2.0% of GDP**

Environment

Forest area **35.6%**
Annual change in forest area **0.0%**
Protected land area **7.1%**
CO2 emissions **5.1 metric tons per capita**

Social Indicators

Infant mortality rate **15 per 1 000 live births**
Life expectancy **74.1**
Literacy rate **97.0%**
Access to safe water **N/A**
Doctors **2.55 per 1 000 people**

The Former Yugoslav Republic of Macedonia is a landlocked state in southern Europe. Lying within the southern Balkan Mountains, it is traversed northwest-southeast by the Vardar valley. The climate is continental. The economy is based on industry, mining and agriculture, but conflicts in the region have reduced trade and caused economic difficulties. Foreign aid and loans are now assisting in modernization and development of the country.

Lake Ohrid, Macedonia

Area Sq Km **587 041**
Area Sq Miles **226 658**

Population **19 625 000**
Capital **Antananarivo**

Currency **Malagasy ariary, Malagasy franc**
Languages **Malagasy, French**

Religions **Traditional beliefs, Christian, Sunni Muslim**
Organizations **SADC, UN**

Population

Total population **19 625 000**
Population change **2.7%**
Urban population **29.5%**
Total fertility rate **4.8 births per woman**
Population aged 0–14 **43.3%**
Population aged over 65 **3.1%**
2050 projected population **43 508 000**

Communications

Main telephone lines **0.7 per 100 people**
Cellular mobile subscribers **5.5 per 100 people**
Internet users **58 per 10 000 people**
International dialling code **261**
Time zone **+3**

Environment

Forest area **22.1%**
Annual change in forest area **-0.3%**
Protected land area **2.6%**
CO_2 emissions **0.2 metric tons per capita**

Economy

Total Gross National Income (GNI) **5 343 US$M**
GNI per capita **410 US$**
Debt service ratio **1.2% of GNI**
Total debt service **67 571 000 US$**
Aid receipts **13.9% of GNI**
Military spending **1.0% of GDP**

Social Indicators

Infant mortality rate **70 per 1 000 live births**
Life expectancy **60.5**
Literacy rate **N/A**
Access to safe water **50%**
Doctors **0.29 per 1 000 people**

Madagascar lies off the east coast of southern Africa. The world's fourth largest island, it is mainly a high plateau, with a coastal strip to the east and scrubby plain to the west. The climate is tropical, with heavy rainfall in the north and east. Most of the population lives on the plateau.

Although the amount of arable land is limited, the economy is based on agriculture. The main industries are agricultural processing, textile manufacturing and oil refining. Foreign aid is important. Exports include coffee, vanilla, cotton cloth, sugar and shrimps. France is the main trading partner.

Boabab trees, Madagascar

Malawi Republic of Malawi

Area Sq Km **118 484**
Area Sq Miles **45 747**

Population **15 263 000**
Capital **Lilongwe**

Currency **Malawian kwacha**
Languages **Chichewa, English, local languages**

Religions **Christian, traditional beliefs, Sunni Muslim**
Organizations **Comm., SADC, UN**

Population

Total population **15 263 000**
Population change **2.5%**
Urban population **18.8%**
Total fertility rate **5.6 births per woman**
Population aged 0–14 **46.4%**
Population aged over 65 **3.1%**
2050 projected population **29 452 000**

Communications

Main telephone lines
0.8 per 100 people
Cellular mobile subscribers
3.3 per 100 people
Internet users
45 per 10 000 people
International dialling code **265**
Time zone **+2**

Environment

Forest area **36.2%**
Annual change in forest area **-0.9%**
Protected land area **19.5%**
CO_2 emissions **0.1 metric tons per capita**

Economy

Total Gross National Income (GNI) **3 143 US$M**
GNI per capita **290 US$**
Debt service ratio **2.9% of GNI**
Total debt service **90 044 000 US$**
Aid receipts **30.5% of GNI**
Military spending **0.5% of GDP**

Social Indicators

Infant mortality rate
71 per 1 000 live births
Life expectancy **48.3**
Literacy rate **71.8%**
Access to safe water **73%**
Doctors **0.02 per 1 000 people**

Kande, Malawi

Landlocked Malawi in central Africa is a narrow hilly country at the southern end of the Great Rift Valley. One-fifth is covered by Lake Nyasa. Most of the population lives in rural areas in the southern regions. The climate is mainly subtropical, with varying rainfall. The economy is predominantly agricultural, with tobacco, tea and sugar the main exports. Malawi is one of the world's least developed countries and relies heavily on foreign aid. South Africa is the main trading partner.

Area Sq Km **332 965**
Area Sq Miles **128 559**

Population **27 468 000**
Capital **Kuala Lumpur/Putrajaya**

Currency **Ringgit**
Languages **Malay, English, Chinese, Tamil, local languages**

Religions **Sunni Muslim, Buddhist, Hindu, Christian, traditional beliefs**
Organizations **APEC, ASEAN, Comm., UN**

Population

Total population **27 468 000**
Population change **1.7%**
Urban population **70.4%**
Total fertility rate **2.6 births per woman**
Population aged 0–14 **30.0%**
Population aged over 65 **4.6%**
2050 projected population **38 924 000**

Communications

Main telephone lines **16.8 per 100 people**
Cellular mobile subscribers **75.5 per 100 people**
Internet users **5 423 per 10 000 people**
International dialling code **60**
Time zone **+8**

Social Indicators

Infant mortality rate **10 per 1 000 live births**
Life expectancy **74.3**
Literacy rate **91.9%**
Access to safe water **99%**
Doctors **0.71 per 1 000 people**

Economy

Total Gross National Income (GNI) **146 754 US$M**
GNI per capita **6 970 US$**
Debt service ratio **5.2% of GNI**
Total debt service **7 630 086 000 US$**
Aid receipts **0.2% of GNI**
Military spending **2.0% of GDP**

Environment

Forest area **63.6%**
Annual change in forest area **-0.7%**
Protected land area **18.2%**
CO_2 emissions **9.3 metric tons per capita**

Malaysia, in southeast Asia, comprises two regions, separated by the South China Sea. The western region occupies the southern Malay Peninsula, which has a chain of mountains dividing the eastern coastal strip from wider plains to the west. East Malaysia, consisting of the states of Sabah and Sarawak in the north of the island of Borneo, is mainly rainforest-covered hills and mountains with mangrove swamps along the coast. Both regions have a tropical climate with heavy rainfall. About eighty per cent of the population lives in Peninsular Malaysia. The country is rich in natural resources and has reserves of minerals and fuels. It is an important producer of tin, oil, natural gas and tropical hardwoods. Agriculture remains a substantial part of the economy, but industry is the most important sector. The main exports are transport and electronic equipment, oil, chemicals, palm oil, wood and rubber. The main trading partners are Japan, the USA and Singapore.

Kuala Lumpur, Malaysia

Maldives Republic of the Maldives

Area Sq Km **298**
Area Sq Miles **115**

Population **309 000**
Capital **Male**

Currency **Rufiyaa**
Languages **Divehi (Maldivian)**

Religions **Sunni Muslim**
Organizations **Comm., UN**

Population

Total population **309 000**
Population change **1.7%**
Urban population **37.9%**
Total fertility rate **2.6 births per woman**
Population aged 0–14 **29.0%**
Population aged over 65 **4.3%**
2050 projected population **682 000**

Communications

Main telephone lines
10.9 per 100 people
Cellular mobile subscribers
87.9 per 100 people
Internet users
664 per 10 000 people
International dialling code **960**
Time zone **+5**

Social Indicators

Infant mortality rate
26 per 1 000 live births
Life expectancy **68.5**
Literacy rate **97.0%**
Access to safe water **83%**
Doctors **0.92 per 1 000 people**

Economy

Total Gross National
Income (GNI) **903 US$M**
GNI per capita **3 630 US$**
Debt service ratio **3.9% of GNI**
Total debt service **34 588 000 US$**
Aid receipts **4.4% of GNI**
Military spending **N/A**

Environment

Forest area **3.0%**
Annual change in
forest area **0.0%**
Protected land area **N/A**
CO_2 emissions **2.4 metric
tons per capita**

The Maldive archipelago comprises
over a thousand coral atolls (around
two hundred of which are inhabited),
in the Indian Ocean, southwest of
India. Over eighty per cent of the land
area is less than one metre above sea
level. The main atolls are North and
South Male and Addu. The climate is
hot, humid and monsoonal. There is
little cultivation and almost all food
is imported. Tourism has expanded
rapidly and is the most important sector
of the economy.

Yellow snappers, Maldives

Area Sq Km **1 240 140**
Area Sq Miles **478 821**

Population **13 010 000**
Capital **Bamako**

Currency **CFA franc**
Languages **French, Bambara, local languages**

Religions **Sunni Muslim, traditional beliefs, Christian**
Organizations **UN**

Population

Total population **13 010 000**
Population change **3.0%**
Urban population **32.2%**
Total fertility rate **6.5 births per woman**
Population aged 0–14 **44.2%**
Population aged over 65 **2.3%**
2050 projected population **41 976 000**

Communications

Main telephone lines **0.6 per 100 people**
Cellular mobile subscribers **10.9 per 100 people**
Internet users **64 per 10 000 people**
International dialling code **223**
Time zone **GMT**

Environment

Forest area **10.3%**
Annual change in forest area **-0.8%**
Protected land area **2.1%**
CO_2 emissions **0.0 metric tons per capita**

Economy

Total Gross National Income (GNI) **5 546 US$M**
GNI per capita **580 US$**
Debt service ratio **1.5% of GNI**
Total debt service **80 175 000 US$**
Aid receipts **13.4% of GNI**
Military spending **2.2% of GDP**

Social Indicators

Infant mortality rate **117 per 1 000 live births**
Life expectancy **54.3**
Literacy rate **26.2%**
Access to safe water **50%**
Doctors **0.08 per 1 000 people**

A landlocked state in west Africa, Mali is generally low-lying. Northern regions lie within the Sahara desert. To the south are marshes and savanna grassland. Rainfall is unreliable. Most of the population lives along the Niger and Falémé rivers. Exports include cotton, livestock and gold. Mali relies heavily on foreign aid.

Mud mosque, Djenne, Mali

Malta Republic of Malta

Area Sq Km **316**
Area Sq Miles **122**

Population **409 000**
Capital **Valletta**

Currency **Euro**
Languages **Maltese, English**

Religions **Roman Catholic**
Organizations **Comm., EU, UN**

Population

Total population **409 000**
Population change **0.5%**
Urban population **94.3%**
Total fertility rate **1.3 births per woman**
Population aged 0–14 **16.0%**
Population aged over 65 **14.0%**
2050 projected population **428 000**

Communications

Main telephone lines
50.1 per 100 people
Cellular mobile subscribers
86.0 per 100 people
Internet users
3 173 per 10 000 people
International dialling code **356**
Time zone **+1**

Economy

Total Gross National
Income (GNI) **6 216 US$M**
GNI per capita **16 680 US$**
Debt service ratio **N/A**
Total debt service **N/A**
Aid receipts **N/A**
Military spending **0.6% of GDP**

Environment

Forest area **0.9%**
Annual change in
forest area **0.0%**
Protected land area **14.1%**
CO_2 emissions **6.3 metric
tons per capita**

Social Indicators

Infant mortality rate
4 per 1 000 live births
Life expectancy **79.6**
Literacy rate **92.4%**
Access to safe water **100%**
Doctors **3.88 per 1 000 people**

The islands of Malta and Gozo lie in the Mediterranean Sea, off the coast of southern Italy. The islands have hot, dry summers and mild winters. The economy depends on foreign trade, tourism and the manufacture of electronics and textiles. Main trading partners are the USA, France and Italy. Malta joined the European Union in May 2004.

Fort St Angelo, Malta

Area Sq Km **181**
Area Sq Miles **70**

Population **62 000**
Capital **Delap-Uliga-Djarrit**

Currency **United States dollar**
Languages **English, Marshallese**

Religions **Protestant, Roman Catholic**
Organizations **UN**

Population

Total population **62 000**
Population change **2.3%**
Urban population **71.1%**
Total fertility rate **N/A**
Population aged 0–14 **N/A**
Population aged over 65 **N/A**
2050 projected population **150 000**

Communications

Main telephone lines **8.3 per 100 people**
Cellular mobile subscribers **1.1 per 100 people**
Internet users **N/A**
International dialling code **692**
Time zone **+12**

Social Indicators

Infant mortality rate **49 per 1 000 live births**
Life expectancy **N/A**
Literacy rate **N/A**
Access to safe water **87%**
Doctors **0.47 per 1 000 people**

Economy

Total Gross National Income (GNI) **195 US$M**
GNI per capita **3 270 US$**
Debt service ratio **N/A**
Total debt service **N/A**
Aid receipts **28.5% of GNI**
Military spending **N/A**

Environment

Forest area **N/A**
Annual change in forest area **0.0%**
Protected land area **N/A**
CO_2 emissions **1.5 metric tons per capita**

The Marshall Islands consist of over a thousand atolls and islands in the north Pacific Ocean. The main atolls are Majuro (home to half the population), Kwajalein, Jaluit, Enewetak and Bikini. The climate is tropical. About half the workforce is employed in farming or fishing. Tourism is a small source of foreign exchange and the islands depend heavily on aid from the USA.

Martinique French Overseas Department

Area Sq Km **1 079**
Area Sq Miles **417**

Currency **Euro**
Languages **French, creole**

Population **405 000**
Capital **Fort-de-France**

Religions **Roman Catholic, traditional beliefs**

Martinique, one of the Caribbean Windward Islands, has volcanic peaks in the north, a populous central plain, and hills and beaches in the south.

Tourism is a major source of income, and substantial aid comes from France. The main trading partners are France and Guadeloupe.

Mount Pelée, Martinique

Mauritania Islamic Arab and African Republic of Mauritania

Area Sq Km **1 030 700**
Area Sq Miles **397 955**

Population **3 291 000**
Capital **Nouakchott**

Currency **Ouguiya**
Languages **Arabic, French, local languages**

Religions **Sunni Muslim**
Organizations **UN**

Population

Total population **3 291 000**
Population change **2.5%**
Urban population **41.0%**
Total fertility rate **4.4 births per woman**
Population aged 0–14 **39.8%**
Population aged over 65 **2.6%**
2050 projected population **7 497 000**

Communications

Main telephone lines
1.1 per 100 people
Cellular mobile subscribers
33.6 per 100 people
Internet users
95 per 10 000 people
International dialling code **222**
Time zone **GMT**

Economy

Total Gross National
Income (GNI) **2 325 US$M**
GNI per capita **840 US$**
Debt service ratio **3.5% of GNI**
Total debt service **97 426 000 US$**
Aid receipts **6.8% of GNI**
Military spending **2.5% of GDP**

Environment

Forest area **0.3%**
Annual change in
forest area **-3.4%**
Protected land area **N/A**
CO_2 emissions **0.6 metric tons per capita**

Social Indicators

Infant mortality rate
75 per 1 000 live births
Life expectancy **64.1**
Literacy rate **55.8%**
Access to safe water **53%**
Doctors **0.11 per 1 000 people**

Mauritania is on the Atlantic coast of northwest Africa and lies almost entirely within the Sahara desert. Oases and a fertile strip along the Senegal river to the south are the only areas suitable for cultivation. The climate is generally hot and dry. About a quarter of Mauritanians live in the capital, Nouakchott. Most of the workforce depends on livestock rearing and subsistence farming. There are large deposits of iron ore which account for more than half of total exports. Mauritania's coastal waters are among the richest fishing grounds in the world. The main trading partners are France, Japan and Italy.

Fort Saganne, Amogjar, Mauritania

Area Sq Km **2 040**
Area Sq Miles **788**

Population **1 288 000**
Capital **Port Louis**

Currency **Mauritius rupee**
Languages **English, creole, Hindi, Bhojpuri, French**

Religions **Hindu, Roman Catholic, Sunni Muslim**
Organizations **Comm., SADC, UN**

Population

Total population **1 288 000**
Population change **0.6%**
Urban population **42.5%**
Total fertility rate **1.7 births per woman**
Population aged 0–14 **23.2%**
Population aged over 65 **7.0%**
2050 projected population **1 465 000**

Social Indicators

Infant mortality rate **13 per 1 000 live births**
Life expectancy **72.4**
Literacy rate **87.4%**
Access to safe water **100%**
Doctors **1.06 per 1 000 people**

Communications

Main telephone lines **28.5 per 100 people**
Cellular mobile subscribers **61.5 per 100 people**
Internet users **2 548 per 10 000 people**
International dialling code **230**
Time zone **+4**

Economy

Total Gross National Income (GNI) **6 812 US$M**
GNI per capita **6 400 US$**
Debt service ratio **4.8% of GNI**
Total debt service **308 955 000 US$**
Aid receipts **0.3% of GNI**
Military spending **0.2% of GDP**

Environment

Forest area **18.2%**
Annual change in forest area **-0.5%**
Protected land area **3.3%**
CO_2 emissions **2.7 metric tons per capita**

The state comprises Mauritius, Rodrigues and some twenty small islands in the Indian Ocean, east of Madagascar. The main island of Mauritius is volcanic in origin and has a coral coast, rising to a central plateau. Most of the population lives on the north and west sides of the island. The climate is warm and humid. The economy is based on sugar production, light manufacturing (chiefly clothing) and tourism.

Salt ponds, Mauritius

Mayotte French Departmental Collectivity

Area Sq Km **373**
Area Sq Miles **144**

Currency **Euro**
Languages **French, Mahorian**

Population **194 000**
Capital **Dzaoudzi**

Religions **Sunni Muslim, Christian**

Lying in the Indian Ocean off the east coast of central Africa, Mayotte is geographically part of the Comoro archipelago.

The economy is based on agriculture, but Mayotte depends heavily on aid from France.

Mexico United Mexican States

Area Sq Km **1 972 545**
Area Sq Miles **761 604**

Population **109 610 000**
Capital **Mexico City**

Currency **Mexican peso**
Languages **Spanish, Amerindian languages**

Religions **Roman Catholic, Protestant**
Organizations **APEC, OECD, UN**

Population

Total population **109 610 000**
Population change **1.0%**
Urban population **77.2%**
Total fertility rate **2.1 births per woman**
Population aged 0–14 **29.1%**
Population aged over 65 **6.2%**
2050 projected population **139 015 000**

Communications

Main telephone lines **18.3 per 100 people**
Cellular mobile subscribers **52.6 per 100 people**
Internet users **1 898 per 10 000 people**
International dialling code **52**
Time zone **-6 to -8**

Economy

Total Gross National Income (GNI) **815 741 US$M**
GNI per capita **9 980 US$**
Debt service ratio **6.8% of GNI**
Total debt service **56 068 050 000 US$**
Aid receipts **0.0% of GNI**
Military spending **0.4% of GDP**

Environment

Forest area **33.0%**
Annual change in forest area **-0.4%**
Protected land area **5.3%**
CO_2 emissions **4.1 metric tons per capita**

Social Indicators

Infant mortality rate **29 per 1 000 live births**
Life expectancy **74.9**
Literacy rate **92.8%**
Access to safe water **97%**
Doctors **1.5 per 1 000 people**

Chichén Itzá, Mexico

The largest country in Central America, Mexico extends south from the USA to Guatemala and Belize. Most of the country is high plateau flanked by the Sierra Madre mountains. The principal lowland is the Yucatán peninsula in the southeast. The climate is hot and humid in the lowlands, warm on the plateau and cool with cold winters in the mountains. The north is arid, while the far south has heavy rainfall. Mexico City is the second largest conurbation in the world and the country's economic centre. Agriculture involves a fifth of the workforce; crops include grains, coffee, cotton and vegetables. Mexico is rich in minerals, including copper, zinc, lead, tin, sulphur, and silver. It is one of the world's largest producers of oil, from vast reserves in the Gulf of Mexico. The oil and petrochemical industries still dominate the economy, but a variety of goods are produced, including iron and steel, motor vehicles, textiles, chemicals and food and tobacco products. Over three-quarters of all trade is with the USA.

Area Sq Km **701**
Area Sq Miles **271**

Population **111 000**
Capital **Palikir**

Currency **United States dollar**
Languages **English, Chuukese, Pohnpeian, local languages**

Religions **Roman Catholic, Protestant**
Organizations **UN**

Population

Total population **111 000**
Population change **0.3%**
Urban population **22.5%**
Total fertility rate **3.7 births per woman**
Population aged 0–14 **37.3%**
Population aged over 65 **3.7%**
2050 projected population **99 000**

Communications

Main telephone lines **11.2 per 100 people**
Cellular mobile subscribers **12.7 per 100 people**
Internet users **1 439 per 10 000 people**
International dialling code **691**
Time zone **+10 to +11**

Social Indicators

Infant mortality rate **33 per 1 000 live births**
Life expectancy **68.5**
Literacy rate **N/A**
Access to safe water **94%**
Doctors **0.55 per 1 000 people**

Economy

Total Gross National Income (GNI) **264 US$M**
GNI per capita **2 340 US$**
Debt service ratio **N/A**
Total debt service **N/A**
Aid receipts **41.4% of GNI**
Military spending **N/A**

Environment

Forest area **90.6%**
Annual change in forest area **0.0%**
Protected land area **7.3%**
CO_2 emissions **N/A**

Micronesia comprises over six hundred atolls and islands of the Caroline Islands in the north Pacific Ocean. A third of the population lives on Pohnpei. The climate is tropical, with heavy rainfall. Fishing and subsistence farming are the main activities. Fish, garments and bananas are the main exports. Income is also derived from tourism and the licensing of foreign fishing fleets. The islands depend heavily on aid from the USA.

Chuuk Lagoon, Micronesia

Moldova Republic of Moldova

Area Sq Km **33 700**
Area Sq Miles **13 012**

Population **3 604 000**
Capital **Chişinău (Kishinev)**

Currency **Moldovan leu**
Languages **Romanian, Ukrainian, Gagauz, Russian**

Religions **Romanian Orthodox, Russian Orthodox**
Organizations **CIS, UN**

Population

Total population **3 604 000**
Population change **-0.9%**
Urban population **41.8%**
Total fertility rate **1.5 births per woman**
Population aged 0–14 **17.2%**
Population aged over 65 **11.1%**
2050 projected population **3 312 000**

Communications

Main telephone lines **24.3 per 100 people**
Cellular mobile subscribers **32.4 per 100 people**
Internet users **1 735 per 10 000 people**
International dialling code **373**
Time zone **+2**

Economy

Total Gross National Income (GNI) **3 650 US$M**
GNI per capita **1 470 US$**
Debt service ratio **8.9% of GNI**
Total debt service **334 842 000 US$**
Aid receipts **6.0% of GNI**
Military spending **0.3% of GDP**

Environment

Forest area **10.0%**
Annual change in forest area **0.2%**
Protected land area **1.4%**
CO_2 emissions **2.1 metric tons per capita**

Social Indicators

Infant mortality rate **16 per 1 000 live births**
Life expectancy **68.5**
Literacy rate **99.2%**
Access to safe water **92%**
Doctors **2.66 per 1 000 people**

Moldova lies between Romania and Ukraine in eastern Europe. It consists of hilly steppe land, drained by the Prut and Dniester rivers. The economy is mainly agricultural, with sugar beet, tobacco, wine and fruit the chief products. Food processing, machinery and textiles are the main industries. The Russian Federation is the main trading partner.

Tiraspol monastery, Moldova

Area Sq Km **2**
Area Sq Miles **1**

Population **33 000**
Capital **Monaco-Ville**

Currency **Euro**
Languages **French, Monégasque, Italian**

Religions **Roman Catholic**
Organizations **UN**

Population

Total population **33 000**
Population change **0.3%**
Urban population **100.0%**
Total fertility rate **N/A**
Population aged 0–14 **N/A**
Population aged over 65 **N/A**
2050 projected population **55 000**

Communications

Main telephone lines
96.8 per 100 people
Cellular mobile subscribers
51.6 per 100 people
Internet users
5 634 per 10 000 people
International dialling code **377**
Time zone **+1**

Economy

Total Gross National Income (GNI) **N/A**
GNI per capita **N/A**
Debt service ratio **N/A**
Total debt service **N/A**
Aid receipts **N/A**
Military spending **N/A**

Environment

Forest area **N/A**
Annual change in forest area **0.0%**
Protected land area **N/A**
CO_2 emissions **N/A**

Social Indicators

Infant mortality rate
3 per 1 000 live births
Life expectancy **N/A**
Literacy rate **N/A**
Access to safe water **100%**
Doctors **N/A**

The principality occupies a rocky peninsula and a strip of land on France's Mediterranean coast. Monaco's economy depends on service industries (chiefly tourism, banking and finance) and light industry.

Oceanographic Museum, Monaco

Mongolia

Area Sq Km **1 565 000**
Area Sq Miles **604 250**

Population **2 671 000**
Capital **Ulan Bator (Ulaanbaatar)**

Currency **Tugrik (Tögrög)**
Languages **Khalka (Mongolian), Kazakh, local languages**

Religions **Buddhist, Sunni Muslim**
Organizations **UN**

Population

Total population **2 671 000**
Population change **0.9%**
Urban population **57.2%**
Total fertility rate **1.9 births per woman**
Population aged 0–14 **26.5%**
Population aged over 65 **3.9%**
2050 projected population **3 625 000**

Communications

Main telephone lines **5.9 per 100 people**
Cellular mobile subscribers **28.9 per 100 people**
Internet users **1 157 per 10 000 people**
International dialling code **976**
Time zone **+8**

Economy

Total Gross National Income (GNI) **2 576 US$M**
GNI per capita **1 680 US$**
Debt service ratio **1.6% of GNI**
Total debt service **48 462 000 US$**
Aid receipts **7.8% of GNI**
Military spending **1.3% of GDP**

Environment

Forest area **6.5%**
Annual change in forest area **-0.8%**
Protected land area **13.9%**
CO_2 emissions **3.4 metric tons per capita**

Social Indicators

Infant mortality rate **35 per 1 000 live births**
Life expectancy **66.8**
Literacy rate **97.3%**
Access to safe water **62%**
Doctors **2.63 per 1 000 people**

Mongolian landscape

Mongolia is a landlocked country in eastern Asia between the Russian Federation and China. Much of it is high steppe land, with mountains and lakes in the west and north. In the south is the Gobi Desert. Mongolia has long, cold winters and short, mild summers. A quarter of the population lives in the capital, Ulan Bator. Livestock breeding and agricultural processing are important. There are substantial mineral resources. Copper and textiles are the main exports.

Area Sq Km **13 812**
Area Sq Miles **5 333**

Population **624 000**
Capital **Podgorica**

Currency **Euro**
Languages **Serbian (Montenegrin), Albanian**

Religions **Montenegrin Orthodox, Sunni Muslim**
Organizations **UN**

Population

Total population **624 000**
Population change **0.2%**
Urban population **60.2%**
Total fertility rate **1.6 births per woman**
Population aged 0–14 **19.6%**
Population aged over 65 **12.8%**
2050 projected population **N/A**

Communications

Main telephone lines **58.9 per 100 people**
Cellular mobile subscribers **107.3 per 100 people**
Internet users **4 434 per 10 000 people**
International dialling code **382**
Time zone **+1**

Social Indicators

Infant mortality rate **9 per 1 000 live births**
Life expectancy **74.2**
Literacy rate **N/A**
Access to safe water **N/A**
Doctors **N/A**

Economy

Total Gross National Income (GNI) **2 481 US$M**
GNI per capita **6 440 US$**
Debt service ratio **0.5% of GNI**
Total debt service **13 260 000 US$**
Aid receipts **4.2% of GNI**
Military spending **N/A**

Environment

Forest area **N/A**
Annual change in forest area **N/A**
Protected land area **N/A**
CO2 emissions **N/A**

Montenegro, previously a constituent republic of the former Yugoslavia, became an independent nation in June 2006 when it opted to split from the state union of Serbia and Montenegro. Montenegro separates the much larger Serbia from the Adriatic coast. The landscape is rugged and mountainous, and the climate Mediterranean.

Crnojevíc river, Montenegro

Montserrat United Kingdom Overseas Territory

Area Sq Km **100**
Area Sq Miles **39**

Population **4 655**
Capital **Brades**

Currency **East Caribbean dollar**
Languages **English**
Religions **Protestant, Roman Catholic**
Organizations **CARICOM**

An island in the Leeward Islands group in the Lesser Antilles, in the Caribbean. From 1995 to 1997 the volcanoes in the Soufrière Hills erupted for the first time since 1630. Over sixty per cent of the island was covered in volcanic ash and Plymouth, the capital, was virtually destroyed. Many people emigrated, and the remaining population moved to the north of the island. Brades has replaced Plymouth as the temporary capital. Reconstruction is being funded by aid from the UK.

Morocco Kingdom of Morocco

Area Sq Km **446 550**
Area Sq Miles **172 414**

Population **31 993 000**
Capital **Rabat**

Currency **Moroccan dirham**
Languages **Arabic, Berber, French**

Religions **Sunni Muslim**
Organizations **UN**

Population

Total population **31 993 000**
Population change **1.2%**
Urban population **56.0%**
Total fertility rate **2.4 births per woman**
Population aged 0–14 **28.8%**
Population aged over 65 **5.3%**
2050 projected population **46 397 000**

Communications

Main telephone lines
4.1 per 100 people
Cellular mobile subscribers
52.1 per 100 people
Internet users
1 985 per 10 000 people
International dialling code **212**
Time zone **GMT**

Economy

Total Gross National
Income (GNI) **65 793 US$M**
GNI per capita **2 580 US$**
Debt service ratio **5.3% of GNI**
Total debt service **3 404 801 000 US$**
Aid receipts **1.8% of GNI**
Military spending **3.7% of GDP**

Environment

Forest area **9.8%**
Annual change in
forest area **0.2%**
Protected land area **1.1%**
CO2 emissions **1.6 metric tons per capita**

Social Indicators

Infant mortality rate
32 per 1 000 live births
Life expectancy **71.1**
Literacy rate **55.6%**
Access to safe water **81%**
Doctors **0.51 per 1 000 people**

Aït Benhaddou, Morocco

Lying in the northwest corner of Africa, Morocco has both Atlantic and Mediterranean coasts. The Atlas Mountains separate the arid south and disputed region of Western Sahara from the fertile regions of the west and north, which have a milder climate. Most Moroccans live on the Atlantic coastal plain. The economy is based on agriculture, phosphate mining and tourism; the most important industries are food processing, textiles and chemicals. France is the main trading partner.

Area Sq Km **799 380**
Area Sq Miles **308 642**

Population **22 894 000**
Capital **Maputo**

Currency **Metical**
Languages **Portuguese, Makua, Tsonga, local languages**

Religions **Traditional beliefs, Roman Catholic, Sunni Muslim**
Organizations **Comm., SADC, UN**

Population

Total population **22 894 000**
Population change **1.9%**
Urban population **36.8%**
Total fertility rate **5.1 births per woman**
Population aged 0–14 **44.1%**
Population aged over 65 **3.2%**
2050 projected population **37 604 000**

Communications

Main telephone lines **0.3 per 100 people**
Cellular mobile subscribers **11.6 per 100 people**
Internet users **90 per 10 000 people**
International dialling code **258**
Time zone **+2**

Environment

Forest area **24.5%**
Annual change in forest area **-0.3%**
Protected land area **5.8%**
CO_2 emissions **0.1 metric tons per capita**

Economy

Total Gross National Income (GNI) **6 453 US$M**
GNI per capita **370 US$**
Debt service ratio **0.9% of GNI**
Total debt service **55 018 000 US$**
Aid receipts **23.3% of GNI**
Military spending **0.0% of GDP**

Social Indicators

Infant mortality rate **115 per 1 000 live births**
Life expectancy **42.1**
Literacy rate **44.4%**
Access to safe water **43%**
Doctors **0.03 per 1 000 people**

Mozambique lies on the east coast of southern Africa. The land is mainly a savanna plateau drained by the Zambezi and Limpopo rivers, with highlands to the north. Most of the population lives on the coast or in the river valleys. In general the climate is tropical with winter rainfall, but droughts occur. The economy is based on subsistence agriculture. Exports include shrimps, cashews, cotton and sugar, but Mozambique relies heavily on aid, and remains one of the least developed countries in the world.

Pemba, Mozambique

Myanmar (Burma) Union of Myanmar

Area Sq Km **676 577**	
Area Sq Miles **261 228**	

Population **50 020 000**
Capital **Nay Pyi Taw/Yangôn (Rangoon)**

Currency **Kyat**
Languages **Burmese, Shan, Karen, local languages**

Religions **Buddhist, Christian, Sunni Muslim**
Organizations **ASEAN, UN**

Population

Total population **50 020 000**
Population change **0.8%**
Urban population **32.6%**
Total fertility rate **2.1 births per woman**
Population aged 0–14 **27.1%**
Population aged over 65 **5.5%**
2050 projected population **63 657 000**

Communications

Main telephone lines **0.9 per 100 people**
Cellular mobile subscribers **0.4 per 100 people**
Internet users **18 per 10 000 people**
International dialling code **95**
Time zone **+6.5**

Social Indicators

Infant mortality rate **74 per 1 000 live births**
Life expectancy **62.1**
Literacy rate **N/A**
Access to safe water **78%**
Doctors **0.36 per 1 000 people**

Economy

Total Gross National Income (GNI) **N/A**
GNI per capita **N/A**
Debt service ratio **N/A**
Total debt service **86 428 000 US$**
Aid receipts **N/A**
Military spending **N/A**

Environment

Forest area **49.0%**
Annual change in forest area **-1.4%**
Protected land area **5.4%**
CO_2 emissions **0.2 metric tons per capita**

Myanmar (Burma) is in southeast Asia, bordering the Bay of Bengal and the Andaman Sea. Most of the population lives in the valley and delta of the Irrawaddy river, which is flanked by mountains and high plateaus. The climate is hot and monsoonal, and rainforest covers much of the land. Most of the workforce is employed in agriculture. Myanmar is rich in minerals, including zinc, lead, copper and silver. Political and social unrest and lack of foreign investment have affected economic development.

Htilominlo Temple, Myanmar

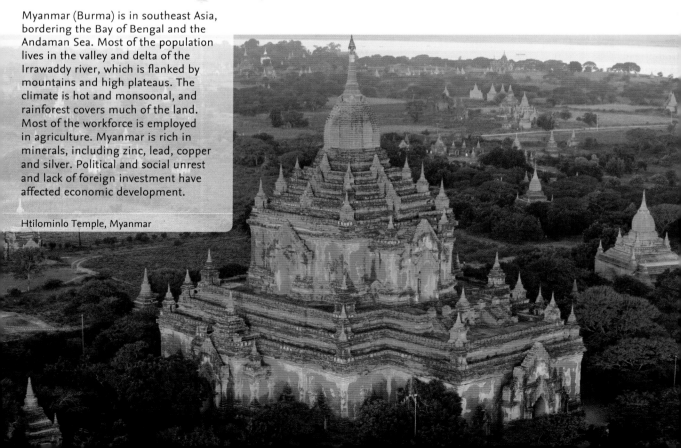

Area Sq Km **824 292**
Area Sq Miles **318 261**

Population **2 171 000**
Capital **Windhoek**

Currency **Namibian dollar**
Languages **English, Afrikaans, German, Ovambo, local languages**

Religions **Protestant, Roman Catholic**
Organizations **Comm., SADC, UN**

Population

Total population **2 171 000**
Population change **1.6%**
Urban population **36.8%**
Total fertility rate **3.6 births per woman**
Population aged 0–14 **37.4%**
Population aged over 65 **3.6%**
2050 projected population **3 060 000**

Communications

Main telephone lines **6.8 per 100 people**
Cellular mobile subscribers **24.4 per 100 people**
Internet users **397 per 10 000 people**
International dialling code **264**
Time zone **+1**

Environment

Forest area **9.3%**
Annual change in forest area **-0.9%**
Protected land area **5.2%**
CO_2 emissions **1.3 metric tons per capita**

Economy

Total Gross National Income (GNI) **6 573 US$M**
GNI per capita **4 200 US$**
Debt service ratio **N/A**
Total debt service **N/A**
Aid receipts **2.3% of GNI**
Military spending **2.9% of GDP**

Social Indicators

Infant mortality rate **47 per 1 000 live births**
Life expectancy **52.8**
Literacy rate **88.0%**
Access to safe water **87%**
Doctors **0.3 per 1 000 people**

Namibia lies on the southern Atlantic coast of Africa. Mountain ranges separate the coastal Namib Desert from the interior plateau, bordered to the south and east by the Kalahari Desert. The country is hot and dry, but some summer rain in the north supports crops and livestock. Employment is in agriculture and fishing, although the economy is based on mineral extraction – diamonds, uranium, lead, zinc and silver. The economy is closely linked to the Republic of South Africa.

Fish River Canyon, Namibia

Nauru Republic of Nauru

Area Sq Km **21**
Area Sq Miles **8**

Population **10 000**
Capital **Yaren**

Currency **Australian dollar**
Languages **Nauruan, English**

Religions **Protestant, Roman Catholic**
Organizations **Comm., UN**

Population

Total population **10 000**
Population change **N/A**
Urban population **N/A**
Total fertility rate **N/A**
Population aged 0–14 **N/A**
Population aged over 65 **N/A**
2050 projected population **18 000**

Communications

Main telephone lines **N/A**
Cellular mobile subscribers **N/A**
Internet users **N/A**
International dialling code **674**
Time zone **+12**

Social Indicators

Infant mortality rate **N/A**
Life expectancy **N/A**
Literacy rate **N/A**
Access to safe water **N/A**
Doctors **N/A**

Economy

Total Gross National Income (GNI) **N/A**
GNI per capita **N/A**
Debt service ratio **N/A**
Total debt service **N/A**
Aid receipts **N/A**
Military spending **N/A**

Environment

Forest area **N/A**
Annual change in forest area **0.0%**
Protected land area **N/A**
CO_2 emissions **N/A**

Nauru is a coral island near the Equator in the Pacific Ocean. It has a fertile coastal strip and a barren central plateau. The climate is tropical. The economy is based on phosphate mining, but reserves are near exhaustion and replacement of this income is a serious long-term problem.

Effect of phosphate mining, Nauru

Area Sq Km **147 181**
Area Sq Miles **56 827**

Population **29 331 000**
Capital **Kathmandu**

Currency **Nepalese rupee**
Languages **Nepali, Maithili, Bhojpuri, English, local languages**

Religions **Hindu, Buddhist, Sunni Muslim**
Organizations **UN**

Population

Total population **29 331 000**
Population change **1.7%**
Urban population **17.2%**
Total fertility rate **3.0 births per woman**
Population aged 0–14 **37.2%**
Population aged over 65 **4.0%**
2050 projected population **51 172 000**

Communications

Main telephone lines **2.2 per 100 people**
Cellular mobile subscribers **4.2 per 100 people**
Internet users **114 per 10 000 people**
International dialling code **977**
Time zone **+5.75**

Economy

Total Gross National Income (GNI) **8 790 US$M**
GNI per capita **400 US$**
Debt service ratio **1.6% of GNI**
Total debt service **139 842 000 US$**
Aid receipts **6.3% of GNI**
Military spending **1.9% of GDP**

Environment

Forest area **25.4%**
Annual change in forest area **-1.4%**
Protected land area **16.0%**
CO_2 emissions **0.1 metric tons per capita**

Social Indicators

Infant mortality rate **43 per 1 000 live births**
Life expectancy **63.7**
Literacy rate **56.5%**
Access to safe water **90%**
Doctors **0.21 per 1 000 people**

Nepal lies in the eastern Himalaya mountains between India and China. High mountains (including Everest) dominate the north. Most people live in the temperate central valleys and subtropical southern plains. The economy is based largely on agriculture and forestry. There is some manufacturing, chiefly of textiles and carpets, and tourism is important. Nepal relies heavily on foreign aid.

Mount Everest, Nepal

Netherlands Kingdom of the Netherlands

Area Sq Km **41 526**
Area Sq Miles **16 033**

Population **16 592 000**
Capital **Amsterdam/ The Hague ('s-Gravenhage)**

Currency **Euro**
Languages **Dutch, Frisian**

Religions **Roman Catholic, Protestant, Sunni Muslim**
Organizations **EU, NATO, OECD, UN**

Population

Total population **16 592 000**
Population change **0.4%**
Urban population **81.8%**
Total fertility rate **1.7 births per woman**
Population aged 0–14 **17.9%**
Population aged over 65 **14.7%**
2050 projected population **17 139 000**

Communications

Main telephone lines **46.6 per 100 people**
Cellular mobile subscribers **106.9 per 100 people**
Internet users **10 998 per 10 000 people**
International dialling code **31**
Time zone **+1**

Economy

Total Gross National Income (GNI) **703 484 US$M**
GNI per capita **50 150 US$**
Debt service ratio **N/A**
Total debt service **N/A**
Aid receipts **N/A**
Military spending **1.5% of GDP**

Environment

Forest area **10.8%**
Annual change in forest area **0.3%**
Protected land area **12.7%**
CO2 emissions **7.7 metric tons per capita**

Social Indicators

Infant mortality rate **4 per 1 000 live births**
Life expectancy **80.2**
Literacy rate **N/A**
Access to safe water **100%**
Doctors **3.71 per 1 000 people**

Tulip farm, Netherlands

The Netherlands lies on the North Sea coast of western Europe. Apart from low hills in the far southeast, the land is flat and low-lying, much of it below sea level. The coastal region includes the delta of five rivers and polders (reclaimed land), protected by sand dunes, dykes and canals. The climate is temperate, with cool summers and mild winters. Rainfall is spread evenly throughout the year. The Netherlands is a densely populated and highly urbanized country, with the majority of the population living in the cities of Amsterdam, Rotterdam and The Hague. Horticulture and dairy farming are important activities, although they employ less than four per cent of the workforce. The Netherlands ranks as the world's third agricultural exporter, and is a leading producer and exporter of natural gas from reserves in the North Sea. The economy is based mainly on international trade and manufacturing industry. The main industries produce food products, chemicals, machinery, electrical and electronic goods and transport equipment. Germany is the main trading partner, followed by other European Union countries.

Area Sq Km **800**
Area Sq Miles **309**

Population **198 000**
Capital **Willemstad**

Currency **Netherlands Antilles guilder**
Languages **Dutch, Papiamento, English**
Religions **Roman Catholic, Protestant**

Dissolved in October 2010, this former territory comprised two island groups: Curaçao and Bonaire off the coast of Venezuela, and Saba, Sint Eustatius and Sint Maarten in the Lesser Antilles. Tourism, oil refining and offshore finance were the mainstays of the economy. The main trading partners were the USA, Venezuela and Mexico. Since late 2010, Curaçao and Sint Maarten have become Self-governing Netherlands Territories, while Bonaire, Saba and Sint Eustatius are now Special Municipalities governed directly from the Netherlands.

Curaçao, now a Self-governing Netherlands Territory, fomerly part of the Netherlands Antilles

---

New Caledonia French Overseas Collectivity

Area Sq Km **19 058**
Area Sq Miles **7 358**

Population **250 000**
Capital **Nouméa**

Currency **CFP franc**
Languages **French, local languages**

Religions **Roman Catholic, Protestant, Sunni Muslim**

An island group lying in the southwest Pacific, with a sub-tropical climate. New Caledonia has over one-fifth of the world's nickel reserves, and the main economic activity is metal mining. Tourism is also important. New Caledonia relies on aid from France.

Crested gecko, New Caledonia

Area Sq Km **270 534**
Area Sq Miles **104 454**

Population **4 266 000**
Capital **Wellington**

Currency **New Zealand dollar**
Languages **English, Maori**

Religions **Protestant, Roman Catholic**
Organizations **APEC, Comm., OECD, UN**

Population

Total population **4 266 000**
Population change **0.9%**
Urban population **86.6%**
Total fertility rate **2.2 births per woman**
Population aged 0–14 **20.7%**
Population aged over 65 **12.5%**
2050 projected population **4 790 000**

Communications

Main telephone lines **44.1 per 100 people**
Cellular mobile subscribers **94.0 per 100 people**
Internet users **7 877 per 10 000 people**
International dialling code **64**
Time zone **+12**

Social Indicators

Infant mortality rate **5 per 1 000 live births**
Life expectancy **80.1**
Literacy rate **N/A**
Access to safe water **N/A**
Doctors **2.2 per 1 000 people**

Economy

Total Gross National Income (GNI) **111 958 US$M**
GNI per capita **27 940 US$**
Debt service ratio **N/A**
Total debt service **N/A**
Aid receipts **N/A**
Military spending **1.0% of GDP**

Environment

Forest area **31.0%**
Annual change in forest area **0.2%**
Protected land area **24.2%**
CO_2 emissions **7.2 metric tons per capita**

Milford Sound, New Zealand

New Zealand comprises two main islands. Both are mountainous. The North Island, with three-quarters of the population, has broad fertile valleys and a central plateau with volcanoes and hot springs. The South Island has the Southern Alps, with the Canterbury Plains the only significant lowland. The climate is temperate, although South Island has colder winters. New Zealand is a leading producer of beef, lamb and mutton, and wool and dairy products; fruit and fish are also important. Hydroelectric and geothermal power provide most energy needs. Other industries produce timber, wood pulp, iron, aluminium, machinery and chemicals. Tourism is growing. Main trading partners are Australia, the USA and Japan.

Area Sq Km **130 000**
Area Sq Miles **50 193**

Population **5 743 000**
Capital **Managua**

Currency **Córdoba**
Languages **Spanish, Amerindian languages**

Religions **Roman Catholic, Protestant**
Organizations **UN**

Population

Total population **5 743 000**
Population change **1.3%**
Urban population **56.7%**
Total fertility rate **2.8 births per woman**
Population aged 0–14 **35.8%**
Population aged over 65 **4.4%**
2050 projected population **9 371 000**

Communications

Main telephone lines **4.4 per 100 people**
Cellular mobile subscribers **32.7 per 100 people**
Internet users **277 per 10 000 people**
International dialling code **505**
Time zone **-6**

Social Indicators

Infant mortality rate **28 per 1 000 live births**
Life expectancy **72.9**
Literacy rate **78.0%**
Access to safe water **79%**
Doctors **0.37 per 1 000 people**

Economy

Total Gross National Income (GNI) **5 163 US$M**
GNI per capita **1 080 US$**
Debt service ratio **2.4% of GNI**
Total debt service **122 997 000 US$**
Aid receipts **13.9% of GNI**
Military spending **0.7% of GDP**

Environment

Forest area **42.7%**
Annual change in forest area **-1.3%**
Protected land area **17.6%**
CO_2 emissions **0.7 metric tons per capita**

Nicaragua lies at the heart of Central America, with both Pacific and Caribbean coasts. Mountain ranges separate the east, which is largely rainforest, from the more developed western regions, which include Lake Nicaragua and some active volcanoes. The highest land is in the north. The climate is tropical. Nicaragua is one of the western hemisphere's poorest countries, and the economy is largely agricultural. Exports include coffee, seafood, cotton and bananas. The USA is the main trading partner. Nicaragua has a huge national debt, and relies heavily on foreign aid.

Granada Cathedral, Nicaragua

Niger Republic of Niger

Area Sq Km **1 267 000**
Area Sq Miles **489 191**

Population **15 290 000**
Capital **Niamey**

Currency **CFA franc**
Languages **French, Hausa, Fulani, local languages**

Religions **Sunni Muslim, traditional beliefs**
Organizations **UN**

Population

Total population **15 290 000**
Population change **3.3%**
Urban population **16.5%**
Total fertility rate **7.0 births per woman**
Population aged 0–14 **49.7%**
Population aged over 65 **2.0%**
2050 projected population **50 156 000**

Communications

Main telephone lines **0.2 per 100 people**
Cellular mobile subscribers **3.4 per 100 people**
Internet users **28 per 10 000 people**
International dialling code **227**
Time zone **+1**

Environment

Forest area **1.0%**
Annual change in forest area **-1.0%**
Protected land area **6.6%**
CO_2 emissions **0.1 metric tons per capita**

Economy

Total Gross National Income (GNI) **3 665 US$M**
GNI per capita **330 US$**
Debt service ratio **5.0% of GNI**
Total debt service **181 178 000 US$**
Aid receipts **11.0% of GNI**
Military spending **1.1% of GDP**

Social Indicators

Infant mortality rate **83 per 1 000 live births**
Life expectancy **56.9**
Literacy rate **28.7%**
Access to safe water **46%**
Doctors **0.02 per 1 000 people**

A landlocked state of west Africa, Niger lies mostly within the Sahara desert, but with savanna in the south and in the Niger valley area. The mountains of the Massif de l'Aïr dominate central regions. Much of the country is hot and dry. The south has some summer rainfall, although droughts occur. The economy depends on subsistence farming and herding, and uranium exports, but Niger is one of the world's least developed countries and relies heavily on foreign aid. France is the main trading partner.

Desert landscape, Niger

Area Sq Km **923 768**
Area Sq Miles **356 669**

Population **154 729 000**
Capital **Abuja**

Currency **Naira**
Languages **English, Hausa, Yoruba, Ibo, Fulani, local languages**

Religions **Sunni Muslim, Christian, traditional beliefs**
Organizations **Comm., OPEC, UN**

Population

Total population **154 729 000**
Population change **2.2%**
Urban population **48.4%**
Total fertility rate **5.3 births per woman**
Population aged 0–14 **42.7%**
Population aged over 65 **3.1%**
2050 projected population **258 108 000**

Communications

Main telephone lines **1.3 per 100 people**
Cellular mobile subscribers **24.1 per 100 people**
Internet users **595 per 10 000 people**
International dialling code **234**
Time zone **+1**

Environment

Forest area **12.2%**
Annual change in forest area **-3.3%**
Protected land area **6.2%**
CO_2 emissions **0.8 metric tons per capita**

Economy

Total Gross National Income (GNI) **90 025 US$M**
GNI per capita **1 160 US$**
Debt service ratio **6.8% of GNI**
Total debt service **6 805 053 000 US$**
Aid receipts **11.1% of GNI**
Military spending **0.7% of GDP**

Social Indicators

Infant mortality rate **97 per 1 000 live births**
Life expectancy **46.8**
Literacy rate **72.0%**
Access to safe water **48%**
Doctors **0.28 per 1 000 people**

Nigeria is in west Africa, on the Gulf of Guinea, and is the most populous country in Africa. The Niger delta dominates coastal areas, fringed with sandy beaches, mangrove swamps and lagoons. Inland is a belt of rainforest which gives way to woodland or savanna on high plateaus. The far north is the semi-desert edge of the Sahara. The climate is tropical, with heavy summer rainfall in the south but low rainfall in the north. Most of the population lives in the coastal lowlands or in the west. About half the workforce is involved in agriculture, mainly growing subsistence crops. Agricultural production, however, has failed to keep up with demand, and Nigeria is now a net importer of food. Cocoa and rubber are the only significant export crops. The economy is heavily dependent on vast oil resources in the Niger delta and in shallow offshore waters, and oil accounts for over ninety per cent of export earnings. Nigeria also has natural gas reserves and some mineral deposits, but these are largely undeveloped. Industry involves mainly oil refining, chemicals (chiefly fertilizers), agricultural processing, textiles, steel manufacture and vehicle assembly. Political instability in the past has left Nigeria with heavy debts, poverty and unemployment.

Nigerian fishermen

 **Niue** Self-governing New Zealand Overseas Territory

Area Sq Km **258**
Area Sq Miles **100**

Currency **New Zealand dollar**
Languages **English, Niuean**

Population **1 625**
Capital **Alofi**

Religions **Christian**

Niue, one of the largest coral islands in the world, lies in the south Pacific Ocean about 500 kilometres (300 miles) east of Tonga. The economy depends on aid and remittances from New Zealand. The population is declining because of migration to New Zealand.

Talava natural arch, Niue

 Norfolk Island Australian External Territory

Area Sq Km **35**
Area Sq Miles **14**

Currency **Australian dollar**
Languages **English**

Population **2 523**
Capital **Kingston**

Religions **Protestant, Roman Catholic**

In the south Pacific Ocean, Norfolk Island lies between Vanuatu and New Zealand. Tourism has increased steadily and is the mainstay of the economy and provides revenues for agricultural development.

Northern Mariana Islands United States Commonwealth

Area Sq Km **477**
Area Sq Miles **184**

Currency **United States dollar**
Languages **English, Chamorro, local languages**

Population **87 000**
Capital **Capitol Hill**

Religions **Roman Catholic**

A chain of islands in the northwest Pacific Ocean, extending over 550 kilometres (350 miles) north to south. The main island is Saipan. Tourism is a major industry, employing approximately half the workforce.

Area Sq Km **120 538**
Area Sq Miles **46 540**

Population **23 906 000**
Capital **P'yŏngyang**

Currency **North Korean won**
Languages **Korean**

Religions **Traditional beliefs,
             Chondoist, Buddhist**
Organizations **UN**

Population

Total population **23 906 000**
Population change **0.3%**
Urban population **62.7%**
Total fertility rate **1.9 births per woman**
Population aged 0–14 **22.2%**
Population aged over 65 **9.4%**
2050 projected population **24 192 000**

Communications

Main telephone lines
4.4 per 100 people
Cellular mobile subscribers **N/A**
Internet users **N/A**
International dialling code **850**
Time zone **+9**

Economy

Total Gross National
Income (GNI) **N/A**
GNI per capita **N/A**
Debt service ratio **N/A**
Total debt service **N/A**
Aid receipts **N/A**
Military spending **N/A**

Environment

Forest area **51.4%**
Annual change in
forest area **-1.9%**
Protected land area **2.6%**
CO_2 emissions **3.5 metric
tons per capita**

Social Indicators

Infant mortality rate
42 per 1 000 live births
Life expectancy **67.1**
Literacy rate **N/A**
Access to safe water **100%**
Doctors **3.29 per 1 000 people**

Occupying the northern half of
the Korean peninsula in eastern
Asia, North Korea is a rugged and
mountainous country. The principal
lowlands and the main agricultural
areas are the plains in the southwest.
More than half the population lives
in urban areas, mainly on the coastal
plains. North Korea has a continental
climate, with cold, dry winters and
hot, wet summers. Approximately
one-third of the workforce is involved
in agriculture, mainly growing food
crops on cooperative farms. Various
minerals, notably iron ore, are mined
and are the basis of the country's heavy
industries. Exports include minerals
(lead, magnesite and zinc) and metal
products (chiefly iron and steel). The
economy declined after 1991, when ties
to the former USSR and eastern bloc
collapsed, and there have been serious
food shortages.

P'yŏngyang, North Korea

Norway Kingdom of Norway

Area Sq Km **323 878**
Area Sq Miles **125 050**

Population **4 812 000**
Capital **Oslo**

Currency **Norwegian krone**
Languages **Norwegian**

Religions **Protestant, Roman Catholic**
Organizations **NATO, OECD, UN**

Population

Total population **4 812 000**
Population change **1.3%**
Urban population **77.5%**
Total fertility rate **1.9 births per woman**
Population aged 0–14 **19.1%**
Population aged over 65 **14.6%**
2050 projected population **5 435 000**

Communications

Main telephone lines **44.3 per 100 people**
Cellular mobile subscribers **108.6 per 100 people**
Internet users **8 168 per 10 000 people**
International dialling code **47**
Time zone **+1**

Economy

Total Gross National Income (GNI) **318 919 US$M**
GNI per capita **87 070 US$**
Debt service ratio **N/A**
Total debt service **N/A**
Aid receipts **N/A**
Military spending **1.5% of GDP**

Environment

Forest area **30.8%**
Annual change in forest area **0.2%**
Protected land area **5.1%**
CO_2 emissions **11.4 metric tons per capita**

Social Indicators

Infant mortality rate **3 per 1 000 live births**
Life expectancy **80.4**
Literacy rate **N/A**
Access to safe water **100%**
Doctors **3.77 per 1 000 people**

Lofoten Islands, Norway

Norway stretches along the north and west coasts of Scandinavia, from the Arctic Ocean to the North Sea. Its extensive coastline is indented with fjords and fringed with many islands. Inland, the terrain is mountainous, with coniferous forests and lakes in the south. The only major lowland areas are along the southern North Sea and Skagerrak coasts, where most of the population lives. The climate is modified by the effect of the North Atlantic Drift ocean current. Norway has vast petroleum and natural gas resources in the North Sea. It is one of western Europe's leading producers of oil and gas, and exports of oil account for approximately half of total export earnings. Related industries include engineering (oil and gas platforms) and petrochemicals. More traditional industries process local raw materials, particularly fish, timber and minerals. Agriculture is limited, but fishing and fish farming are important. Norway is the world's leading exporter of farmed salmon. Merchant shipping and tourism are major sources of foreign exchange.

Area Sq Km **309 500**
Area Sq Miles **119 499**

Population **2 845 000**
Capital **Muscat (Masqaṭ)**

Currency **Omani riyal**
Languages **Arabic, Baluchi, Indian languages**

Religions **Ibadhi Muslim, Sunni Muslim**
Organizations **UN**

Population

Total population **2 845 000**
Population change **2.1%**
Urban population **71.6%**
Total fertility rate **3.1 births per woman**
Population aged 0–14 **32.0%**
Population aged over 65 **2.9%**
2050 projected population **4 958 000**

Communications

Main telephone lines
10.3 per 100 people
Cellular mobile subscribers
69.6 per 100 people
Internet users
1 222 per 10 000 people
International dialling code **968**
Time zone **+4**

Economy

Total Gross National
Income (GNI) **27 887 US$M**
GNI per capita **12 270 US$**
Debt service ratio **5.1% of GNI**
Total debt service **310 065 000 US$**
Aid receipts **N/A**
Military spending **11.8% of GDP**

Environment

Forest area **0.0%**
Annual change in
forest area **0.0%**
Protected land area **0.1%**
CO_2 emissions **12.0 metric tons per capita**

Social Indicators

Infant mortality rate
11 per 1 000 live births
Life expectancy **76.0**
Literacy rate **84.4%**
Access to safe water **N/A**
Doctors **1.67 per 1 000 people**

In southwest Asia, Oman occupies the east and southeast coasts of the Arabian Peninsula and an enclave north of the United Arab Emirates. Most of the land is desert, with mountains in the north and south. The climate is hot and mainly dry. Most of the population lives on the coastal strip on the Gulf of Oman. The majority depend on farming and fishing, but the oil and gas industries dominate the economy with around eighty per cent of export revenues coming from oil.

Mountain landscape, Oman

Area Sq Km **803 940**
Area Sq Miles **310 403**

Population **180 808 000**
Capital **Islamabad**

Currency **Pakistani rupee**
Languages **Urdu, Punjabi, Sindhi, Pushtu, English**

Religions **Sunni Muslim, Shi'a Muslim, Christian, Hindu**
Organizations **Comm., UN**

Population

Total population **180 808 000**
Population change **2.2%**
Urban population **36.2%**
Total fertility rate **3.9 births per woman**
Population aged 0–14 **37.3%**
Population aged over 65 **4.0%**
2050 projected population **304 700 000**

Communications

Main telephone lines **3.3 per 100 people**
Cellular mobile subscribers **22.0 per 100 people**
Internet users **764 per 10 000 people**
International dialling code **92**
Time zone **+5**

Economy

Total Gross National Income (GNI) **126 711 US$M**
GNI per capita **980 US$**
Debt service ratio **1.8% of GNI**
Total debt service **2 282 421 000 US$**
Aid receipts **1.7% of GNI**
Military spending **3.8% of GDP**

Environment

Forest area **2.5%**
Annual change in forest area **-2.1%**
Protected land area **8.5%**
CO_2 emissions **0.9 metric tons per capita**

Social Indicators

Infant mortality rate **73 per 1 000 live births**
Life expectancy **65.5**
Literacy rate **54.2%**
Access to safe water **91%**
Doctors **0.8 per 1 000 people**

Pakistan is in the northwest part of the Indian subcontinent in south Asia, on the Arabian Sea. The east and south are dominated by the great basin of the Indus river system. This is the main agricultural area and contains most of the predominantly rural population. To the north the land rises to the mountains of the Karakoram, Hindu Kush and Himalaya. The west is semi-desert plateaus and mountain ranges. The climate ranges between dry desert, and arctic tundra on the mountain tops. Temperatures are generally warm and rainfall is monsoonal. Agriculture is the main sector of the economy, employing approximately half of the workforce, and is based on extensive irrigation schemes. Pakistan is one of the world's leading producers of cotton and a major exporter of rice. Pakistan produces natural gas and has a variety of mineral deposits including coal and gold, but they are little developed. The main industries are textiles and clothing manufacture and food processing, with fabrics and ready-made clothing the leading exports. Pakistan also produces leather goods, fertilizers, chemicals, paper and precision instruments. The country depends heavily on foreign aid and remittances from workers abroad.

Badshahi Mosque, Lahore, Pakistan

Area Sq Km **497**
Area Sq Miles **192**

Population **20 000**
Capital **Melekeok**

Currency **United States dollar**
Languages **Palauan, English**

Religions **Roman Catholic, Protestant, traditional beliefs**
Organizations **UN**

Population

Total population **20 000**
Population change **0.6%**
Urban population **80.5%**
Total fertility rate **N/A**
Population aged 0–14 **N/A**
Population aged over 65 **N/A**
2050 projected population **21 000**

Communications

Main telephone lines **N/A**
Cellular mobile subscribers **N/A**
Internet users **N/A**
International dialling code **680**
Time zone **+9**

Social Indicators

Infant mortality rate **9 per 1 000 live births**
Life expectancy **69**
Literacy rate **N/A**
Access to safe water **85%**
Doctors **1.58 per 1 000 people**

Economy

Total Gross National Income (GNI) **161 US$M**
GNI per capita **8 650 US$**
Debt service ratio **N/A**
Total debt service **N/A**
Aid receipts **23.5% of GNI**
Military spending **N/A**

Environment

Forest area **87.6%**
Annual change in forest area **0.4%**
Protected land area **0.0%**
CO_2 emissions **5.7 metric tons per capita**

Palau comprises over three hundred islands in the western Caroline Islands, in the west Pacific Ocean. The climate is tropical. The economy is based on farming, fishing and tourism, but Palau is heavily dependent on aid from the USA.

Beach in Palau

Panama Republic of Panama

Area Sq Km **77 082**
Area Sq Miles **29 762**

Population **3 454 000**
Capital **Panama City**

Currency **Balboa**
Languages **Spanish, English, Amerindian languages**

Religions **Roman Catholic, Protestant, Sunni Muslim**
Organizations **UN**

Population
Total population **3 454 000**
Population change **1.6%**
Urban population **73.2%**
Total fertility rate **2.6 births per woman**
Population aged 0–14 **29.5%**
Population aged over 65 **6.4%**
2050 projected population **5 093 000**

Communications
Main telephone lines **14.9 per 100 people**
Cellular mobile subscribers **66.1 per 100 people**
Internet users **669 per 10 000 people**
International dialling code **507**
Time zone **-5**

Social Indicators
Infant mortality rate **18 per 1 000 live births**
Life expectancy **75.6**
Literacy rate **93.4%**
Access to safe water **90%**
Doctors **1.5 per 1 000 people**

Economy
Total Gross National Income (GNI) **16 442 US$M**
GNI per capita **6 180 US$**
Debt service ratio **21.5% of GNI**
Total debt service **3 458 784 000 US$**
Aid receipts **0.2% of GNI**
Military spending **N/A**

Environment
Forest area **57.7%**
Annual change in forest area **-0.1%**
Protected land area **10.2%**
CO_2 emissions **1.8 metric tons per capita**

Panama is the most southerly state in central America and has Pacific and Caribbean coasts. It is hilly, with mountains in the west and jungle near the Colombian border. The climate is tropical. Most of the population lives on the drier Pacific side. The economy is based mainly on services related to the Panama Canal: shipping, banking and tourism. Exports include bananas, shrimps, coffee, clothing and fish products. The USA is the main trading partner.

Gatun Locks, Panama Canal, Panama

Area Sq Km **462 840**
Area Sq Miles **178 704**

Population **6 732 000**
Capital **Port Moresby**

Currency **Kina**
Languages **English, Tok Pisin (creole), local languages**

Religions **Protestant, Roman Catholic, traditional beliefs**
Organizations **APEC, Comm., UN**

Population

Total population **6 732 000**
Population change **2.0%**
Urban population **12.5%**
Total fertility rate **3.8 births per woman**
Population aged 0–14 **40.1%**
Population aged over 65 **2.4%**
2050 projected population **10 619 000**

Communications

Main telephone lines **1.1 per 100 people**
Cellular mobile subscribers **1.3 per 100 people**
Internet users **183 per 10 000 people**
International dialling code **675**
Time zone **+10**

Social Indicators

Infant mortality rate **50 per 1 000 live births**
Life expectancy **57.4**
Literacy rate **57.8%**
Access to safe water **39%**
Doctors **0.05 per 1 000 people**

Economy

Total Gross National Income (GNI) **4 603 US$M**
GNI per capita **1 010 US$**
Debt service ratio **5.8% of GNI**
Total debt service **293 913 000 US$**
Aid receipts **5.5% of GNI**
Military spending **0.5% of GDP**

Environment

Forest area **65.0%**
Annual change in forest area **-0.5%**
Protected land area **8.0%**
CO_2 emissions **0.7 metric tons per capita**

Papua New Guinea occupies the eastern half of the island of New Guinea and includes many island groups. It has a forested and mountainous interior, bordered by swampy plains, and a tropical monsoon climate. Most of the workforce are farmers. Timber, copra, coffee and cocoa are important, but exports are dominated by minerals, chiefly gold and copper. The country depends on foreign aid. Australia, Japan and Singapore are the main trading partners.

Lesser bird-of-paradise, Papua New Guinea

Paraguay Republic of Paraguay

Area Sq Km **406 752**
Area Sq Miles **157 048**

Population **6 349 000**
Capital **Asunción**

Currency **Guaraní**
Languages **Spanish, Guaraní**

Religions **Roman Catholic, Protestant**
Organizations **UN**

Population

Total population **6 349 000**
Population change **1.7%**
Urban population **60.3%**
Total fertility rate **3.1 births per woman**
Population aged 0–14 **34.4%**
Population aged over 65 **5.0%**
2050 projected population **12 095 000**

Communications

Main telephone lines
5.3 per 100 people
Cellular mobile subscribers
51.3 per 100 people
Internet users
413 per 10 000 people
International dialling code **595**
Time zone **-4**

Social Indicators

Infant mortality rate
24 per 1 000 live births
Life expectancy **71.8**
Literacy rate **94.6%**
Access to safe water **86%**
Doctors **1.11 per 1 000 people**

Economy

Total Gross National
Income (GNI) **8 461 US$M**
GNI per capita **2 180 US$**
Debt service ratio **4.5% of GNI**
Total debt service **420 751 000 US$**
Aid receipts **0.6% of GNI**
Military spending **0.8% of GDP**

Environment

Forest area **46.5%**
Annual change in
forest area **-0.9%**
Protected land area **5.9%**
CO2 emissions **0.7 metric tons per capita**

Presidential Palace, Asunción, Paraguay

Paraguay is a landlocked country in central South America, bordering Bolivia, Brazil and Argentina. The Paraguay river separates a sparsely populated western zone of marsh and flat alluvial plains from a more developed, hilly and forested region to the east and south. The climate is subtropical. Virtually all electricity is produced by hydroelectric plants, and surplus power is exported to Brazil and Argentina. The hydroelectric dam at Itaipú is one of the largest in the world. The mainstay of the economy is agriculture and related industries. Exports include cotton, soya bean and edible oil products, timber and meat. Brazil and Argentina are the main trading partners.

Area Sq Km **1 285 216**
Area Sq Miles **496 225**

Population **29 165 000**
Capital **Lima**

Currency **Sol**
Languages **Spanish, Quechua, Aymara**

Religions **Roman Catholic, Protestant**
Organizations **APEC, UN**

Population

Total population **29 165 000**
Population change **1.1%**
Urban population **71.4%**
Total fertility rate **2.6 births per woman**
Population aged 0–14 **30.7%**
Population aged over 65 **5.7%**
2050 projected population **42 552 000**

Communications

Main telephone lines
8.5 per 100 people
Cellular mobile subscribers
30.9 per 100 people
Internet users
2 581 per 10 000 people
International dialling code **51**
Time zone **-5**

Social Indicators

Infant mortality rate
17 per 1 000 live births
Life expectancy **73.3**
Literacy rate **89.6%**
Access to safe water **83%**
Doctors **N/A**

Economy

Total Gross National
Income (GNI) **82 201 US$M**
GNI per capita **3 990 US$**
Debt service ratio **4.4% of GNI**
Total debt service **3 745 566 000 US$**
Aid receipts **0.6% of GNI**
Military spending **1.2% of GDP**

Environment

Forest area **53.7%**
Annual change in
forest area **-0.1%**
Protected land area **13.7%**
CO_2 emissions **1.3 metric tons per capita**

Peru lies on the Pacific coast of South America. Most Peruvians live on the coastal strip and on the plateaus of the high Andes mountains. East of the Andes is the Amazon rainforest. The coast is temperate with low rainfall while the east is hot, humid and wet. Agriculture involves one-third of the workforce and fishing is also important. Agriculture and fishing have both been disrupted by the El Niño climatic effect in recent years. Sugar, cotton, coffee and, illegally, coca are the main cash crops. Copper and copper products, fishmeal, zinc products, coffee, petroleum and its products, and textiles are the main exports. The USA and the European Union are the main trading partners.

Machu Picchu, Peru

Philippines Republic of the Philippines

Area Sq Km **300 000**
Area Sq Miles **115 831**

Population **91 983 000**
Capital **Manila**

Currency **Philippine peso**
Languages **English, Filipino, Tagalog, Cebuano, local languages**

Religions **Roman Catholic, Protestant, Sunni Muslim**
Organizations **APEC, ASEAN, UN**

Population

Total population **91 983 000**
Population change **1.8%**
Urban population **64.9%**
Total fertility rate **3.1 births per woman**
Population aged 0–14 **34.3%**
Population aged over 65 **4.1%**
2050 projected population **127 068 000**

Social Indicators

Infant mortality rate **23 per 1 000 live births**
Life expectancy **71.9**
Literacy rate **93.4%**
Access to safe water **85%**
Doctors **1.15 per 1 000 people**

Communications

Main telephone lines **4.3 per 100 people**
Cellular mobile subscribers **50.8 per 100 people**
Internet users **548 per 10 000 people**
International dialling code **63**
Time zone **+8**

Economy

Total Gross National Income (GNI) **120 190 US$M**
GNI per capita **1 890 US$**
Debt service ratio **10.7% of GNI**
Total debt service **13 680 640 000 US$**
Aid receipts **0.4% of GNI**
Military spending **0.9% of GDP**

Environment

Forest area **24.0%**
Annual change in forest area **-2.1%**
Protected land area **10.1%**
CO2 emissions **0.9 metric tons per capita**

The Philippines, in southeast Asia, consists of over seven thousand islands and atolls lying between the South China Sea and the Pacific Ocean. The islands of Luzon and Mindanao account for two-thirds of the land area. They and nine other fairly large islands are mountainous and forested. There are active volcanoes, and earthquakes and tropical storms are common. Most of the population lives in the plains on the larger islands or on the coastal strips. The climate is hot and humid with heavy monsoonal rainfall. Rice, coconuts, sugar cane, pineapples and bananas are the main agricultural crops, and fishing is also important. Main exports are electronic equipment, machinery and transport equipment, garments and coconut products. Foreign aid and remittances from workers abroad are important to the economy, which faces problems of high population growth rate and high unemployment. The USA and Japan are the main trading partners.

Jeepney, Philippines

Pitcairn Islands United Kingdom Overseas Territory

Area Sq Km **45**
Area Sq Miles **17**

Currency **New Zealand dollar**
Languages **English**

Population **66**
Capital **Adamstown**

Religions **Protestant**

An island group in the southeast Pacific Ocean consisting of Pitcairn Island and three uninhabited islands.

It was originally settled by mutineers from *HMS Bounty* in 1790.

Area Sq Km **312 683**
Area Sq Miles **120 728**

Population **38 074 000**
Capital **Warsaw (Warszawa)**

Currency **Złoty**
Languages **Polish, German**

Religions **Roman Catholic, Polish Orthodox**
Organizations **EU, NATO, OECD, UN**

Population

Total population **38 074 000**
Population change **0.0%**
Urban population **61.3%**
Total fertility rate **1.3 births per woman**
Population aged 0–14 **15.2%**
Population aged over 65 **13.3%**
2050 projected population **31 916 000**

Communications

Main telephone lines **29.8 per 100 people**
Cellular mobile subscribers **95.5 per 100 people**
Internet users **3 658 per 10 000 people**
International dialling code **48**
Time zone **+1**

Economy

Total Gross National Income (GNI) **312 994 US$M**
GNI per capita **11 880 US$**
Debt service ratio **11.1% of GNI**
Total debt service **36 044 403 000 US$**
Aid receipts **N/A**
Military spending **2.0% of GDP**

Environment

Forest area **30.0%**
Annual change in forest area **0.3%**
Protected land area **24.6%**
CO_2 emissions **7.9 metric tons per capita**

Social Indicators

Infant mortality rate **6 per 1 000 live births**
Life expectancy **75.1**
Literacy rate **99.3%**
Access to safe water **N/A**
Doctors **1.97 per 1 000 people**

Poland lies on the Baltic coast of eastern Europe. The Oder (Odra) and Vistula (Wisła) river deltas dominate the coast. Inland, much of the country is low-lying, with woods and lakes. In the south the land rises to the Sudeten Mountains and the western part of the Carpathian Mountains, which form the borders with the Czech Republic and Slovakia respectively. The climate is continental. Around a quarter of the workforce is involved in agriculture, and exports include livestock products and sugar. The economy is heavily industrialized, with mining and manufacturing accounting for forty per cent of national income. Poland is one of the world's major producers of coal, and also produces copper, zinc, lead, sulphur and natural gas. The main industries are machinery and transport equipment, shipbuilding, and metal and chemical production. Exports include machinery and transport equipment, manufactured goods, food and live animals. Germany is the main trading partner. Poland joined the European Union in May 2004.

Poznań, Poland

Portugal Portuguese Republic

Area Sq Km **88 940**
Area Sq Miles **34 340**

Population **10 707 000**
Capital **Lisbon (Lisboa)**

Currency **Euro**
Languages **Portuguese**

Religions **Roman Catholic, Protestant**
Organizations **EU, NATO, OECD, UN**

Population

Total population **10 707 000**
Population change **0.2%**
Urban population **59.5%**
Total fertility rate **1.3 births per woman**
Population aged 0–14 **15.4%**
Population aged over 65 **17.5%**
2050 projected population **10 723 000**

Communications

Main telephone lines **40.2 per 100 people**
Cellular mobile subscribers **116.0 per 100 people**
Internet users **3 025 per 10 000 people**
International dialling code **351**
Time zone **GMT**

Economy

Total Gross National Income (GNI) **189 017 US$M**
GNI per capita **20 560 US$**
Debt service ratio **N/A**
Total debt service **N/A**
Aid receipts **N/A**
Military spending **2.1% of GDP**

Environment

Forest area **41.3%**
Annual change in forest area **1.1%**
Protected land area **5.0%**
CO2 emissions **5.9 metric tons per capita**

Social Indicators

Infant mortality rate **3 per 1 000 live births**
Life expectancy **78.3**
Literacy rate **94.9%**
Access to safe water **N/A**
Doctors **3.44 per 1 000 people**

Portugal lies in the west of the Iberian peninsula in southwest Europe. The island groups of the Azores and Madeira are parts of Portugal. The climate in the he south is warmer, with dry, mild winters. Most Portuguese live near the coast, particularly around Lisbon (Lisboa). Agriculture, fishing and forestry involve only a tenth of the workforce: mining and manufacturing are the main economic sectors, producing kaolin, copper, tin, zinc, tungsten and salt. Exports include textiles, clothing and footwear, electrical machinery and transport equipment, cork and wood products, and chemicals. Tourism and banking are important, as are remittances from workers abroad. Most trade is with other EU countries.

Monument to the Discoveries, Lisbon, Portugal

Area Sq Km **9 104**
Area Sq Miles **3 515**

Currency **United States dollar**
Languages **Spanish, English**

Population **3 982 000**
Capital **San Juan**

Religions **Roman Catholic,
Protestant**

The Caribbean island of Puerto Rico has a forested, hilly interior, coastal plains and a tropical climate. Half of the population lives in the San Juan area. The economy is based on manufacturing (chiefly chemicals, electronics and food), tourism and agriculture. The USA is the main trading partner.

El Morro, San Juan, Puerto Rico

Qatar State of Qatar

Area Sq Km **11 437**
Area Sq Miles **4 416**

Population **1 409 000**
Capital **Doha (Ad Dawḥah)**

Currency **Qatari riyal**
Languages **Arabic**

Religions **Sunni Muslim**
Organizations **OPEC, UN**

Population

Total population **1 409 000**
Population change **11.9%**
Urban population **95.6%**
Total fertility rate **2.4 births per woman**
Population aged 0–14 **16.2%**
Population aged over 65 **1.1%**
2050 projected population **1 330 000**

Communications

Main telephone lines
27.2 per 100 people
Cellular mobile subscribers
109.6 per 100 people
Internet users
3 455 per 10 000 people
International dialling code **974**
Time zone **+3**

Social Indicators

Infant mortality rate
12 per 1 000 live births
Life expectancy **76.0**
Literacy rate **93.1%**
Access to safe water **100%**
Doctors **2.64 per 1 000 people**

Economy

Total Gross National Income (GNI) **N/A**
GNI per capita **N/A**
Debt service ratio **N/A**
Total debt service **N/A**
Aid receipts **N/A**
Military spending **N/A**

Environment

Forest area **N/A**
Annual change in forest area **0.0%**
Protected land area **0.0%**
CO2 emissions **56.3 metric tons per capita**

Qatar occupies a peninsula in southwest Asia that extends northwards from east-central Saudi Arabia into The Gulf. The land is flat and barren with sand dunes and salt pans. The climate is hot and mainly dry. Most people live in the area of the capital, Doha. The economy is heavily dependent on oil and natural gas production and the oil-refining industry. Income also comes from overseas investment. Japan is the largest trading partner.

Réunion French Overseas Department

Area Sq Km **2 551**	Currency **Euro**
Area Sq Miles **985**	Languages **French, creole**

Population **827 000**	Religions **Roman Catholic**
Capital **St-Denis**	

The Indian Ocean island of Réunion is mountainous, with coastal lowlands and a warm climate. The economy depends on tourism, French aid, and exports of sugar. In

2005 France transferred the administration of various small uninhabited islands in the seas around Madagascar from Réunion to the French Southern and Antarctic Lands.

Trois Bassin waterfall, Réunion

Romania

Area Sq Km **237 500**	Population **21 275 000**
Area Sq Miles **91 699**	Capital **Bucharest (Bucureşti)**

Currency **Romanian leu**
Languages **Romanian, Hungarian**

Religions **Romanian Orthodox, Protestant, Roman Catholic**
Organizations **EU, NATO, UN**

Population

Total population **21 275 000**
Population change **-0.2%**
Urban population **54.2%**
Total fertility rate **1.3 births per woman**
Population aged 0–14 **15.2%**
Population aged over 65 **14.9%**
2050 projected population **16 757 000**

Communications

Main telephone lines
19.4 per 100 people
Cellular mobile subscribers
80.5 per 100 people
Internet users
5 224 per 10 000 people
International dialling code **40**
Time zone **+2**

Social Indicators

Infant mortality rate
13 per 1 000 live births
Life expectancy **72.6**
Literacy rate **97.6%**
Access to safe water **57%**
Doctors **1.92 per 1 000 people**

Economy

Total Gross National Income (GNI) **104 382 US$M**
GNI per capita **7 930 US$**
Debt service ratio **7.3% of GNI**
Total debt service **8 678 183 000 US$**
Aid receipts **N/A**
Military spending **1.9% of GDP**

Environment

Forest area **27.7%**
Annual change in forest area **N/A**
Protected land area **2.2%**
CO2 emissions **4.1 metric tons per capita**

Romania lies in eastern Europe, on the northwest coast of the Black Sea. The climate is continental. Romania has mineral resources (zinc, lead, silver and gold) and oil and natural gas reserves. Economic development has been slow and sporadic, but measures to accelerate change were introduced in 1999. Agriculture employs over one-third of the workforce. The main exports are textiles, mineral products, chemicals, machinery and footwear. The main trading partners are Germany and Italy.

Area Sq Km **17 075 400**
Area Sq Miles **6 592 849**

Population **140 874 000**
Capital **Moscow (Moskva)**

Currency **Russian rouble**
Languages **Russian, Tatar, Ukrainian, local languages**

Religions **Russian Orthodox, Sunni Muslim, Protestant**
Organizations **APEC, CIS, UN**

Population

Total population **140 874 000**
Population change **-0.2%**
Urban population **72.8%**
Total fertility rate **1.4 births per woman**
Population aged 0–14 **14.7%**
Population aged over 65 **13.3%**
2050 projected population **111 752 000**

Environment

Forest area **49.4%**
Annual change in forest area **N/A**
Protected land area **6.8%**
CO_2 emissions **10.5 metric tons per capita**

Economy

Total Gross National Income (GNI) **822 328 US$M**
GNI per capita **9 620 US$**
Debt service ratio **5.2% of GNI**
Total debt service **50 222 974 000 US$**
Aid receipts **N/A**
Military spending **4.0% of GDP**

Communications

Main telephone lines **30.8 per 100 people**
Cellular mobile subscribers **105.7 per 100 people**
Internet users **1 802 per 10 000 people**
International dialling code **7**
Time zone **+2 to +12**

Social Indicators

Infant mortality rate **13 per 1 000 live births**
Life expectancy **67.6**
Literacy rate **99.5%**
Access to safe water **97%**
Doctors **4.31 per 1 000 people**

The Russian Federation occupies much of eastern Europe and all of northern Asia, and is the world's largest country. It borders fourteen countries to the west and south and has long coastlines on the Arctic and Pacific Oceans to the north and east. European Russia lies west of the Ural Mountains. To the south the land rises to uplands and the Caucasus mountains on the border with Georgia and Azerbaijan. East of the Urals lies the flat West Siberian Plain and the Central Siberian Plateau. In the south-east is Lake Baikal, the world's deepest lake, and the Sayan ranges on the border with Kazakhstan and Mongolia. Eastern Siberia is rugged and mountainous, with many active volcanoes in the Kamchatka Peninsula. The country's major rivers are the Volga in the west and the Ob', Irtysh, Yenisey, Lena and Amur in Siberia. The climate and vegetation range between arctic tundra in the north and semi-arid steppe towards the Black and Caspian Sea coasts in the south. In general, the climate is continental with extreme temperatures. The majority of the population (the eighth largest in the world), and industry and agriculture are concentrated in European Russia.

The economy is dependent on exploitation of raw materials and on heavy industry. Russia has a wealth of mineral resources, although they are often difficult to exploit because of climate and remote locations. It is one of the world's leading producers of petroleum, natural gas and coal as well as iron ore, nickel, copper, bauxite, and many precious and rare metals. Forests cover over forty per cent of the land area and supply an important timber, paper and pulp industry. Approximately eight per cent of the land is suitable for cultivation, but farming is generally inefficient and food, especially grains, must be imported. Fishing is important and Russia has a large fleet operating around the world. The transition to a market economy has been slow and difficult, with considerable underemployment. As well as mining and extractive industries there is a wide range of manufacturing industry, from steel mills to aircraft and space vehicles, shipbuilding, synthetic fabrics, plastics, cotton fabrics, consumer durables,

chemicals and fertilizers. Exports include fuels, metals, machinery, chemicals and forest products. The most important trading partners include Germany, the USA and Belarus.

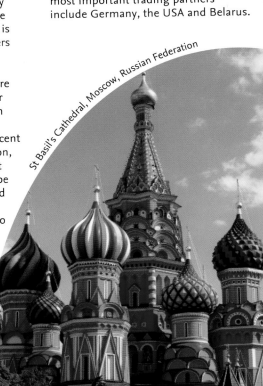

St Basil's Cathedral, Moscow, Russian Federation

Rwanda Republic of Rwanda

Area Sq Km **26 338**
Area Sq Miles **10 169**

Population **9 998 000**
Capital **Kigali**

Currency **Rwandan franc**
Languages **Kinyarwanda,
French, English**

Religions **Roman Catholic,
traditional beliefs,
Protestant**
Organizations **UN**

Population

Total population **9 998 000**
Population change **2.8%**
Urban population **18.3%**
Total fertility rate **5.4 births per woman**
Population aged 0–14 **42.2%**
Population aged over 65 **2.5%**
2050 projected population **18 153 000**

Communications

Main telephone lines
0.2 per 100 people
Cellular mobile subscribers
3.4 per 100 people
Internet users
55 per 10 000 people
International dialling code **250**
Time zone **+2**

Social Indicators

Infant mortality rate
109 per 1 000 live births
Life expectancy **50.2**
Literacy rate **N/A**
Access to safe water **74%**
Doctors **0.05 per 1 000 people**

Economy

Total Gross National
Income (GNI) **2 341 US$M**
GNI per capita **410 US$**
Debt service ratio **1.2% of GNI**
Total debt service **30 612 000 US$**
Aid receipts **23.6% of GNI**
Military spending **2.7% of GDP**

Environment

Forest area **19.5%**
Annual change in
forest area **6.9%**
Protected land area **8.1%**
CO_2 emissions **0.1 metric
tons per capita**

Rwanda, the most densely populated
country in Africa, is situated in the
mountains and plateaus to the east
of the western branch of the Great
Rift Valley in east Africa. The climate
is warm with a summer dry season.
Rwanda depends on subsistence
farming, coffee and tea exports, light
industry and foreign aid. The country is
slowly recovering from serious internal
conflict which caused devastation in the
early 1990s.

L'Hoest monkey, Rwanda

St Helena Part of the United Kingdom Overseas Territory of St Helena, Ascension and Tristan da Cunha

Area Sq Km **121**
Area Sq Miles **47**

Currency **St Helena pound**
Languages **English**

Population **4 255**
Capital **Jamestown**

Religions **Protestant, Roman
Catholic**

St Helena is the largest constituent
part of the UK Overseas dependent
Territory, St Helena, Ascension
and Tristan da Cunha, a group of
isolated islands lying in the south

Atlantic Ocean. The economy relies
on financial aid from the UK. Main
trading partners are the UK and
South Africa.

Area Sq Km **261**	Population **52 000**	Currency **East Caribbean dollar**	Religions **Protestant, Roman**
Area Sq Miles **101**	Capital **Basseterre**	Languages **English, creole**	**Catholic**

Organizations **CARICOM, Comm., UN**

Social Indicators

Infant mortality rate
16 per 1 000 live births
Life expectancy **N/A**
Literacy rate
N/A
Access to
safe water **100%**
Doctors **1.1 per 1 000 people**

Population

Total population **52 000**
Population change **0.8%**
Urban population **32.3%**
Total fertility rate **N/A**
Population aged 0–14 **N/A**
Population aged over 65 **N/A**
2050 projected population **59 000**

Communications

Main telephone lines
59.3 per 100 people
Cellular mobile subscribers
23.7 per 100 people
Internet users
2 428 per 10 000 people
International dialling code **1 869**
Time zone **-4**

Economy

Total Gross National
Income (GNI) **406 US$M**
GNI per capita **10 960 US$**
Debt service ratio **12.3% of GNI**
Total debt service **46 585 000 US$**
Aid receipts **1.2% of GNI**
Military spending **N/A**

Environment

Forest area **20.4%**
Annual change in
forest area **0.0%**
Protected land area **0.0%**
CO_2 emissions **2.8 metric
tons per capita**

St Kitts and Nevis are in the Leeward Islands, in the Caribbean. Both volcanic islands are mountainous and forested, with sandy beaches and a warm, wet climate. About three-quarters of the population lives on St Kitts. Agriculture is the main activity, with sugar the main product. Tourism and manufacturing (chiefly garments and electronic components) and offshore banking are important activities.

St Lucia

Area Sq Km **616**	Population **172 000**	Currency **East Caribbean dollar**	Religions **Roman Catholic,**
Area Sq Miles **238**	Capital **Castries**	Languages **English, creole**	**Protestant**

Organizations **CARICOM, Comm., UN**

Social Indicators

Infant mortality rate
14 per 1 000 live births
Life expectancy **74.4**
Literacy rate
N/A
Access to
safe water **98%**
Doctors **N/A**

Population

Total population **172 000**
Population change **1.2%**
Urban population **27.8%**
Total fertility rate **2.1 births per woman**
Population aged 0–14 **26.8%**
Population aged over 65 **6.8%**
2050 projected population **188 000**

Communications

Main telephone lines
32.6 per 100 people
Cellular mobile subscribers
65.7 per 100 people
Internet users
6 169 per 10 000 people
International dialling code **1 758**
Time zone **-4**

Economy

Total Gross National
Income (GNI) **833 US$M**
GNI per capita **5 530 US$**
Debt service ratio **4.1% of GNI**
Total debt service **34 456 000 US$**
Aid receipts **2.2% of GNI**
Military spending **N/A**

Environment

Forest area **27.9%**
Annual change in
forest area **0.0%**
Protected land area **15.4%**
CO_2 emissions **2.2 metric
tons per capita**

St Lucia, one of the Windward Islands in the Caribbean Sea, is a volcanic island with forested mountains, hot springs, sandy beaches and a wet tropical climate. Agriculture is the main activity, with bananas accounting for approximately forty per cent of export earnings. Tourism, agricultural processing and light manufacturing are increasingly important.

St Vincent and the Grenadines

Area Sq Km **389**
Area Sq Miles **150**

Population **109 000**
Capital **Kingstown**

Currency **East Caribbean dollar**
Languages **English, creole**

Religions **Protestant, Roman Catholic**
Organizations **CARICOM, Comm., UN**

Social Indicators
Infant mortality rate **17 per 1 000 live births**
Life expectancy **71.8**
Literacy rate **N/A**
Access to safe water **N/A**
Doctors **0.75 per 1 000 people**

Population
Total population **109 000**
Population change **0.1%**
Urban population **47.0%**
Total fertility rate **2.1 births per woman**
Population aged 0–14 **27.3%**
Population aged over 65 **6.9%**
2050 projected population **105 000**

Communications
Main telephone lines **19.0 per 100 people**
Cellular mobile subscribers **73.6 per 100 people**
Internet users **840 per 10 000 people**
International dialling code **1 784**
Time zone **-4**

Economy
Total Gross National Income (GNI) **395 US$M**
GNI per capita **5 140 US$**
Debt service ratio **7.0% of GNI**
Total debt service **35 627 000 US$**
Aid receipts **1.0% of GNI**
Military spending **N/A**

Environment
Forest area **27.4%**
Annual change in forest area **0.8%**
Protected land area **11.3%**
CO2 emissions **1.8 metric tons per capita**

St Vincent, whose territory includes islets and cays in the Grenadines, is in the Windward Islands, in the Caribbean. St Vincent itself is forested and mountainous, with an active volcano, Soufrière. The climate is tropical and wet. The economy is based mainly on agriculture and tourism. Bananas account for approximately one-third of export earnings and arrowroot is also important. Most trade is with the USA and other CARICOM countries.

Samoa Independent State of Samoa

Area Sq Km **2 831**
Area Sq Miles **1 093**

Population **179 000**
Capital **Apia**

Currency **Tala**
Languages **Samoan, English**

Religions **Protestant, Roman Catholic**
Organizations **Comm., UN**

Population
Total population **179 000**
Population change **0.1%**
Urban population **23.0%**
Total fertility rate **3.9 births per woman**
Population aged 0–14 **40.0%**
Population aged over 65 **4.8%**
2050 projected population **157 000**

Communications
Main telephone lines **10.9 per 100 people**
Cellular mobile subscribers **25.4 per 100 people**
Internet users **446 per 10 000 people**
International dialling code **685**
Time zone **-11**

Social Indicators
Infant mortality rate **22 per 1 000 live births**
Life expectancy **71.6**
Literacy rate **98.7%**
Access to safe water **88%**
Doctors **0.28 per 1 000 people**

Economy
Total Gross National Income (GNI) **421 US$M**
GNI per capita **2 780 US$**
Debt service ratio **7.0% of GNI**
Total debt service **29 506 000 US$**
Aid receipts **11.3% of GNI**
Military spending **N/A**

Environment
Forest area **60.4%**
Annual change in forest area **0.0%**
Protected land area **2.0%**
CO2 emissions **0.8 metric tons per capita**

Samoa consists of two larger mountainous and forested islands, Savai'i and Upolu, and seven smaller islands, in the south Pacific Ocean. Over half the population lives on Upolu. The climate is tropical. The economy is based on agriculture, with some fishing and light manufacturing. Traditional exports are coconut products, fish and beer. Tourism is increasing, but the islands depend on workers' remittances and foreign aid.

Area Sq Km **61**
Area Sq Miles **24**

Population **31 000**
Capital **San Marino**

Currency **Euro**
Languages **Italian**

Religions **Roman Catholic**
Organizations **UN**

Population

Total population **31 000**
Population change **1.4%**
Urban population **94.2%**
Total fertility rate **N/A**
Population aged 0–14 **N/A**
Population aged over 65 **N/A**
2050 projected population **30 000**

Communications

Main telephone lines **77.8 per 100 people**
Cellular mobile subscribers **64.4 per 100 people**
Internet users **5 704 per 10 000 people**
International dialling code **378**
Time zone **+1**

Social Indicators

Infant mortality rate **4 per 1 000 live births**
Life expectancy **82**
Literacy rate **N/A**
Access to safe water **N/A**
Doctors **N/A**

Economy

Total Gross National Income (GNI) **1 291 US$M**
GNI per capita **46 770 US$**
Debt service ratio **N/A**
Total debt service **N/A**
Aid receipts **N/A**
Military spending **N/A**

Environment

Forest area **1.7%**
Annual change in forest area **0.0%**
Protected land area **N/A**
CO_2 emissions **N/A**

Landlocked San Marino lies in northeast Italy. A third of the people live in the capital. There is some agriculture and light industry, but most income comes from tourism. Italy is the main trading partner.

São Tomé and Príncipe Democratic Republic of São Tomé and Príncipe

Area Sq Km **964**
Area Sq Miles **372**

Population **163 000**
Capital **São Tomé**

Currency **Dobra**
Languages **Portuguese, creole**

Religions **Roman Catholic, Protestant**
Organizations **UN**

Social Indicators

Infant mortality rate **64 per 1 000 live births**
Life expectancy **65.4**
Literacy rate **87.9%**
Access to safe water **79%**
Doctors **0.49 per 1 000 people**

Population

Total population **163 000**
Population change **1.8%**
Urban population **60.6%**
Total fertility rate **3.9 births per woman**
Population aged 0–14 **40.9%**
Population aged over 65 **4.1%**
2050 projected population **295 000**

Communications

Main telephone lines **4.7 per 100 people**
Cellular mobile subscribers **11.5 per 100 people**
Internet users **1 811 per 10 000 people**
International dialling code **239**
Time zone **GMT**

Economy

Total Gross National Income (GNI) **124 US$M**
GNI per capita **1 020 US$**
Debt service ratio **7.8% of GNI**
Total debt service **9 337 000 US$**
Aid receipts **18.0% of GNI**
Military spending **N/A**

Environment

Forest area **28.5%**
Annual change in forest area **0.0%**
Protected land area **N/A**
CO_2 emissions **0.7 metric tons per capita**

The two main islands and adjacent islets lie off the coast of west Africa in the Gulf of Guinea. São Tomé is the larger island, with over ninety per cent of the population. Both São Tomé and Príncipe are mountainous and tree-covered, and have a hot and humid climate. The economy is heavily dependent on cocoa, which accounts for around ninety per cent of export earnings.

Saudi Arabia Kingdom of Saudi Arabia

Area Sq Km **2 200 000**
Area Sq Miles **849 425**

Population **25 721 000**
Capital **Riyadh (Ar Riyāḍ)**

Currency **Saudi Arabian riyal**
Languages **Arabic**

Religions **Sunni Muslim, Shi'a Muslim**
Organizations **OPEC, UN**

Population

Total population **25 721 000**
Population change **2.0%**
Urban population **82.4%**
Total fertility rate **3.4 births per woman**
Population aged 0–14 **32.9%**
Population aged over 65 **2.9%**
2050 projected population **49 464 000**

Communications

Main telephone lines
15.7 per 100 people
Cellular mobile subscribers
78.1 per 100 people
Internet users
1 866 per 10 000 people
International dialling code **966**
Time zone **+3**

Economy

Total Gross National Income (GNI) **331 041 US$M**
GNI per capita **15 500 US$**
Debt service ratio **N/A**
Total debt service **N/A**
Aid receipts **N/A**
Military spending **8.5% of GDP**

Environment

Forest area **1.4%**
Annual change in forest area **0.0%**
Protected land area **38.1%**
CO2 emissions **16.5 metric tons per capita**

Social Indicators

Infant mortality rate
20 per 1 000 live births
Life expectancy **73.0**
Literacy rate **85.0%**
Access to safe water **N/A**
Doctors **1.37 per 1 000 people**

Saudi Arabia occupies most of the Arabian Peninsula in southwest Asia. The terrain is desert or semi-desert plateaus, which rise to mountains running parallel to the Red Sea in the west and slope down to plains in the southeast and along The Gulf in the east. Over eighty per cent of the population lives in urban areas. There are around four million foreign workers in Saudi Arabia, employed mainly in the oil and service industries. Summers are hot, winters are warm and rainfall is low. Saudi Arabia has the world's largest reserves of oil and significant natural gas reserves, both onshore and in The Gulf. Crude oil and refined products account for over ninety per cent of export earnings. Other industries and irrigated agriculture are being encouraged, but most food and raw materials are imported. Saudi Arabia has important banking and commercial interests. Japan and the USA are the main trading partners.

Nabatean tombs, Saudi Arabia

Area Sq Km **196 720**
Area Sq Miles **75 954**

Population **12 534 000**
Capital **Dakar**

Currency **CFA franc**
Languages **French, Wolof, Fulani, local languages**

Religions **Sunni Muslim, Roman Catholic, traditional beliefs**
Organizations **UN**

Population

Total population **12 534 000**
Population change **2.6%**
Urban population **42.4%**
Total fertility rate **5.0 births per woman**
Population aged 0–14 **43.8%**
Population aged over 65 **2.4%**
2050 projected population **23 108 000**

Environment

Forest area **45.0%**
Annual change in forest area **-0.5%**
Protected land area **11.2%**
CO2 emissions **0.4 metric tons per capita**

Communications

Main telephone lines **2.4 per 100 people**
Cellular mobile subscribers **25.0 per 100 people**
Internet users **545 per 10 000 people**
International dialling code **221**
Time zone **GMT**

Economy

Total Gross National Income (GNI) **9 117 US$M**
GNI per capita **970 US$**
Debt service ratio **2.2% of GNI**
Total debt service **202 197 000 US$**
Aid receipts **9.3% of GNI**
Military spending **1.6% of GDP**

Social Indicators

Infant mortality rate **59 per 1 000 live births**
Life expectancy **55.7**
Literacy rate **41.9%**
Access to safe water **76%**
Doctors **0.06 per 1 000 people**

Senegal lies on the Atlantic coast of west Africa. The north is arid semi-desert, while the south is mainly fertile savanna bushland. The climate is tropical with summer rains, although droughts occur. One-fifth of the population lives in and around Dakar, the capital and main port. Fish, groundnuts and phosphates are the main exports. France is the main trading partner.

Mosque de Oukama, Dakar, Senegal

Serbia Republic of Serbia

Area Sq Km **77 453**
Area Sq Miles **29 904**

Population **9 850 000**
Capital **Belgrade (Beograd)**

Currency **Serbian dinar**
Languages **Serbian, Hungarian**

Religions **Serbian Orthodox, Roman Catholic, Sunni Muslim**
Organizations **UN**

Population

Total population **9 850 448**
Population change **-0.4%**
Urban population **52.0%**
Total fertility rate **1.4 births per woman**
Population aged 0–14 **17.8%**
Population aged over 65 **14.5%**
2050 projected population **N/A**

Communications

Main telephone lines **25.9 per 100 people**
Cellular mobile subscribers **63.3 per 100 people**
Internet users **1 334 per 10 000 people**
International dialling code **381**
Time zone **+1**

Economy

Total Gross National Income (GNI) **29 961 US$M**
GNI per capita **5 700 US$**
Debt service ratio **8.5% of GNI**
Total debt service **2 679 730 000 US$**
Aid receipts **5.1% of GNI**
Military spending **2.1% of GDP**

Environment

Forest area **N/A**
Annual change in forest area **N/A**
Protected land area **N/A**
CO2 emissions **N/A**

Social Indicators

Infant mortality rate **7 per 1 000 live births**
Life expectancy **73.4**
Literacy rate **N/A**
Access to safe water **N/A**
Doctors **N/A**

St. George's Church, Topola, Serbia

Following ethnic conflict and the break-up of Yugoslavia through the 1990s, the state union of Serbia and Montenegro retained the name Yugoslavia until 2003. The two then became separate independent countries in 2006. The southern Serbian province of Kosovo declared its independence from Serbia in February 2008. The landscape is rugged, mountainous and forested in the south, while the north is low-lying and drained by the Danube river system.

Area Sq Km **455**
Area Sq Miles **176**

Population **84 000**
Capital **Victoria**

Currency **Seychelles rupee**
Languages **English, French, creole**

Religions **Roman Catholic, Protestant**
Organizations **Comm., SADC, UN**

Population

Total population **84 000**
Population change **1.5%**
Urban population **54.3%**
Total fertility rate **2.1 births per woman**
Population aged 0–14 **N/A**
Population aged over 65 **N/A**
2050 projected population **99 000**

Communications

Main telephone lines **25.4 per 100 people**
Cellular mobile subscribers **86.5 per 100 people**
Internet users **3 567 per 10 000 people**
International dialling code **248**
Time zone **+4**

Social Indicators

Infant mortality rate **12 per 1 000 live births**
Life expectancy **73**
Literacy rate **N/A**
Access to safe water **88%**
Doctors **1.51 per 1 000 people**

Economy

Total Gross National Income (GNI) **751 US$M**
GNI per capita **10 290 US$**
Debt service ratio **24.8% of GNI**
Total debt service **181 083 000 US$**
Aid receipts **2.0% of GNI**
Military spending **1.8% of GDP**

Environment

Forest area **87.0%**
Annual change in forest area **0.0%**
Protected land area **8.3%**
CO_2 emissions **7.0 metric tons per capita**

The Seychelles comprises an archipelago of over one hundred granitic and coral islands in the western Indian Ocean. Over ninety per cent of the population lives on the main island, Mahé. The climate is hot and humid with heavy rainfall. The economy is based mainly on tourism, fishing and light manufacturing.

Giant tortoise, Seychelles

Sierra Leone Republic of Sierra Leone

Area Sq Km **71 740**
Area Sq Miles **27 699**

Population **5 696 000**
Capital **Freetown**

Currency **Leone**
Languages **English, creole, Mende, Temne, local languages**

Religions **Sunni Muslim, traditional beliefs**
Organizations **Comm., UN**

Population

Total population **5 696 000**
Population change **2.5%**
Urban population **37.8%**
Total fertility rate **5.2 births per woman**
Population aged 0–14 **43.3%**
Population aged over 65 **1.9%**
2050 projected population **13 786 000**

Communications

Main telephone lines
0.5 per 100 people
Cellular mobile subscribers
2.2 per 100 people
Internet users
19 per 10 000 people
International dialling code **232**
Time zone **GMT**

Environment

Forest area **38.5%**
Annual change in forest area **-0.7%**
Protected land area **4.1%**
CO_2 emissions **0.2 metric tons per capita**

Economy

Total Gross National Income (GNI) **1 353 US$M**
GNI per capita **320 US$**
Debt service ratio **2.4% of GNI**
Total debt service **33 899 000 US$**
Aid receipts **25.7% of GNI**
Military spending **1.0% of GDP**

Social Indicators

Infant mortality rate
155 per 1 000 live births
Life expectancy **47.7**
Literacy rate **38.1%**
Access to safe water **57%**
Doctors **0.03 per 1 000 people**

Sierra Leone lies on the Atlantic coast of west Africa. Its coastline is heavily indented and is lined with mangrove swamps. Inland is a forested area rising to savanna plateaus, with mountains to the northeast. The climate is tropical and rainfall is heavy. Most of the workforce is involved in subsistence farming. Cocoa and coffee are the main cash crops. Diamonds and rutile (titanium ore) are the main exports. Sierra Leone is one of the world's poorest countries, and the economy relies on substantial foreign aid.

Freetown, Sierra Leone

Area Sq Km **639**
Area Sq Miles **247**

Population **4 737 000**
Capital **Singapore**

Currency **Singapore dollar**
Languages **Chinese, English, Malay, Tamil**

Religions **Buddhist, Taoist, Sunni Muslim, Christian, Hindu**
Organizations **APEC, ASEAN, Comm., UN**

Population

Total population **4 737 000**
Population change **5.3%**
Urban population **100.0%**
Total fertility rate **1.3 births per woman**
Population aged 0–14 **17.1%**
Population aged over 65 **9.4%**
2050 projected population **5 213 000**

Communications

Main telephone lines **42.3 per 100 people**
Cellular mobile subscribers **109.3 per 100 people**
Internet users **4 362 per 10 000 people**
International dialling code **65**
Time zone **+8**

Social Indicators

Infant mortality rate **2 per 1 000 live births**
Life expectancy **80.5**
Literacy rate **94.4%**
Access to safe water **100%**
Doctors **1.5 per 1 000 people**

Economy

Total Gross National Income (GNI) **128 816 US$M**
GNI per capita **34 760 US$**
Debt service ratio **N/A**
Total debt service **N/A**
Aid receipts **N/A**
Military spending **4.7% of GDP**

Environment

Forest area **3.3%**
Annual change in forest area **0.0%**
Protected land area **4.2%**
CO_2 emissions **13.2 metric tons per capita**

The state comprises the main island of Singapore and over fifty other islands, lying off the southern tip of the Malay Peninsula in southeast Asia. Singapore is generally low-lying and includes land reclaimed from swamps and the sea. It is hot and humid, with heavy rainfall throughout the year. There are fish farms and vegetable gardens in the north and east of the island, but most food is imported. Singapore also lacks mineral and energy resources. Manufacturing industries and services are the main sectors of the economy. Their rapid development has fuelled the nation's impressive economic growth during recent decades. Main industries include electronics, oil refining, chemicals, pharmaceuticals, ship repair, food processing and textiles. Singapore is also a major financial centre.

Its port is one of the world's largest and busiest and acts as an entrepôt for neighbouring states. Tourism is also important. Japan, the USA and Malaysia are the main trading partners.

Sri Srinivasa Perumal Temple, Singapore

Slovakia Slovak Republic

Area Sq Km **49 035**
Area Sq Miles **18 933**

Population **5 406 000**
Capital **Bratislava**

Currency **Euro**
Languages **Slovak, Hungarian, Czech**

Religions **Roman Catholic, Protestant, Orthodox**
Organizations **EU, NATO, OECD, UN**

Population

Total population **5 406 000**
Population change **0.2%**
Urban population **56.6%**
Total fertility rate **1.3 births per woman**
Population aged 0–14 **15.6%**
Population aged over 65 **12.0%**
2050 projected population **4 612 000**

Communications

Main telephone lines **21.6 per 100 people**
Cellular mobile subscribers **90.6 per 100 people**
Internet users **4 176 per 10 000 people**
International dialling code **421**
Time zone **+1**

Economy

Total Gross National Income (GNI) **51 807 US$M**
GNI per capita **14 540 US$**
Debt service ratio **7.8% of GNI**
Total debt service **4 125 305 000 US$**
Aid receipts **N/A**
Military spending **1.7% of GDP**

Environment

Forest area **40.1%**
Annual change in forest area **0.1%**
Protected land area **20.0%**
CO_2 emissions **6.8 metric tons per capita**

Social Indicators

Infant mortality rate **7 per 1 000 live births**
Life expectancy **74.2**
Literacy rate **N/A**
Access to safe water **100%**
Doctors **3.12 per 1 000 people**

A landlocked country in central Europe, Slovakia is mountainous in the north, but low-lying in the southwest. The climate is continental. There is a range of manufacturing industries, and the main exports are machinery and transport equipment, but in recent years there have been economic difficulties and growth has been slow. Slovakia joined the European Union in May 2004. Most trade is with other EU countries, especially the Czech Republic.

Spišský Hrad, Slovakia

Area Sq Km **20 251**
Area Sq Miles **7 819**

Population **2 020 000**
Capital **Ljubljana**

Currency **Euro**
Languages **Slovene, Croatian, Serbian**

Religions **Roman Catholic, Protestant**
Organizations **EU, NATO, UN**

Population

Total population **2 020 000**
Population change **1.0%**
Urban population **48.6%**
Total fertility rate **1.4 births per woman**
Population aged 0–14 **13.9%**
Population aged over 65 **16.0%**
2050 projected population **1 630 000**

Economy

Total Gross National Income (GNI) **37 445 US$M**
GNI per capita **24 010 US$**
Debt service ratio **N/A**
Total debt service **N/A**
Aid receipts **N/A**
Military spending **1.7% of GDP**

Environment

Forest area **62.8%**
Annual change in forest area **0.4%**
Protected land area **6.7%**
CO2 emissions **7.4 metric tons per capita**

Communications

Main telephone lines **42.6 per 100 people**
Cellular mobile subscribers **92.6 per 100 people**
Internet users **6 362 per 10 000 people**
International dialling code **386**
Time zone **+1**

Social Indicators

Infant mortality rate **3 per 1 000 live births**
Life expectancy **77.7**
Literacy rate **99.7%**
Access to safe water **N/A**
Doctors **2.4 per 1 000 people**

Slovenia lies in the northwest Balkan Mountains of southern Europe and has a short coastline on the Adriatic Sea. It is mountainous and hilly, with lowlands on the coast and in the Sava and Drava river valleys. The climate is generally continental inland and Mediterranean nearer the coast. The main agricultural products are potatoes, grain and sugar beet; the main industries include metal processing, electronics and consumer goods. Trade has been re-orientated towards western markets and the main trading partners are Germany and Italy. Slovenia joined the European Union in May 2004.

Lake Bled, Slovenia

Solomon Islands

Area Sq Km **28 370**
Area Sq Miles **10 954**

Population **523 000**
Capital **Honiara**

Currency **Solomon Islands dollar**
Languages **English, creole, local languages**

Religions **Protestant, Roman Catholic**
Organizations **Comm., UN**

Population

Total population **523 000**
Population change **2.3%**
Urban population **18.0%**
Total fertility rate **3.9 births per woman**
Population aged 0–14 **39.5%**
Population aged over 65 **3.1%**
2050 projected population **921 000**

Communications

Main telephone lines **1.6 per 100 people**
Cellular mobile subscribers **1.3 per 100 people**
Internet users **163 per 10 000 people**
International dialling code **677**
Time zone **+11**

Social Indicators

Infant mortality rate **53 per 1 000 live births**
Life expectancy **63.6**
Literacy rate **N/A**
Access to safe water **70%**
Doctors **0.13 per 1 000 people**

Economy

Total Gross National Income (GNI) **333 US$M**
GNI per capita **1 180 US$**
Debt service ratio **1.3% of GNI**
Total debt service **4 276 000 US$**
Aid receipts **60.6% of GNI**
Military spending **N/A**

Environment

Forest area **77.6%**
Annual change in forest area **-1.7%**
Protected land area **0.7%**
CO_2 emissions **0.4 metric tons per capita**

The state consists of the Solomon, Santa Cruz and Shortland Islands in the southwest Pacific Ocean. The six main islands are volcanic, mountainous and forested, although Guadalcanal, the most populous, has a large lowland area. The climate is generally hot and humid. Subsistence farming, forestry and fishing predominate. Exports include timber products, fish, copra and palm oil. The islands depend on foreign aid.

Dive boats, Solomon Islands

Area Sq Km **637 657**
Area Sq Miles **246 201**

Population **9 133 000**
Capital **Mogadishu (Muqdisho)**

Currency **Somali shilling**
Languages **Somali, Arabic**

Religions **Sunni Muslim**
Organizations **UN**

Population

Total population **9 133 000**
Population change **2.9%**
Urban population **36.5%**
Total fertility rate **6.0 births per woman**
Population aged 0–14 **44.9%**
Population aged over 65 **2.7%**
2050 projected population **21 329 000**

Communications

Main telephone lines
1.2 per 100 people
Cellular mobile subscribers
6.1 per 100 people
Internet users
111 per 10 000 people
International dialling code **252**
Time zone **+3**

Environment

Forest area **11.4%**
Annual change in
forest area **-1.0%**
Protected land area **0.3%**
CO2 emissions **0.1 metric
tons per capita**

Economy

Total Gross National
Income (GNI) **N/A**
GNI per capita **N/A**
Debt service ratio **N/A**
Total debt service **19 000 US$**
Aid receipts **N/A**
Military spending **N/A**

Social Indicators

Infant mortality rate
88 per 1 000 live births
Life expectancy **48.1**
Literacy rate **N/A**
Access to safe water **29%**
Doctors **N/A**

Somalia is in northeast Africa, on the Gulf of Aden and Indian Ocean. It consists of a dry scrubby plateau, rising to highlands in the north. The climate is hot and dry, but coastal areas and the Jubba and Webi Shabeelle river valleys support crops and most of the population. Subsistence farming and livestock rearing are the main activities. Exports include livestock and bananas. Frequent drought and civil war have prevented economic development. Somalia is one of the poorest, most unstable and least developed countries in the world.

Waller's gazelle, Somalia

South Africa, Republic of

Area Sq Km **1 219 090**
Area Sq Miles **470 689**

Population **50 110 000**
Capital **Pretoria (Tshwane)/ Cape Town**

Currency **Rand**
Languages **Afrikaans, English, nine other official languages**

Religions **Protestant, Roman Catholic, Sunni Muslim, Hindu**
Organizations **Comm., SADC, UN**

Population

Total population **50 110 000**
Population change **1.7%**
Urban population **60.7%**
Total fertility rate **2.7 births per woman**
Population aged 0–14 **30.8%**
Population aged over 65 **4.4%**
2050 projected population **48 660 000**

Communications

Main telephone lines **10.0 per 100 people**
Cellular mobile subscribers **83.3 per 100 people**
Internet users **1 075 per 10 000 people**
International dialling code **27**
Time zone **+2**

Environment

Forest area **7.6%**
Annual change in forest area **0.0%**
Protected land area **6.1%**
CO_2 emissions **8.7 metric tons per capita**

Economy

Total Gross National Income (GNI) **255 389 US$M**
GNI per capita **5 820 US$**
Debt service ratio **2.2% of GNI**
Total debt service **5 472 200 000 US$**
Aid receipts **0.3% of GNI**
Military spending **1.4% of GDP**

Social Indicators

Infant mortality rate **46 per 1 000 live births**
Life expectancy **50.5**
Literacy rate **88.0%**
Access to safe water **88%**
Doctors **0.77 per 1 000 people**

The Republic of South Africa occupies most of the southern part of Africa. It surrounds Lesotho and has a long coastline on the Atlantic and Indian Oceans. Much of the land is a vast plateau, covered with grassland or bush and drained by the Orange and Limpopo river systems. A fertile coastal plain rises to mountain ridges in the south and east, including Table Mountain near Cape Town and the Drakensberg range in the east. Gauteng is the most populous province, with Johannesburg and Pretoria its main cities. South Africa has warm summers and mild winters. Most of the country has the majority of its rainfall in summer, but the coast around Cape Town has winter rains. South Africa has the largest economy in Africa, although wealth is unevenly distributed and unemployment is very high. Agriculture employs approximately one-third of the workforce, and produce includes fruit, wine, wool and maize. The country is the world's leading producer of gold and chromium and an important producer of diamonds. Many other minerals are also mined. The main industries are mineral and food processing, chemicals, electrical equipment, textiles and motor vehicles. Financial services are also important.

Meerkats, Kalahari Desert, South Africa

Area Sq Km **99 274**
Area Sq Miles **38 330**

Population **48 333 000**
Capital **Seoul (Sŏul)**

Currency **South Korean won**
Languages **Korean**

Religions **Buddhist, Protestant, Roman Catholic**
Organizations **APEC, OECD, UN**

Population

Total population **48 333 000**
Population change **0.3%**
Urban population **81.5%**
Total fertility rate **1.3 births per woman**
Population aged 0–14 **17.4%**
Population aged over 65 **10.4%**
2050 projected population **44 629 000**

Communications

Main telephone lines **49.8 per 100 people**
Cellular mobile subscribers **83.8 per 100 people**
Internet users **7 275 per 10 000 people**
International dialling code **82**
Time zone **+9**

Economy

Total Gross National Income (GNI) **856 565 US$M**
GNI per capita **21 530 US$**
Debt service ratio **N/A**
Total debt service **N/A**
Aid receipts **N/A**
Military spending **2.7% of GDP**

Environment

Forest area **63.5%**
Annual change in forest area **-0.1%**
Protected land area **3.5%**
CO_2 emissions **9.4 metric tons per capita**

Social Indicators

Infant mortality rate **4 per 1 000 live births**
Life expectancy **79.0**
Literacy rate **N/A**
Access to safe water **92%**
Doctors **1.57 per 1 000 people**

The state consists of the southern half of the Korean Peninsula in eastern Asia and many islands lying off the western and southern coasts in the Yellow Sea. The terrain is mountainous, although less rugged than that of North Korea. Population density is high and the country is highly urbanized; most of the population lives on the western coastal plains and in the river basins of the Han-gang in the northwest and the Naktong-gang in the southeast. The climate is continental, with hot, wet summers and dry, cold winters. Arable land is limited by the mountainous terrain, but because of intensive farming South Korea is nearly self-sufficient in food. Sericulture (silk) is important, as is fishing, which contributes to exports. South Korea has few mineral resources, except for coal and tungsten. It has achieved high economic growth based mainly on export manufacturing. The main manufactured goods are cars, electronic and electrical goods, ships, steel, chemicals and toys, as well as textiles, clothing, footwear and food products. The USA and Japan are the main trading partners.

Gyeongbok Palace, Seoul, South Korea

South Sudan Republic of South Sudan

Area Sq Km **644 329**
Area Sq Miles **248 775**

Population **8 260 490**
Capital **Juba**

Currency **Sudanese Pound (Sudani)**
Languages **Arabic, Dinka, local languages**

Religions **Traditional beliefs, Christian**
Organizations **N/A**

A landlocked country in central Africa, South Sudan voted for independence from Sudan in January 2011. Sudan had previously been the largest country in Africa and even after the split both parts of the old country remain two of the largest by area in the continent. Civil wars throughout most of the late 20th century, have left their mark so the country has some of the poorest levels of infrastructure in the world. Most of the roads are unpaved, and communication throughout the area is difficult. South Sudan's economy is built on agriculture with subsistance farming being the main way of life for most inhabitants. The area is thought to be rich in many minerals as yet largely untouched, although oil exploration and timber exporting began when under Sudanese rule. Recent years have seen a greater degree of urbanisation, a trend which is expected to increase under independence. Major trading partners are Sudan and Uganda.

Juba Bridge, South Sudan

Area Sq Km **504 782**
Area Sq Miles **194 897**

Population **44 904 000**
Capital **Madrid**

Currency **Euro**
Languages **Castilian, Catalan, Galician, Basque**

Religions **Roman Catholic**
Organizations **EU, NATO, OECD, UN**

Population

Total population **44 904 000**
Population change **1.5%**
Urban population **77.1%**
Total fertility rate **1.4 births per woman**
Population aged 0–14 **14.7%**
Population aged over 65 **16.9%**
2050 projected population **42 541 000**

Communications

Main telephone lines
42.4 per 100 people
Cellular mobile subscribers
106.4 per 100 people
Internet users
4 283 per 10 000 people
International dialling code **34**
Time zone **+1**

Economy

Total Gross National Income (GNI) **1 206 169 US$M**
GNI per capita **31 960 US$**
Debt service ratio **N/A**
Total debt service **N/A**
Aid receipts **N/A**
Military spending **1.0% of GDP**

Environment

Forest area **35.9%**
Annual change in forest area **1.7%**
Protected land area **8.3%**
CO_2 emissions **7.9 metric tons per capita**

Social Indicators

Infant mortality rate
4 per 1 000 live births
Life expectancy **80.9**
Literacy rate **97.9%**
Access to safe water **100%**
Doctors **3.3 per 1 000 people**

Spain occupies the greater part of the Iberian peninsula in southwest Europe, with coastlines on the Atlantic Ocean and Mediterranean Sea. It includes the Balearic Islands in the Mediterranean, the Canary Islands in the Atlantic, and two enclaves in north Africa (Ceuta and Melilla). Much of the mainland is a high plateau drained by the Douro (Duero), Tagus (Tajo) and Guadiana rivers. The plateau is interrupted by a low mountain range and bounded to the east and north also by mountains, including the Pyrenees, which form the border with France and Andorra. The main lowland areas are the Ebro basin in the northeast, the eastern coastal plains and the Guadalquivir basin in the southwest.

Over three-quarters of the population lives in urban areas. The plateau experiences hot summers and cold winters. Conditions are cooler and wetter to the north, and warmer and drier to the south. Agriculture involves about ten per cent of the workforce, and fruit, vegetables and wine are exported. Fishing is an important industry, and Spain has a large fishing fleet. Mineral resources include lead, copper, mercury and fluorspar. Some oil is produced, but Spain has to import most energy needs. The economy is based mainly on manufacturing and services. The principal products are machinery, transport equipment, motor vehicles and food products, with a wide variety of other manufactured goods. With approximately fifty million visitors a year, tourism is a major industry. Banking and commerce are also important. Approximately seventy per cent of trade is with other European Union countries.

Plaza of the Virgin, Valencia, Spain

Sri Lanka Democratic Socialist Republic of Sri Lanka

Area Sq Km **65 610**
Area Sq Miles **25 332**

Population **20 238 000**
Capital **Sri Jayewardenepura Kotte**

Currency **Sri Lankan rupee**
Languages **Sinhalese, Tamil, English**

Religions **Buddhist, Hindu, Sunni Muslim, Roman Catholic**
Organizations **Comm., UN**

Population

Total population **20 238 000**
Population change **0.7%**
Urban population **15.1%**
Total fertility rate **1.9 births per woman**
Population aged 0–14 **24.3%**
Population aged over 65 **7.3%**
2050 projected population **23 554 000**

Communications

Main telephone lines **9.0 per 100 people**
Cellular mobile subscribers **25.9 per 100 people**
Internet users **169 per 10 000 people**
International dialling code **94**
Time zone **+5.5**

Social Indicators

Infant mortality rate **17 per 1 000 live births**
Life expectancy **72.4**
Literacy rate **90.8%**
Access to safe water **79%**
Doctors **0.55 per 1 000 people**

Economy

Total Gross National Income (GNI) **26 001 US$M**
GNI per capita **1 780 US$**
Debt service ratio **3.6% of GNI**
Total debt service **957 927 000 US$**
Aid receipts **3.0% of GNI**
Military spending **2.4% of GDP**

Environment

Forest area **29.9%**
Annual change in forest area **-1.5%**
Protected land area **17.5%**
CO2 emissions **0.6 metric tons per capita**

Sri Lanka lies in the Indian Ocean off the southeast coast of India in south Asia. It has rolling coastal plains, with mountains in the centre-south. The climate is hot and monsoonal. Most people live on the west coast. Manufactures (chiefly textiles and clothing), tea, rubber, copra and gems are exported. The economy relies on foreign aid and workers' remittances. The USA and the UK are the main trading partners.

Kiri Vihara, Polonnaruwa, Sri Lanka

Area Sq Km **1 861 484**
Area Sq Miles **718 725**

Population **36 371 510**
Capital **Khartoum**

Currency **Sudanese pound (Sudani)**
Languages **Arabic, Dinka, Nubian, Beja, Nuer, local languages**

Religions **Sunni Muslim, traditional beliefs, Christian**
Organizations **UN**

Population

Total population **36 371 510**
Population change **2.2%**
Urban population **43.4%**
Total fertility rate **4.2 births per woman**
Population aged 0–14 **39.5%**
Population aged over 65 **3.6%**
2050 projected population **66 705 000**

Environment

Forest area **28.4%**
Annual change in forest area **-0.8%**
Protected land area **4.8%**
CO2 emissions **0.3 metric tons per capita**

Communications

Main telephone lines **1.7 per 100 people**
Cellular mobile subscribers **12.7 per 100 people**
Internet users **946 per 10 000 people**
International dialling code **249**
Time zone **+3**

Economy

Total Gross National Income (GNI) **30 086 US$M**
GNI per capita **1 130 US$**
Debt service ratio **0.8% of GNI**
Total debt service **292 431 000 US$**
Aid receipts **6.0% of GNI**
Military spending **2.2% of GDP**

Social Indicators

Infant mortality rate **69 per 1 000 live births**
Life expectancy **58.3**
Literacy rate **N/A**
Access to safe water **70%**
Doctors **0.3 per 1 000 people**

No longer Africa's largest country after the South voted for independence in 2011, the Sudan is in the northeast of the continent, on the Red Sea. It lies within the upper Nile basin, much of which is arid plain but with swamps to the south. Mountains lie to the northeast, west and south. The climate is hot and arid with light summer rainfall, and droughts occur. Most people live along the Nile and are farmers and herders. Cotton, gum arabic, livestock and other agricultural products are exported. The government is working with foreign investors to develop oil resources, but civil war has restricted the growth of the economy in recent years. Main trading partners are Saudi Arabia, China and Libya.

Meroe Pyramids, Sudan

Suriname Republic of Suriname

Area Sq Km **163 820**
Area Sq Miles **63 251**

Population **520 000**
Capital **Paramaribo**

Currency **Suriname guilder**
Languages **Dutch, Surinamese, English, Hindi**

Religions **Hindu, Roman Catholic, Protestant, Sunni Muslim**
Organizations **CARICOM, UN**

Population

Total population **520 000**
Population change **0.9%**
Urban population **74.9%**
Total fertility rate **2.4 births per woman**
Population aged 0–14 **29.2%**
Population aged over 65 **6.3%**
2050 projected population **429 000**

Communications

Main telephone lines **18.0 per 100 people**
Cellular mobile subscribers **70.8 per 100 people**
Internet users **712 per 10 000 people**
International dialling code **597**
Time zone **-3**

Social Indicators

Infant mortality rate **27 per 1 000 live births**
Life expectancy **69.1**
Literacy rate **90.4%**
Access to safe water **92%**
Doctors **0.45 per 1 000 people**

Economy

Total Gross National Income (GNI) **1 918 US$M**
GNI per capita **4 990 US$**
Debt service ratio **N/A**
Total debt service **N/A**
Aid receipts **4.1% of GNI**
Military spending **N/A**

Environment

Forest area **94.7%**
Annual change in forest area **0.0%**
Protected land area **11.8%**
CO_2 emissions **4.8 metric tons per capita**

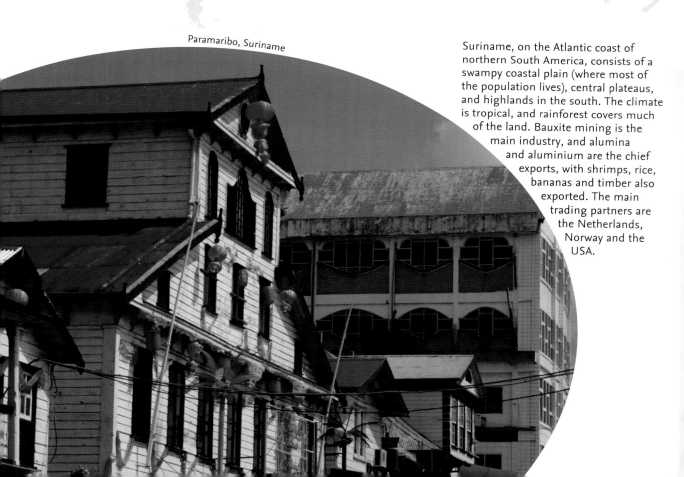

Paramaribo, Suriname

Suriname, on the Atlantic coast of northern South America, consists of a swampy coastal plain (where most of the population lives), central plateaus, and highlands in the south. The climate is tropical, and rainforest covers much of the land. Bauxite mining is the main industry, and alumina and aluminium are the chief exports, with shrimps, rice, bananas and timber also exported. The main trading partners are the Netherlands, Norway and the USA.

Area Sq Km **17 364**
Area Sq Miles **6 704**

Population **1 185 000**
Capital **Mbabane**

Currency **Emalangeni, South African rand**
Languages **Swazi, English**

Religions **Christian, traditional beliefs**
Organizations **Comm., SADC, UN**

Population

Total population **1 185 000**
Population change **1.4%**
Urban population **24.9%**
Total fertility rate **3.6 births per woman**
Population aged 0–14 **40.0%**
Population aged over 65 **3.3%**
2050 projected population **1 026 000**

Communications

Main telephone lines **4.3 per 100 people**
Cellular mobile subscribers **24.3 per 100 people**
Internet users **408 per 10 000 people**
International dialling code **268**
Time zone **+2**

Environment

Forest area **31.5%**
Annual change in forest area **0.9%**
Protected land area **3.1%**
CO_2 emissions **0.9 metric tons per capita**

Economy

Total Gross National Income (GNI) **2 737 US$M**
GNI per capita **2 520 US$**
Debt service ratio **1.7% of GNI**
Total debt service **44 704 000 US$**
Aid receipts **1.3% of GNI**
Military spending **1.9% of GDP**

Social Indicators

Infant mortality rate **66 per 1 000 live births**
Life expectancy **46.4**
Literacy rate **N/A**
Access to safe water **62%**
Doctors **0.16 per 1 000 people**

Landlocked Swaziland in southern Africa lies between Mozambique and the Republic of South Africa. Savanna plateaus descend from mountains in the west towards hill country in the east. The climate is subtropical, but temperate in the mountains. Subsistence farming predominates. Asbestos and diamonds are mined. Exports include sugar, fruit and wood pulp. Tourism and workers' remittances are important to the economy. Most trade is with South Africa.

Phophonyane Falls, Swaziland

Sweden Kingdom of Sweden

Area Sq Km **449 964**
Area Sq Miles **173 732**

Population **9 249 000**
Capital **Stockholm**

Currency **Swedish krona**
Languages **Swedish**

Religions **Protestant, Roman Catholic**
Organizations **EU, OECD, UN**

Population

Total population **9 249 000**
Population change **0.8%**
Urban population **84.5%**
Total fertility rate **1.9 births per woman**
Population aged 0–14 **16.7%**
Population aged over 65 **17.7%**
2050 projected population **10 054 000**

Communications

Main telephone lines **59.5 per 100 people**
Cellular mobile subscribers **105.9 per 100 people**
Internet users **7 697 per 10 000 people**
International dialling code **46**
Time zone **+1**

Economy

Total Gross National Income (GNI) **395 411 US$M**
GNI per capita **50 940 US$**
Debt service ratio **N/A**
Total debt service **N/A**
Aid receipts **N/A**
Military spending **1.4% of GDP**

Environment

Forest area **67.1%**
Annual change in forest area **N/A**
Protected land area **10.3%**
CO_2 emissions **5.4 metric tons per capita**

Social Indicators

Infant mortality rate **3 per 1 000 live births**
Life expectancy **80.9**
Literacy rate **N/A**
Access to safe water **100%**
Doctors **3.28 per 1 000 people**

Sweden occupies the eastern part of the Scandinavian peninsula in northern Europe and borders the Baltic Sea, the Gulf of Bothnia, and the Kattegat and Skagerrak, connecting with the North Sea. Forested mountains cover the northern half, part of which lies within the Arctic Circle. The southern part of the country is a lowland lake region where most of the population lives. Sweden has warm summers and cold winters, which are more severe in the north. Natural resources include coniferous forests, mineral deposits and water resources. Some dairy products, meat, cereals and vegetables are produced in the south. The forests supply timber for export and for the important pulp, paper and furniture industries. Sweden is an important producer of iron ore and copper. Zinc, lead, silver and gold are also mined. Machinery and transport equipment, chemicals, pulp and wood, and telecommunications equipment are the main exports. The majority of trade is with other European Union countries.

Stockholm, Sweden

Area Sq Km **41 293**
Area Sq Miles **15 943**

Population **7 568 000**
Capital **Bern (Berne)**

Currency **Swiss franc**
Languages **German, French, Italian, Romansch**

Religions **Roman Catholic, Protestant**
Organizations **OECD, UN**

Population

Total population **7 568 000**
Population change **1.1%**
Urban population **73.5%**
Total fertility rate **1.5 births per woman**
Population aged 0–14 **15.5%**
Population aged over 65 **16.7%**
2050 projected population **7 252 000**

Communications

Main telephone lines **66.9 per 100 people**
Cellular mobile subscribers **99.0 per 100 people**
Internet users **5 807 per 10 000 people**
International dialling code **41**
Time zone **+1**

Economy

Total Gross National Income (GNI) **434 844 US$M**
GNI per capita **65 330 US$**
Debt service ratio **N/A**
Total debt service **N/A**
Aid receipts **N/A**
Military spending **0.9% of GDP**

Environment

Forest area **30.5%**
Annual change in forest area **0.4%**
Protected land area **29.5%**
CO_2 emissions **5.5 metric tons per capita**

Social Indicators

Infant mortality rate **4 per 1 000 live births**
Life expectancy **81.7**
Literacy rate **N/A**
Access to safe water **100%**
Doctors **3.97 per 1 000 people**

Switzerland is a mountainous landlocked country in west central Europe. The southern regions lie within the Alps, while the northwest is dominated by the Jura mountains. The rest of the land is a high plateau, where most of the population lives. The climate varies greatly, depending on altitude and relief, but in general summers are mild and winters are cold with heavy snowfalls. Switzerland has one of the highest standards of living in the world, yet it has few mineral resources, and most food and industrial raw materials are imported. Manufacturing makes the largest contribution to the economy. Engineering is the most important industry, producing precision instruments and heavy machinery. Other important industries are chemicals and pharmaceuticals. Banking and financial services are very important, and Zürich is one of the world's leading banking cities. Tourism, and international organizations based in Switzerland, are also major foreign currency earners. Germany is the main trading partner.

View from Braunwald, Switzerland

Area Sq Km **185 180**
Area Sq Miles **71 498**

Population **21 906 000**
Capital **Damascus (Dimashq)**

Currency **Syrian pound**
Languages **Arabic, Kurdish, Armenian**

Religions **Sunni Muslim, Shi'a Muslim, Christian**
Organizations **UN**

Population

Total population **21 906 000**
Population change **3.5%**
Urban population **54.2%**
Total fertility rate **3.3 births per woman**
Population aged 0–14 **35.3%**
Population aged over 65 **3.2%**
2050 projected population **35 935 000**

Communications

Main telephone lines **16.6 per 100 people**
Cellular mobile subscribers **24.0 per 100 people**
Internet users **794 per 10 000 people**
International dialling code **963**
Time zone **+2**

Economy

Total Gross National Income (GNI) **30 333 US$M**
GNI per capita **2 090 US$**
Debt service ratio **0.6% of GNI**
Total debt service **186 679 000 US$**
Aid receipts **0.1% of GNI**
Military spending **3.8% of GDP**

Environment

Forest area **2.5%**
Annual change in forest area **1.3%**
Protected land area **0.7%**
CO2 emissions **3.6 metric tons per capita**

Social Indicators

Infant mortality rate **15 per 1 000 live births**
Life expectancy **74.3**
Literacy rate **83.1%**
Access to safe water **93%**
Doctors **0.53 per 1 000 people**

Syria is in southwest Asia, has a short coastline on the Mediterranean Sea, and stretches inland to a plateau traversed northwest-southeast by the Euphrates river. Mountains flank the southwest borders with Lebanon and Israel. The climate is Mediterranean in coastal regions, hotter and drier inland. Most Syrians live on the coast or in the river valleys. Cotton, cereals and fruit are important products, but the main exports are petroleum and related products, and textiles.

Palmyra, Syria

Area Sq Km **143 100**
Area Sq Miles **55 251**

Population **6 952 000**
Capital **Dushanbe**

Currency **Somoni**
Languages **Tajik, Uzbek, Russian**

Religions **Sunni Muslim**
Organizations **CIS, UN**

Population

Total population **6 952 000**
Population change **1.6%**
Urban population **26.5%**
Total fertility rate **3.5 births per woman**
Population aged 0–14 **37.5%**
Population aged over 65 **3.7%**
2050 projected population **10 423 000**

Communications

Main telephone lines
4.3 per 100 people
Cellular mobile subscribers
4.1 per 100 people
Internet users
30 per 10 000 people
International dialling code **992**
Time zone **+5**

Economy

Total Gross National
Income (GNI) **2 572 US$M**
GNI per capita **600 US$**
Debt service ratio **5.0% of GNI**
Total debt service **136 859 000 US$**
Aid receipts **8.8% of GNI**
Military spending **2.2% of GDP**

Environment

Forest area **2.9%**
Annual change in
forest area **0.0%**
Protected land area **14.0%**
CO_2 emissions **0.8 metric
tons per capita**

Social Indicators

Infant mortality rate
57 per 1 000 live births
Life expectancy **66.9**
Literacy rate **99.6%**
Access to safe water **59%**
Doctors **2.01 per 1 000 people**

Landlocked Tajikistan in central Asia is a mountainous country, dominated by the mountains of the Alai Range and the Pamir. In the less mountainous western areas summers are warm, although winters are cold. Agriculture is the main sector of the economy, chiefly cotton growing and cattle breeding. Mineral deposits include lead, zinc, and uranium. Processed metals, textiles and clothing are the main manufactured goods; the main exports are aluminium and cotton. Uzbekistan, Kazakhstan and the Russian Federation are the main trading partners.

Kulikalon Wall, Tajikistan

Tanzania United Republic of Tanzania

Area Sq Km **945 087**
Area Sq Miles **364 900**

Population **43 739 000**
Capital **Dodoma**

Currency **Tanzanian shilling**
Languages **Swahili, English, Nyamwezi, local languages**

Religions **Shi'a Muslim, Sunni Muslim, traditional beliefs, Christian**
Organizations **Comm., SADC, UN**

Population

Total population **43 739 000**
Population change **2.9%**
Urban population **25.5%**
Total fertility rate **5.6 births per woman**
Population aged 0–14 **44.7%**
Population aged over 65 **3.1%**
2050 projected population **66 845 000**

Communications

Main telephone lines **0.4 per 100 people**
Cellular mobile subscribers **14.8 per 100 people**
Internet users **100 per 10 000 people**
International dialling code **255**
Time zone **+3**

Environment

Forest area **39.8%**
Annual change in forest area **-1.1%**
Protected land area **38.7%**
CO2 emissions **0.1 metric tons per capita**

Economy

Total Gross National Income (GNI) **13 404 US$M**
GNI per capita **440 US$**
Debt service ratio **0.9% of GNI**
Total debt service **113 148 000 US$**
Aid receipts **14.5% of GNI**
Military spending **1.1% of GDP**

Social Indicators

Infant mortality rate **73 per 1 000 live births**
Life expectancy **55.9**
Literacy rate **72.3%**
Access to safe water **62%**
Doctors **0.02 per 1 000 people**

Tanzania lies on the coast of east Africa and includes the island of Zanzibar in the Indian Ocean. Most of the mainland is a savanna plateau lying east of the Great Rift Valley. In the north, near the border with Kenya, is Kilimanjaro, the highest mountain in Africa. The climate is tropical. The economy is predominantly based on agriculture, which employs an estimated ninety per cent of the workforce. Agricultural processing and gold and diamond mining are the main industries, although tourism is growing. Coffee, cotton, cashew nuts and tobacco are the main exports, with cloves from Zanzibar. Most export trade is with India and the UK. Tanzania depends heavily on foreign aid.

Ngorongoro Crater, Tanzania

Area Sq Km **513 115**
Area Sq Miles **198 115**

Population **67 764 000**
Capital **Bangkok (Krung Thep)**

Currency **Baht**
Languages **Thai, Lao, Chinese, Malay, Mon-Khmer languages**

Religions **Buddhist, Sunni Muslim**
Organizations **APEC, ASEAN, UN**

Population

Total population **67 764 000**
Population change **0.6%**
Urban population **33.3%**
Total fertility rate **1.8 births per woman**
Population aged 0–14 **22.0%**
Population aged over 65 **7.4%**
2050 projected population **74 594 000**

Communications

Main telephone lines **10.9 per 100 people**
Cellular mobile subscribers **62.9 per 100 people**
Internet users **1 307 per 10 000 people**
International dialling code **66**
Time zone **+7**

Social Indicators

Infant mortality rate **6 per 1 000 live births**
Life expectancy **69.0**
Literacy rate **94.1%**
Access to safe water **99%**
Doctors **0.37 per 1 000 people**

Economy

Total Gross National Income (GNI) **193 734 US$M**
GNI per capita **2 840 US$**
Debt service ratio **7.3% of GNI**
Total debt service **14 685 762 000 US$**
Aid receipts **-0.1% of GNI**
Military spending **1.1% of GDP**

Environment

Forest area **28.4%**
Annual change in forest area **-0.4%**
Protected land area **19.9%**
CO_2 emissions **4.1 metric tons per capita**

The largest country in the Indo-China peninsula, Thailand has coastlines on the Gulf of Thailand and Andaman Sea. Central Thailand is dominated by the Chao Phraya river basin, which contains Bangkok, the capital city and centre of most economic activity. To the east is a dry plateau drained by tributaries of the Mekong river, while to the north, west and south, extending down most of the Malay peninsula, are forested hills and mountains. Many small islands line the coast. The climate is hot, humid and monsoonal. About half the workforce is involved in agriculture. Fishing and fish processing are important. Thailand produces natural gas, some oil and lignite, minerals (chiefly tin, tungsten and baryte) and gemstones. Manufacturing is the largest contributor to national income, with electronics, textiles, clothing and footwear, and food processing the main industries. With around seven million visitors a year, tourism is the major source of foreign exchange. Thailand is one of the world's leading exporters of rice and rubber, and a major exporter of maize and tapioca. Japan and the USA are the main trading partners.

Grand Palace, Bangkok, Thailand

Togo Republic of Togo

Area Sq Km **56 785**
Area Sq Miles **21 925**

Population **6 619 000**
Capital **Lomé**

Currency **CFA franc**
Languages **French, Ewe, Kabre, local languages**

Religions **Traditional beliefs, Christian, Sunni Muslim**
Organizations **UN**

Social Indicators

Infant mortality rate
65 per 1 000 live births
Life expectancy **62.7**
Literacy rate **N/A**
Access to safe water **52%**
Doctors
0.04 per 1 000 people

Population

Total population **6 619 000**
Population change **2.5%**
Urban population **42.0%**
Total fertility rate **4.3 births per woman**
Population aged 0–14 **40.2%**
Population aged over 65 **3.5%**
2050 projected population **13 544 000**

Communications

Main telephone lines
1.3 per 100 people
Cellular mobile subscribers
11.2 per 100 people
Internet users
507 per 10 000 people
International dialling code **228**
Time zone **GMT**

Economy

Total Gross National Income (GNI) **2 265 US$M**
GNI per capita **400 US$**
Debt service ratio **0.7% of GNI**
Total debt service **15 432 000 US$**
Aid receipts **3.6% of GNI**
Military spending **1.6% of GDP**

Environment

Forest area **7.1%**
Annual change in forest area **-4.5%**
Protected land area **11.1%**
CO2 emissions **0.2 metric tons per capita**

Togo is a long narrow country in west Africa with a short coastline on the Gulf of Guinea. The interior consists of plateaus rising to mountainous areas. The climate is tropical, and is drier inland. Agriculture is the mainstay of the economy. Phosphate mining and food processing are the main industries. Cotton, phosphates, coffee and cocoa are the main exports. Lomé, the capital, is an entrepôt trade centre.

Phosphate mine, Togo

Tokelau New Zealand Overseas Territory

Area Sq Km **10**
Area Sq Miles **4**

Currency **New Zealand dollar**
Languages **English, Tokelauan**

Population **1 466**

Religions **Christian**

Tokelau consists of three atolls, Atafu, Nukunonu and Fakaofa, in the Pacific Ocean. Subsistence agriculture is the main activity, and the islands rely on aid from New Zealand and remittances from workers overseas.

Area Sq Km **748**
Area Sq Miles **289**

Population **104 000**
Capital **Nuku'alofa**

Currency **Pa'anga**
Languages **Tongan, English**

Religions **Protestant, Roman Catholic**
Organizations **Comm., UN**

Population

Total population **104 000**
Population change **0.5%**
Urban population **24.8%**
Total fertility rate **4.0 births per woman**
Population aged 0–14 **37.5%**
Population aged over 65 **5.8%**
2050 projected population **75 000**

Communications

Main telephone lines **13.7 per 100 people**
Cellular mobile subscribers **29.8 per 100 people**
Internet users **302 per 10 000 people**
International dialling code **676**
Time zone **+13**

Social Indicators

Infant mortality rate **19 per 1 000 live births**
Life expectancy **71.9**
Literacy rate **99.2%**
Access to safe water **100%**
Doctors **0.29 per 1 000 people**

Economy

Total Gross National Income (GNI) **225 US$M**
GNI per capita **2 560 US$**
Debt service ratio **1.4% of GNI**
Total debt service **3 203 000 US$**
Aid receipts **9.6% of GNI**
Military spending **1.1% of GDP**

Environment

Forest area **5.0%**
Annual change in forest area **0.0%**
Protected land area **8.6%**
CO_2 emissions **1.2 metric tons per capita**

Tonga comprises some one hundred and seventy islands in the south Pacific Ocean, northeast of New Zealand. The three main groups are Tongatapu (where sixty per cent of Tongans live), Ha'apai and Vava'u. The climate is warm and wet, and the economy relies heavily on agriculture. Tourism and light industry are also important to the economy. Exports include squash, fish, vanilla beans and root crops. Most trade is with New Zealand, Japan and Australia.

Trinidad and Tobago Republic of Trinidad and Tobago

Area Sq Km **5 130**
Area Sq Miles **1 981**

Population **1 339 000**
Capital **Port of Spain**

Currency **Trinidad and Tobago dollar**
Languages **English, creole, Hindi**

Religions **Roman Catholic, Hindu, Protestant, Sunni Muslim**
Organizations **CARICOM, Comm., UN**

Social Indicators

Infant mortality rate **31 per 1 000 live births**
Life expectancy **69.7**
Literacy rate **98.7%**
Access to safe water **91%**
Doctors **N/A**

Population

Total population **1 339 000**
Population change **0.3%**
Urban population **13.2%**
Total fertility rate **1.6 births per woman**
Population aged 0–14 **20.8%**
Population aged over 65 **6.6%**
2050 projected population **1 230 000**

Communications

Main telephone lines **24.9 per 100 people**
Cellular mobile subscribers **126.4 per 100 people**
Internet users **1 248 per 10 000 people**
International dialling code **1 868**
Time zone **-4**

Economy

Total Gross National Income (GNI) **16 612 US$M**
GNI per capita **16 540 US$**
Debt service ratio **N/A**
Total debt service **N/A**
Aid receipts **0.1% of GNI**
Military spending **N/A**

Environment

Forest area **44.1%**
Annual change in forest area **-0.2%**
Protected land area **4.7%**
CO_2 emissions **24.7 metric tons per capita**

Trinidad, the most southerly Caribbean island, lies off the Venezuelan coast. It is hilly in the north, with a central plain. Tobago, to the northeast, is smaller, more mountainous and less developed. The climate is tropical. The main crops are cocoa, sugar cane, coffee, fruit and vegetables. Oil and petrochemical industries dominate the economy. Tourism is also important. The USA is the main trading partner.

Tristan da Cunha Part of the United Kingdom Overseas Territory of St Helena, Ascension and Tristan da Cunha

Area Sq Km **98**
Area Sq Miles **38**

Population **264**
Capital **Settlement of Edinburgh**

A group of volcanic islands in the south Atlantic Ocean: the other main islands in the group are Nightingale Island and Inaccessible Island. The group is over 2 000 kilometres (1 250 miles) south of St Helena. Once part of the dependancy of St Helena, a consititutional change in September 2009 saw Tristan da Cunha (along with Ascension), become recognised in the territory's name in its own right. The economy is based on fishing, fish processing and agriculture. Ectourism is increasingly important.

Tunisia Tunisian Republic

Area Sq Km **164 150**
Area Sq Miles **63 379**

Population **10 272 000**
Capital **Tunis**

Currency **Tunisian dinar**
Languages **Arabic, French**

Religions **Sunni Muslim**
Organizations **UN**

Social Indicators

Infant mortality rate
18 per 1 000 live births
Life expectancy **74.3**
Literacy rate **77.7%**
Access to safe water **93%**
Doctors **1.34 per 1 000 people**

Population

Total population **10 272 000**
Population change **1.0%**
Urban population **66.5%**
Total fertility rate **2.0 births per woman**
Population aged 0–14 **23.7%**
Population aged over 65 **6.7%**
2050 projected population **12 927 000**

Communications

Main telephone lines
12.4 per 100 people
Cellular mobile subscribers
71.9 per 100 people
Internet users
1 268 per 10 000 people
International dialling code **216**
Time zone **+1**

Economy

Total Gross National
Income (GNI) **30 091 US$M**
GNI per capita **3 290 US$**
Debt service ratio **8.8% of GNI**
Total debt service **2 520 202 000 US$**
Aid receipts **1.5% of GNI**
Military spending **1.4% of GDP**

Environment

Forest area **6.8%**
Annual change in
forest area **1.9%**
Protected land area **1.5%**
CO2 emissions **2.2 metric
tons per capita**

Tunisia is on the Mediterranean coast of north Africa. The north is mountainous with valleys and coastal plains, has a Mediterranean climate and is the most populous area. The south is hot and arid. Oil and phosphates are the main resources, and the main crops are olives and citrus fruit. Tourism is an important industry. Exports include petroleum products, textiles, fruit and phosphorus. Most trade is with European Union countries.

Sbeitla, Tunisia

Area Sq Km **779 452**
Area Sq Miles **300 948**

Population **74 816 000**
Capital **Ankara**

Currency **Lira**
Languages **Turkish, Kurdish**

Religions **Sunni Muslim, Shi'a Muslim**
Organizations **NATO, OECD, UN**

Population

Total population **74 816 000**
Population change **1.2%**
Urban population **68.7%**
Total fertility rate **2.1 births per woman**
Population aged 0–14 **27.2%**
Population aged over 65 **5.8%**
2050 projected population **101 208 000**

Communications

Main telephone lines
25.4 per 100 people
Cellular mobile subscribers
71.0 per 100 people
Internet users
1 773 per 10 000 people
International dialling code **90**
Time zone **+2**

Economy

Total Gross National Income (GNI) **393 903 US$M**
GNI per capita **9 340 US$**
Debt service ratio **10.1% of GNI**
Total debt service **40 511 288 000 US$**
Aid receipts **0.1% of GNI**
Military spending **2.9% of GDP**

Environment

Forest area **13.2%**
Annual change in forest area **0.2%**
Protected land area **1.6%**
CO2 emissions **3.5 metric tons per capita**

Social Indicators

Infant mortality rate
21 per 1 000 live births
Life expectancy **72.0**
Literacy rate **88.7**
Access to safe water **96%**
Doctors **1.56 per 1 000 people**

Turkey occupies a large peninsula of southwest Asia and has coastlines on the Black, Mediterranean and Aegean Seas. It includes eastern Thrace, which is in southeastern Europe and separated from the rest of the country by the Bosporus, the Sea of Marmara and the Dardanelles. The Asian mainland consists of the semi-arid Anatolian plateau, flanked to the north, south and east by mountains. Over forty per cent of Turks live in central Anatolia and on the Marmara and Aegean coastal plains. The coast has a Mediterranean climate, but inland conditions are more extreme with hot, dry summers and cold, snowy winters. Agriculture involves about forty per cent of the workforce, and products include cotton, grain, tobacco, fruit, nuts and livestock. Turkey is a leading producer of chromium, iron ore, lead, tin, borate, and baryte. Coal is also mined. The main manufactured goods are clothing, textiles, food products, steel and vehicles. Tourism is a major industry, with nine million visitors a year. Germany and the USA are the main trading partners. Remittances from workers abroad are important to the economy.

Istanbul, Turkey

Turkmenistan Republic of Turkmenistan

Area Sq Km **488 100**
Area Sq Miles **188 456**

Population **5 110 000**
Capital **Aşgabat (Ashkhabad)**

Currency **Turkmen manat**
Languages **Turkmen, Uzbek, Russian**

Religions **Sunni Muslim, Russian Orthodox**
Organizations **UN**

Population

Total population **5 110 000**
Population change **1.3%**
Urban population **48.6%**
Total fertility rate **2.5 births per woman**
Population aged 0–14 **30.1%**
Population aged over 65 **4.3%**
2050 projected population **6 780 000**

Communications

Main telephone lines **8.2 per 100 people**
Cellular mobile subscribers **4.4 per 100 people**
Internet users **132 per 10 000 people**
International dialling code **993**
Time zone **+5**

Economy

Total Gross National Income (GNI) **N/A**
GNI per capita **2 840 US$**
Debt service ratio **2.6% of GNI**
Total debt service **254 770 000 US$**
Aid receipts **0.3% of GNI**
Military spending **N/A**

Environment

Forest area **8.8%**
Annual change in forest area **0.0%**
Protected land area **2.7%**
CO2 emissions **8.6 metric tons per capita**

Social Indicators

Infant mortality rate **45 per 1 000 live births**
Life expectancy **63.2**
Literacy rate **99.5%**
Access to safe water **72%**
Doctors **2.49 per 1 000 people**

Aşgabat, Turkmenistan

Turkmenistan, in central Asia, comprises the plains of the Karakum Desert, the foothills of the Kopet Dag mountains in the south, the Amudar'ya valley in the north and the Caspian Sea plains in the west. The climate is dry, with extreme temperatures. The economy is based mainly on irrigated agriculture (chiefly cotton growing), and natural gas and oil. Main exports are natural gas, oil and cotton fibre. Ukraine, Iran, Turkey and the Russian Federation are the main trading partners.

Area Sq Km **430**
Area Sq Miles **166**

Currency **US dollar**
Languages **English**

Population **33 000**
Capital **Grand Turk**
(**Cockburn Town**)

Religions **Protestant**

The state consists of over forty low-lying islands and cays in the northern Caribbean. Only eight islands are inhabited, and two-fifths of the people live on Grand Turk and Salt Cay. The climate is tropical, and the economy is based on tourism, fishing and offshore banking.

Grand Turk, Turks and Caicos Islands

Tuvalu

Area Sq Km **25**
Area Sq Miles **10**

Population **10 000**
Capital **Vaiaku**

Currency **Australian dollar**
Languages **Tuvaluan, English**

Religions **Protestant**
Organizations **Comm., UN**

Population

Total population **10 000**
Population change **N/A**
Urban population **N/A**
Total fertility rate **N/A**
Population aged 0–14 **N/A**
Population aged over 65 **N/A**
2050 projected population **12 000**

Communications

Main telephone lines **10.3 per 100 people**
Cellular mobile subscribers **15 per 100 people**
Internet users **4 673 per 10 000 people**
International dialling code **688**
Time zone **+12**

Social Indicators

Infant mortality rate **N/A**
Life expectancy **N/A**
Literacy rate **N/A**
Access to safe water **100%**
Doctors **N/A**

Economy

Total Gross National Income (GNI) **N/A**
GNI per capita **N/A**
Debt service ratio **N/A**
Total debt service **N/A**
Aid receipts **N/A**
Military spending **N/A**

Environment

Forest area **N/A**
Annual change in forest area **0.0%**
Protected land area **N/A**
CO2 emissions **N/A**

Tuvalu comprises nine low-lying coral atolls in the south Pacific Ocean. One-third of the population lives on Funafuti, and most people depend on subsistence farming and fishing. The islands export copra, stamps and clothing, but rely heavily on foreign aid. Most trade is with Fiji, Australia and New Zealand.

Uganda Republic of Uganda

Area Sq Km **241 038**
Area Sq Miles **93 065**

Population **32 710 000**
Capital **Kampala**

Currency **Ugandan shilling**
Languages **English, Swahili, Luganda, local languages**

Religions **Roman Catholic, Protestant, Muslim, trad. beliefs**
Organizations **Comm., UN**

Population
Total population **32 710 000**
Population change **3.3%**
Urban population **13.0%**
Total fertility rate **6.4 births per woman**
Population aged 0–14 **49.0%**
Population aged over 65 **2.6%**
2050 projected population **126 950 000**

Communications
Main telephone lines **0.4 per 100 people**
Cellular mobile subscribers **6.7 per 100 people**
Internet users **251 per 10 000 people**
International dialling code **256**
Time zone **+3**

Environment
Forest area **18.4%**
Annual change in forest area **-2.2%**
Protected land area **31.9%**
CO2 emissions **0.1 metric tons per capita**

Economy
Total Gross National Income (GNI) **8 996 US$M**
GNI per capita **420 US$**
Debt service ratio **1.2% of GNI**
Total debt service **114 694 000 US$**
Aid receipts **16.9% of GNI**
Military spending **2.1% of GDP**

Social Indicators
Infant mortality rate **82 per 1 000 live births**
Life expectancy **53.0**
Literacy rate **73.6%**
Access to safe water **60%**
Doctors **0.08 per 1 000 people**

A landlocked country in east Africa, Uganda consists of a savanna plateau with mountains and lakes. The climate is warm and wet. Most people live in the southern half of the country. Agriculture employs around eighty per cent of the workforce and dominates the economy. Coffee, tea, fish and fish products are the main exports. Uganda relies heavily on aid.

Hippopotamus, Uganda

Area Sq Km **603 700**
Area Sq Miles **233 090**

Population **45 708 000**
Capital **Kiev (Kyiv)**

Currency **Hryvnia**
Languages **Ukrainian, Russian**

Religions **Ukrainian Orthodox,
Ukrainian Catholic,
Roman Catholic**
Organizations **CIS, UN**

Population

Total population **45 708 000**
Population change **-0.5%**
Urban population **68.0%**
Total fertility rate **1.2 births per woman**
Population aged 0–14 **13.9%**
Population aged over 65 **15.9%**
2050 projected population **26 393 000**

Communications

Main telephone lines
26.8 per 100 people
Cellular mobile subscribers
106.7 per 100 people
Internet users
1 206 per 10 000 people
International dialling code **380**
Time zone **+2**

Economy

Total Gross National
Income (GNI) **90 740 US$M**
GNI per capita **3 210 US$**
Debt service ratio **9.0% of GNI**
Total debt service **9 388 953 000 US$**
Aid receipts **0.5% of GNI**
Military spending **2.1% of GDP**

Environment

Forest area **16.5%**
Annual change in
forest area **0.1%**
Protected land area **3.3%**
CO_2 emissions **6.9 metric
tons per capita**

Social Indicators

Infant mortality rate
20 per 1 000 live births
Life expectancy **68.2**
Literacy rate **99.7%**
Access to safe water **96%**
Doctors **3.13 per 1 000 people**

The country lies on the Black Sea coast of eastern Europe. Much of the land is steppe, generally flat and treeless, but with rich black soil, and it is drained by the river Dnieper. Along the border with Belarus are forested, marshy plains. The only uplands are the Carpathian Mountains in the west and smaller ranges on the Crimean peninsula. Summers are warm and winters are cold, with milder conditions in the Crimea. About a quarter of the population lives in the mainly industrial areas around Donets'k, Kiev and Dnipropetrovs'k. The Ukraine is rich in natural resources: fertile soil, substantial mineral and natural gas deposits, and forests. Agriculture and livestock rearing are important, but mining and manufacturing are the dominant sectors of the economy. Coal, iron and manganese mining, steel and metal production, machinery, chemicals and food processing are the main industries. The Russian Federation is the main trading partner.

St Michael's Cathedral, Kiev, Ukraine

United Arab Emirates Federation of Emirates

Area Sq Km **77 700**
Area Sq Miles **30 000**

Population **4 599 000**
Capital **Abu Dhabi (Abū Ẓabī)**

Currency **United Arab Emirates dirham**
Languages **Arabic, English**

Religions **Sunni Muslim, Shi'a Muslim**
Organizations **OPEC, UN**

Population

Total population **4 599 000**
Population change **2.7%**
Urban population **77.9%**
Total fertility rate **2.3 births per woman**
Population aged 0–14 **19.2%**
Population aged over 65 **1.0%**
2050 projected population **9 056 000**

Communications

Main telephone lines
28.1 per 100 people
Cellular mobile subscribers
118.5 per 100 people
Internet users
3 669 per 10 000 people
International dialling code **971**
Time zone **+4**

Economy

Total Gross National Income (GNI) **N/A**
GNI per capita **26 270 US$**
Debt service ratio **N/A**
Total debt service **N/A**
Aid receipts **N/A**
Military spending **2.0% of GDP**

Environment

Forest area **3.7%**
Annual change in forest area **0.1%**
Protected land area **0.2%**
CO2 emissions **30.1 metric tons per capita**

Social Indicators

Infant mortality rate
7 per 1 000 live births
Life expectancy **79.3**
Literacy rate **90.0%**
Access to safe water **100%**
Doctors **1.69 per 1 000 people**

The UAE lies on the Gulf coast of the Arabian Peninsula. Six emirates are on The Gulf, while the seventh, Fujairah, is on the Gulf of Oman. Most of the land is flat desert with sand dunes and salt pans. The only hilly area is in the northeast. Over eighty per cent of the population lives in three of the emirates - Abu Dhabi, Dubai and Sharjah. Summers are hot and winters are mild, with occasional rainfall in coastal areas. Fruit and vegetables are grown in oases and irrigated areas, but the Emirates' wealth is based on hydrocarbons found in Abu Dhabi, Dubai, Sharjah and Ras al Khaimah. The UAE is one of the major oil producers in the Middle East. Dubai is an important entrepôt trade centre. The main trading partner is Japan.

Dubai, United Arab Emirates

Area Sq Km **243 609**
Area Sq Miles **94 058**

Population **61 565 000**
Capital **London**

Currency **Pound sterling**
Languages **English, Welsh, Gaelic**

Religions **Protestant, Roman Catholic, Muslim**
Organizations **Comm., EU, NATO, OECD, UN**

Population

Total population **61 565 000**
Population change **0.6%**
Urban population **89.9%**
Total fertility rate **1.9 births per woman**
Population aged 0–14 **17.5%**
Population aged over 65 **16.3%**
2050 projected population **67 143 000**

Communications

Main telephone lines **56.2 per 100 people**
Cellular mobile subscribers **116.6 per 100 people**
Internet users **6 316 per 10 000 people**
International dialling code **44**
Time zone **GMT**

Economy

Total Gross National Income (GNI) **2 455 691 US$M**
GNI per capita **45 390 US$**
Debt service ratio **N/A**
Total debt service **N/A**
Aid receipts **N/A**
Military spending **2.6% of GDP**

Environment

Forest area **11.8%**
Annual change in forest area **0.4%**
Protected land area **19.6%**
CO2 emissions **9.1 metric tons per capita**

Social Indicators

Infant mortality rate **5 per 1 000 live births**
Life expectancy **79.3**
Literacy rate **N/A**
Access to safe water **100%**
Doctors **2.2 per 1 000 people**

The United Kingdom, in northwest Europe, occupies the island of Great Britain, part of Ireland, and many small adjacent islands. Great Britain comprises England, Scotland and Wales. England covers over half the land area and supports over four-fifths of the population, at its densest in the southeast. The English landscape is flat or rolling with some uplands, notably the Cheviot Hills on the Scottish border, the Pennines in the centre-north, and the hills of the Lake District in the northwest. Scotland consists of southern uplands, central lowlands, the Highlands (which include the UK's highest peak) and many islands. Wales is a land of hills, mountains and river valleys. Northern Ireland contains uplands, plains and the UK's largest lake, Lough Neagh. The climate of the UK is mild, wet and variable. There are few mineral deposits, but important energy resources. Agricultural activities involve sheep and cattle rearing, dairy farming, and crop and fruit growing in the east and southeast. Productivity is high, but approximately one-third of food is imported. The UK produces petroleum and natural gas from reserves in the North Sea and is self-sufficient in energy in net terms. Major manufactures are food and drinks, motor vehicles and parts, aerospace equipment, machinery, electronic and electrical equipment, and chemicals and chemical products. However, the economy is dominated by service industries, including banking, insurance, finance and business services. London, the capital, is one of the world's major financial centres. Tourism is also a major industry, with approximately twenty-five million visitors a year. International trade is also important, equivalent to one-third of national income. Over half of the UK's trade is with other European Union countries.

Stonehenge, United Kingdom

United States of America Federal Republic

Area Sq Km **9 826 635**
Area Sq Miles **3 794 085**

Population **314 659 000**
Capital **Washington D.C.**

Currency **United States dollar**
Languages **English, Spanish**

Religions **Protestant, Roman Catholic, Sunni Muslim, Jewish**
Organizations **APEC, NATO, OECD, UN**

Population
Total population **314 659 000**
Population change **0.9%**
Urban population **81.7%**
Total fertility rate **2.1 births per woman**
Population aged 0–14 **20.4%**
Population aged over 65 **12.6%**
2050 projected population **394 976 000**

Communications
Main telephone lines **57.2 per 100 people**
Cellular mobile subscribers **77.4 per 100 people**
Internet users **6 983 per 10 000 people**
International dialling code **1**
Time zone **-5 to -10**

Economy
Total Gross National Income (GNI) **13 386 875 US$M**
GNI per capita **47 580 US$**
Debt service ratio **N/A**
Total debt service **N/A**
Aid receipts **N/A**
Military spending **4.1% of GDP**

Environment
Forest area **33.1%**
Annual change in forest area **0.1%**
Protected land area **15.1%**
CO2 emissions **19.5 metric tons per capita**

Social Indicators
Infant mortality rate **7 per 1 000 live births**
Life expectancy **78.0**
Literacy rate **N/A**
Access to safe water **100%**
Doctors **2.3 per 1 000 people**

The USA comprises forty-eight contiguous states in North America, bounded by Canada and Mexico, plus the states of Alaska, to the northwest of Canada, and Hawaii, in the north Pacific Ocean. The populous eastern states cover the Atlantic coastal plain (which includes the Florida peninsula and the Gulf of Mexico coast) and the Appalachian Mountains. The central states occupy a vast interior plain drained by the Mississippi-Missouri river system. To the west lie the Rocky Mountains, separated from the Pacific coastal ranges by intermontane plateaus. The Pacific coastal zone is also mountainous, and prone to earthquakes. Hawaii is a group of some twenty volcanic islands. Climatic conditions range between arctic in Alaska to desert in the intermontane plateaus. Most of the USA has a temperate climate, although the interior has continental conditions. There are abundant natural resources, including major reserves of minerals and energy resources. The USA has the largest and most technologically advanced economy in the world, based on manufacturing and services. Although agriculture accounts for approximately two per cent of national income, productivity is high and the USA is a net exporter of food, chiefly grains and fruit. Cotton is the major industrial crop. The USA produces iron ore, copper, lead, zinc, and many other minerals. It is a major producer of coal, petroleum and natural gas, although being the world's biggest energy user it imports significant quantities of petroleum and its products. Manufacturing is diverse. The main industries are petroleum, steel, motor vehicles, aerospace, telecommunications, electronics, food processing, chemicals and consumer goods. Tourism is a major foreign currency earner, with approximately forty-five million visitors a year. Other important service industries are banking and finance, Wall Street in New York being one of the world's major stock exchanges. Canada and Mexico are the main trading partners.

Grand Canyon, United States of America

Area Sq Km **176 215**
Area Sq Miles **68 037**

Population **3 361 000**
Capital **Montevideo**

Currency **Uruguayan peso**
Languages **Spanish**

Religions **Roman Catholic, Protestant, Jewish**
Organizations **UN**

Population

Total population **3 361 000**
Population change **0.3%**
Urban population **92.3%**
Total fertility rate **2.0 births per woman**
Population aged 0–14 **23.0%**
Population aged over 65 **13.7%**
2050 projected population **4 043 000**

Communications

Main telephone lines **28.3 per 100 people**
Cellular mobile subscribers **66.8 per 100 people**
Internet users **2 055 per 10 000 people**
International dialling code **598**
Time zone **-3**

Social Indicators

Infant mortality rate **12 per 1 000 live births**
Life expectancy **75.9**
Literacy rate **97.9%**
Access to safe water **100%**
Doctors **3.65 per 1 000 people**

Economy

Total Gross National Income (GNI) **17 591 US$M**
GNI per capita **8 260 US$**
Debt service ratio **30.3% of GNI**
Total debt service **5 689 614 000 US$**
Aid receipts **0.1% of GNI**
Military spending **1.2% of GDP**

Environment

Forest area **8.6%**
Annual change in forest area **1.3%**
Protected land area **0.3%**
CO2 emissions **1.7 metric tons per capita**

Uruguay, on the Atlantic coast of central South America, is a low-lying land of prairies. The coast and the River Plate estuary in the south are fringed with lagoons and sand dunes. Almost half the population lives in the capital, Montevideo. Uruguay has warm summers and mild winters.

The economy is based on cattle and sheep ranching, and the main industries produce food products, textiles, and petroleum products. Meat, wool, hides, textiles and agricultural products are the main exports. Brazil and Argentina are the main trading partners.

Montevideo, Uruguay

Uzbekistan Republic of Uzbekistan

Area Sq Km **447 400**
Area Sq Miles **172 742**

Population **27 488 000**
Capital **Tashkent (Toshkent)**

Currency **Uzbek som**
Languages **Uzbek, Russian, Tajik, Kazakh**

Religions **Sunni Muslim, Russian Orthodox**
Organizations **CIS, UN**

Population
Total population **27 488 000**
Population change **1.6%**
Urban population **36.8%**
Total fertility rate **2.4 births per woman**
Population aged 0–14 **30.1%**
Population aged over 65 **4.6%**
2050 projected population **38 665 000**

Communications
Main telephone lines
6.7 per 100 people
Cellular mobile subscribers
9.3 per 100 people
Internet users
630 per 10 000 people
International dialling code **998**
Time zone **+5**

Economy
Total Gross National
Income (GNI) **16 179 US$M**
GNI per capita **910 US$**
Debt service ratio **5.4% of GNI**
Total debt service **923 830 000 US$**
Aid receipts **0.9% of GNI**
Military spending **0.5% of GDP**

Environment
Forest area **7.7%**
Annual change in
forest area **0.5%**
Protected land area **2.0%**
CO2 emissions **4.3 metric tons per capita**

Social Indicators
Infant mortality rate
36 per 1 000 live births
Life expectancy **67.1**
Literacy rate **N/A**
Access to safe water **82%**
Doctors **2.65 per 1 000 people**

A landlocked country of central Asia, Uzbekistan consists mainly of the flat Kyzylkum Desert. High mountains and valleys are found towards the southeast borders with Kyrgyzstan and Tajikistan. Most settlement is in the Fergana basin. The climate is hot and dry. The economy is based mainly on irrigated agriculture, chiefly cotton production. Uzbekistan is rich in minerals, including gold, copper, lead, zinc and uranium, and it has one of the largest gold mines in the world. Industry specializes in fertilizers and machinery for cotton harvesting and textile manufacture. The Russian Federation is the main trading partner.

Samarkand, Uzbekistan

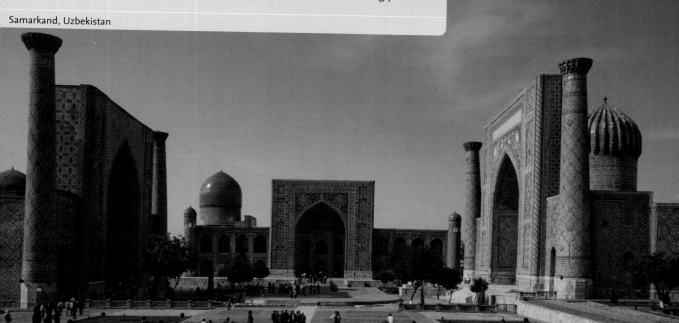

Area Sq Km **12 190**
Area Sq Miles **4 707**

Population **240 000**
Capital **Port Vila**

Currency **Vatu**
Languages **English, Bislama (creole), French**

Religions **Protestant, Roman Catholic, traditional beliefs**
Organizations **Comm., UN**

Population
Total population **240 000**
Population change **2.3%**
Urban population **24.8%**
Total fertility rate **3.7 births per woman**
Population aged 0–14 **39.0%**
Population aged over 65 **3.3%**
2050 projected population **375 000**

Communications
Main telephone lines **3.2 per 100 people**
Cellular mobile subscribers **5.9 per 100 people**
Internet users **346 per 10 000 people**
International dialling code **678**
Time zone **+11**

Social Indicators
Infant mortality rate **28 per 1 000 live births**
Life expectancy **70.1**
Literacy rate **78.1%**
Access to safe water **60%**
Doctors **0.14 per 1 000 people**

Economy
Total Gross National Income (GNI) **373 US$M**
GNI per capita **2 330 US$**
Debt service ratio **1.0% of GNI**
Total debt service **3 725 000 US$**
Aid receipts **13.6% of GNI**
Military spending **N/A**

Environment
Forest area **36.1%**
Annual change in forest area **0.0%**
Protected land area **0.7%**
CO2 emissions **0.4 metric tons per capita**

Vanuatu occupies an archipelago of approximately eighty islands in the southwest Pacific. Many of the islands are mountainous, of volcanic origin and densely forested. The climate is tropical, with heavy rainfall. Half of the population lives on the main islands of Éfaté and Espíritu Santo, and the majority of people are employed in agriculture. Copra, beef, timber, vegetables, and cocoa are the main exports. Tourism is becoming important to the economy. Australia, Japan and Germany are the main trading partners.

Vatican City Vatican City State or Holy See

Area Sq Km **0.5**
Area Sq Miles **0.2**

Population **557**
Capital **Vatican City (Città del Vaticano)**

Currency **Euro**
Languages **Italian**

Religions **Roman Catholic**

Social Indicators
Infant mortality rate **N/A**
Life expectancy **N/A**
Literacy rate **N/A**
Access to safe water **N/A**
Doctors **N/A**

Population
Total population **557**
Population change **N/A**
Urban population **N/A**
Total fertility rate **N/A**
Population aged 0–14 **N/A**
Population aged over 65 **N/A**
2050 projected population **1 000**

Communications
Main telephone lines **N/A**
Cellular mobile subscribers **N/A**
Internet users **N/A**
International dialling code **39**
Time zone **+1**

Economy
Total Gross National Income (GNI) **N/A**
GNI per capita **N/A**
Debt service ratio **N/A**
Total debt service **N/A**
Aid receipts **N/A**
Military spending **N/A**

Environment
Forest area **N/A**
Annual change in forest area **0.0%**
Protected land area **N/A**
CO2 emissions **N/A**

The world's smallest sovereign state, the Vatican City occupies a hill to the west of the river Tiber within the Italian capital, Rome. It is the headquarters of the Roman Catholic church, and income comes from investments, voluntary contributions and tourism.

Venezuela Republic of Venezuela

Area Sq Km **912 050**
Area Sq Miles **352 144**

Population **28 583 000**
Capital **Caracas**

Currency **Bolívar fuerte**
Languages **Spanish, Amerindian languages**

Religions **Roman Catholic, Protestant**
Organizations **OPEC, UN**

Population
Total population **28 583 000**
Population change **1.7%**
Urban population **93.3%**
Total fertility rate **2.6 births per woman**
Population aged 0–14 **30.2%**
Population aged over 65 **5.3%**
2050 projected population **41 991 000**

Communications
Main telephone lines
15.8 per 100 people
Cellular mobile subscribers
69.0 per 100 people
Internet users
1 521 per 10 000 people
International dialling code **58**
Time zone **-4.5**

Social Indicators
Infant mortality rate
17 per 1 000 live births
Life expectancy **73.6**
Literacy rate **95.2%**
Access to safe water **83%**
Doctors **1.94 per 1 000 people**

Economy
Total Gross National
Income (GNI) **163 959 US$M**
GNI per capita **9 230 US$**
Debt service ratio **5.5% of GNI**
Total debt service **9 964 936 000 US$**
Aid receipts **0.0% of GNI**
Military spending **1.1% of GDP**

Environment
Forest area **54.1%**
Annual change in
forest area **-0.6%**
Protected land area **72.3%**
CO_2 emissions **5.6 metric tons per capita**

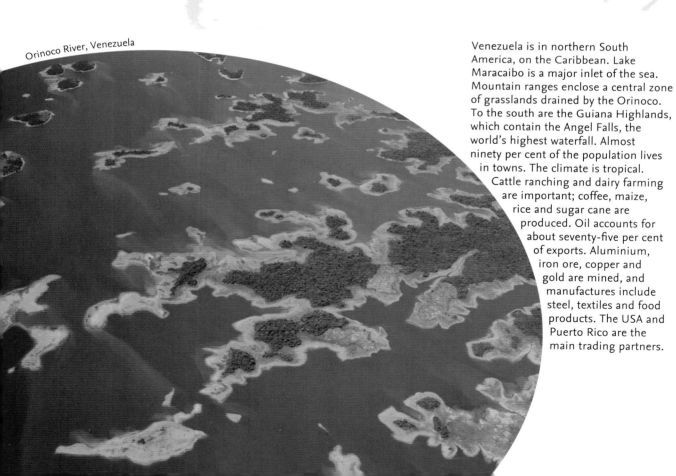

Orinoco River, Venezuela

Venezuela is in northern South America, on the Caribbean. Lake Maracaibo is a major inlet of the sea. Mountain ranges enclose a central zone of grasslands drained by the Orinoco. To the south are the Guiana Highlands, which contain the Angel Falls, the world's highest waterfall. Almost ninety per cent of the population lives in towns. The climate is tropical. Cattle ranching and dairy farming are important; coffee, maize, rice and sugar cane are produced. Oil accounts for about seventy-five per cent of exports. Aluminium, iron ore, copper and gold are mined, and manufactures include steel, textiles and food products. The USA and Puerto Rico are the main trading partners.

Area Sq Km **329 565**
Area Sq Miles **127 246**

Population **88 069 000**
Capital **Hanoi (Ha Nôi)**

Currency **Dong**
Languages **Vietnamese, Thai, Khmer, Chinese, local languages**

Religions **Buddhist, Taoist, Roman Catholic, Cao Dai, Hoa Hao**
Organizations **APEC, ASEAN, UN**

Population

Total population **88 069 000**
Population change **1.2%**
Urban population **27.8%**
Total fertility rate **2.1 births per woman**
Population aged 0–14 **26.5%**
Population aged over 65 **6.3%**
2050 projected population **116 654 000**

Communications

Main telephone lines **18.8 per 100 people**
Cellular mobile subscribers **18.2 per 100 people**
Internet users **1 721 per 10 000 people**
International dialling code **84**
Time zone **+7**

Social Indicators

Infant mortality rate **13 per 1 000 live births**
Life expectancy **74.2**
Literacy rate **N/A**
Access to safe water **85%**
Doctors **0.56 per 1 000 people**

Economy

Total Gross National Income (GNI) **58 506 US$M**
GNI per capita **890 US$**
Debt service ratio **1.5% of GNI**
Total debt service **918 307 000 US$**
Aid receipts **3.1% of GNI**
Military spending **N/A**

Environment

Forest area **41.7%**
Annual change in forest area **2.0%**
Protected land area **5.2%**
CO_2 emissions **1.2 metric tons per capita**

Ha Long Bay, Vietnam

Vietnam lies in southeast Asia on the west coast of the South China Sea. The Red River delta lowlands in the north are separated from the huge Mekong delta in the south by long, narrow coastal plains backed by the mountainous and forested terrain of the Annam Highlands. Most of the population lives in the river deltas. The climate is tropical, with summer monsoon rains. Over three-quarters of the workforce is involved in agriculture, forestry and fishing. Coffee, tea and rubber are important cash crops, but Vietnam is the world's second largest rice exporter. Oil, coal and copper are produced, and other main industries are food processing, clothing and footwear, cement and fertilizers. Exports include oil, coffee, rice, clothing, fish and fish products. Japan and Singapore are the main trading partners.

Virgin Islands (U.K.) United Kingdom Overseas Territory

Area Sq Km **153**
Area Sq Miles **59**

Currency **United States dollar**
Languages **English**

Population **23 000**
Capital **Road Town**

Religions **Protestant, Roman Catholic**

The Caribbean territory comprises four main islands and over thirty islets at the eastern end of the Virgin Islands group. Apart from the flat coral atoll of Anegada, the islands are volcanic in origin and hilly. The climate is subtropical, and tourism is the main industry.

 Virgin Islands (U.S.A.) United States Unincorporated Territory

Area Sq Km **352**
Area Sq Miles **136**

Currency **United States dollar**
Languages **English, Spanish**

Population **110 000**
Capital **Charlotte Amalie**

Religions **Protestant, Roman Catholic**

The territory consists of three main islands and over fifty islets in the Caribbean's western Virgin Islands. The islands are hilly, of volcanic origin, and the climate is subtropical. The economy is based on tourism and some manufacturing.

 **Wallis and Futuna Islands** French Overseas Collectivity

Area Sq Km **274**
Area Sq Miles **106**

Currency **CFP franc**
Languages **French, Wallisian, Futunian**

Population **15 000**
Capital **Matā'utu**

Religions **Roman Catholic**

The territory comprises of the Wallis archipelago and the Hoorn Islands. The climate is tropical. The islands depend on subsistence farming, the sale of licences to foreign fishing fleets, workers' remittances from abroad and French aid.

West Bank Disputed Territory

Area Sq Km **5 860**
Area Sq Miles **2 263**

Languages **Arabic, Hebrew**
Religions **Sunni Muslim, Jewish, Shi'a Muslim, Christian**

Population **2 448 433**
Currency **Jordanian dinar, Israeli shekel**

The territory consists of the west bank of the river Jordan and parts of Judea and Samaria. Annexed by Israel in 1967, some areas have been granted autonomy under agreements between Israel and the Palestinian Authority. Conflict continues to restrict economic growth.

Area Sq Km **266 000**
Area Sq Miles **102 703**

Currency **Moroccan dirhamr**
Languages **Arabic**

Population **513 000**
Capital **Laâyoune**

Religions **Sunni Muslim**

Situated on the northwest coast of Africa, the territory of the Western Sahara is now effectively controlled by Morocco. The land is low, flat desert with higher land in the northeast. There is little cultivation and only about twenty per cent of the land is pasture. Livestock herding, fishing and phosphate mining are the main activities. All trade is controlled by Morocco.

Desert landscape, Western Sahara

Yemen Republic of Yemen

Area Sq Km **527 968**
Area Sq Miles **203 850**

Population **23 580 000**
Capital **Şan'ā'**

Currency **Yemeni riyal**
Languages **Arabic**

Religions **Sunni Muslim, Shi'a Muslim**
Organizations **UN**

Population

Total population **23 580 000**
Population change **3.0%**
Urban population **30.6%**
Total fertility rate **5.5 births per woman**
Population aged 0–14 **44.2%**
Population aged over 65 **2.4%**
2050 projected population **59 454 000**

Communications

Main telephone lines **4.5 per 100 people**
Cellular mobile subscribers **13.8 per 100 people**
Internet users **125 per 10 000 people**
International dialling code **967**
Time zone **+3**

Social Indicators

Infant mortality rate **55 per 1 000 live births**
Life expectancy **62.7**
Literacy rate **58.9%**
Access to safe water **67%**
Doctors **0.33 per 1 000 people**

Economy

Total Gross National Income (GNI) **16 444 US$M**
GNI per capita **950 US$**
Debt service ratio **1.3% of GNI**
Total debt service **225 869 000 US$**
Aid receipts **1.6% of GNI**
Military spending **6.0% of GDP**

Environment

Forest area **1.0%**
Annual change in forest area **0.0%**
Protected land area **0.0%**
CO2 emissions **1.0 metric tons per capita**

Yemen occupies the southwestern part of the Arabian Peninsula, on the Red Sea and the Gulf of Aden. Beyond the Red Sea coastal plain the land rises to a mountain range and then descends to desert plateaus. Much of the country is hot and arid, but there is more rainfall in the west, where most of the population lives. Farming and fishing are the main activities, with cotton the main cash crop. The main exports are crude oil, fish, coffee and dried fruit. Despite some oil resources Yemen is one of the poorest countries in the Arab world. Main trading partners are Thailand, China, South Korea and Saudi Arabia.

Zambia Republic of Zambia

Area Sq Km **752 614**
Area Sq Miles **290 586**

Population **12 935 000**
Capital **Lusaka**

Currency **Zambian kwacha**
Languages **English, Bemba, Nyanja, Tonga, local languages**

Religions **Christian, traditional beliefs**
Organizations **Comm., SADC, UN**

Population

Total population **12 935 000**
Population change **2.5%**
Urban population **35.4%**
Total fertility rate **5.9 births per woman**
Population aged 0–14 **46.2%**
Population aged over 65 **3.0%**
2050 projected population **22 781 000**

Communications

Main telephone lines **0.8 per 100 people**
Cellular mobile subscribers **14.0 per 100 people**
Internet users **422 per 10 000 people**
International dialling code **260**
Time zone **+2**

Environment

Forest area **57.1%**
Annual change in forest area **-1.0%**
Protected land area **40.4%**
CO2 emissions **0.2 metric tons per capita**

Economy

Total Gross National Income (GNI) **7 413 US$M**
GNI per capita **950 US$**
Debt service ratio **1.6% of GNI**
Total debt service **153 699 000 US$**
Aid receipts **14.3% of GNI**
Military spending **2.3% of GDP**

Social Indicators

Infant mortality rate **103 per 1 000 live births**
Life expectancy **45.9**
Literacy rate **70.6%**
Access to safe water **58%**
Doctors **0.12 per 1 000 people**

A landlocked state in south central Africa, Zambia consists principally of high savanna plateaus and is bordered by the Zambezi river in the south. Most people live in the Copperbelt area in the centre-north. The climate is tropical, with a rainy season from November to May. Agriculture employs approximately eighty per cent of the workforce, but is mainly at subsistence level. Copper mining is the mainstay of the economy, although reserves are declining. Copper and cobalt are the main exports. Most trade is with South Africa.

Victoria Falls, Zambia

Area Sq Km **390 759**
Area Sq Miles **150 873**

Population **12 523 000**
Capital **Harare**

Currency **Zimbabwean dollar**
Languages **English, Shona, Ndebele**

Religions **Christian, traditional beliefs**
Organizations **SADC, UN**

Population

Total population **12 523 000**
Population change **0.1%**
Urban population **37.3%**
Total fertility rate **3.5 births per woman**
Population aged 0–14 **40.2%**
Population aged over 65 **4.0%**
2050 projected population **15 805 000**

Communications

Main telephone lines **2.6 per 100 people**
Cellular mobile subscribers **6.5 per 100 people**
Internet users **932 per 10 000 people**
International dialling code **263**
Time zone **+2**

Environment

Forest area **45.3%**
Annual change in forest area **-1.7%**
Protected land area **14.8%**
CO2 emissions **0.9 metric tons per capita**

Economy

Total Gross National Income (GNI) **4 466 US$M**
GNI per capita **360 US$**
Debt service ratio **7.0% of GNI**
Total debt service **83 389 000 US$**
Aid receipts **N/A**
Military spending **0.0% of GDP**

Social Indicators

Infant mortality rate **59 per 1 000 live births**
Life expectancy **45.1**
Literacy rate **91.2%**
Access to safe water **81%**
Doctors **0.16 per 1 000 people**

Zimbabwe, a landlocked state in south-central Africa, consists of high plateaus flanked by the Zambezi river valley and Lake Kariba in the north and the Limpopo river in the south. Most of the population lives in the centre of the country. There are significant mineral resources, including gold, nickel, copper, asbestos, platinum and chromium. Agriculture is a major sector of the economy, with crops including tobacco, maize, sugar cane and cotton. Beef cattle are also important. Exports include tobacco, gold, ferroalloys, nickel and cotton. South Africa is the main trading partner. The economy has suffered recently through significant political unrest and instability.

The Great Enclosure, Zimbabwe

All 195 independent countries and selected dependent and disputed territories are included in this list of the states and territories of the world; the list is arranged in alphabetical order by the conventional name form. For independent states, the full name is given below the conventional name, if this is different; for territories, the status is given.

Area and population statistics are the latest available and include estimates. The information on languages and religions is based on the latest information on 'de facto' speakers of the language or 'de facto' adherents of the religion. This varies greatly from country to country because some countries include questions in censuses while others do not, in which case best estimates are used. The order of the languages and religions reflects their relative importance within the country; generally, languages or religions are included when more than one per cent of the population are estimated to be speakers or adherents.

Membership of selected international organizations is shown by the abbreviations below; dependent territories do not normally have separate memberships of these organizations.

APEC	Asia-Pacific Economic Cooperation
ASEAN	Association of Southeast Asian Nations
CARICOM	Caribbean Community
CIS	Commonwealth of Independent States
Comm.	The Commonwealth
EU	European Union
NATO	North Atlantic Treaty Organization
OECD	Organisation for Economic Co-operation and Development
OPEC	Organization of Petroleum Exporting Countries
SADC	Southern African Development Community
UN	United Nations

Acknowledgements

Shutterstock: 2 Bruno Pagnanelli; **3** Netfalls; **4** WitR; **6** urosr; **7** Robert Koss; **8** Rafael Martin-Gaitero; **9** photo-mania; **10** Jerry Sharp; **10** kwest; **11** tororo reaction; **12** Aleksi Markku; **13** Alexey Averiyanov; **15** Keith Allen Hughes; **16** Graham Tomlin; **17** Tim Arbaev; **18** Andrjuss; **19** Ramunas Bruzas; **20** Eric Isselée; **21** Keith Muratori; **22** Danny Warren; **23** John A. Anderson; **24** Mogens Trolle; **25** Mark Schwettmann; **27** Holger Mette; **28** Ferderic B; **30** Luciano Mortula; **32** Phil Emmerson; **33** Ocean Image Photography; **35** Ecoimages; **36** Andrzej Gibasiewicz; **37** Mikhail Nekrasov; **38** Juan Camilo Bernal; **39** Leksele; **40** neelsky; **41** Pyrus; **42** gmwnz; **44** Holger Mette; **45** Natascha Louwet; **46** Ioannis Ioannou; **47** Ionia; **48** Yarygin; **51** rj lerich; **52** sculpies; **53** L. Kragt Bakker; **56** Pavel Reband; **57** Galyna Andrushko; **58** kwest; **59** Tatiana Edrenkina; **60** Max Topchii; **61** (French Guiana) Nina B, **61** (French Polynesia) urosr; **63** Bernhard Richter; **64** A_Sh; **65** Dainis Derics; **66** Albert Barr; **67** dr. Le Thanh Hung; **69** (Guadeloupe) Fouquin; **69** (Guam) Leksele; **70** Jo Chambers; **72** Vladimir Melnik; **74** posztos (colorlab.hu); **75** Hannamariah; **76** Krishna.Wu; **77** Maugli; **78** Massimiliano Lamagna; **79** homeros; **80** walshphotos; **81** Graham Taylor; **82** Andrejs Pidjass; **83** R. Gino Santa Maria; **84** Hiroshi Ichikawa; **85** Steve Beer; **86** Postnikova Kristina; **87** Paul Banton; **88** Vlas2000; **89** Orhan Çam; **90** Tracing Tea; **91** taboga; **92** Dainis Derics; **93** diak; **94** Leksele; **96** WitR; **97** ElenaGaak; **98** tfrisch99; **99** Sandra Voogt; **100** Anatema; **101** Nazzu; **102** Jiri Haureljuk; **103** Hu Xiao Fang; **104** Specta; **105** Attila JÁNDI; **106** Alexander Maksimenko; **107** Albert Barr; **108** Jam.si; **109** Arnon Ayal; **110** paul prescott; **111** A Cotton Photo; **112** Attila JÁNDI; **113** Vladimir Melnik; **114** Pichugin Dmitry; **115** Vladimir Popovic; **116** apdesign; **117** Jaco van Rensburg; **118** Luciano Mortula; **119** Pichugin Dmitry; **121** my-summit; **122** Rob Ahrens; **123** (Netherlands Antilles) Angels at Work, **123** (New Caledonia) taboga; **124** Martin Maun; **125** Holger Mette; **126** Ecoimages; **127** Francois van der Merwe; **128** Chris Burt; **129** Maxim Tupikov; **130** Igor Plotnikov; **131** Anna Omelchenko; **132** Naiyyer; **133** Axel Siefert; **134** Robert Young; **135** aspen rock; **136** Alexander Chaikin; **137** Worldoctopus; **138** Hugo Maes; **139** Pawel Kielpinski; **140** Matt Trommer; **141** J Donoghue II; **142** AMA; **143** Alexey Usov; **144** Willem Tims; **148** Salem Alforaih; **149** Lukas Hlavac; **150** Elena Elisseeva; **151** Tian Zhan; **152** LEONARDO VITI; **153** Sam DCruz; **154** Danielus48; **155** Adrian Zenz; **156** Dennis Sabo; **157** brianhumek; **158** EcoPrint; **159** yabu; **161** Rob Wilson; **162** Dmitry Rukhlenko; **163** urosr; **164** bart acke; **165** Leksele; **166** Aleksi Markku; **167** Peter Wey; **168** WitR; **169** Andrey Plis; **170** Sam DCruz; **171** Mikhail Nekrasov; **174** parkisland; **175** Clara; **176** Alexey Averiyanov; **177** Ivan Cholakov Gostock-dot-net; **178** Pichugin Dmitry; **179** Sergey Kamshylin; **180** haider; **181** SueC; **182** Alexey Stiop; **183** jorisvo; **184** javarman; **186** Vladinir Melnik; **187** Nickolay Stanev; **189** Nils Volkmer; **190** Pichugin Dmitry; **191** Lakis Fourouklas.

Wikipedia: 5 Eric Guinther; **26** Jgrimmer; **29** Tequendamia; **31** J. et M.F. Ostorero; **34** Pete Chirico, USGS; **43** Zenman stitched by Marku1988; **54** Ipisking; **55** Charles Fred; **62** B.navez; **95** Sahmeditor; **120** Atmospheric Radiation Measurement Program, U.S. Department of Energy; **160** DEMOSH; **172** Alexandra Pugachevsky.

Country pages 64-255
United Nations World Population Prospects 2009
UNESCO Education Data Centre
UN Human Development Report
World Bank World Development Indicators
OECD: Development Co-operation Report
UNICEF: The State of the World's Children
Food and Agriculture Organization
World Resources Institute Biodiversity and Protected Areas Database
International Telecommunications Union (ITU)

Collins
An imprint of HarperCollins Publishers
Westerhill Road, Bishopbriggs, Glasgow, G64 2QT

First Published 2011

Copyright © HarperCollins Publishers 2011

Collins ® is a registered trademark of HarperCollins Publishers Ltd

Printed in China

Imp 001

Front Cover graphic: © Worldoctopus / shutterstock

www.collinsmaps.com